To safety and health professionals
working for a better life for others
and to John G., Etta J.,
Martha,
and the little ones, Andrew D., Colin J., and Karin Emily

CONTENTS

PREFACE

Many books stress the need for the Occupational Safety and Health Administration (OSHA). Some criticize OSHA for being too weak. Others decry overregulation of the workplace. And still others use statistical methods to analyze OSHA's effectiveness. But this is the first book that describes firsthand an inspector's view of OSHA enforcement.

Statistics do not begin to describe the thousands of people each year who, as a result of OSHA enforcement, will not suffer hearing loss from working in a noisy factory, a disease from exposure to a harmful chemical, or disabling workplace-related injuries. Nor do statistics begin to describe the plight of the thousands of workers who, in spite of OSHA's goals, continue to work in dangerous premises in which management takes no responsibility for safety and health.

What are the legal responsibilities, political pressures, and personal limitations an inspector faces in trying to do his or her job? What can an inspector accomplish? And how could OSHA be improved, given the problems it has in reaching its goal of assuring every working man and woman a safe and healthful workplace? These are some of the questions *Dangerous Premises* addresses.

Dangerous Premises is based on my experiences as an OSHA health inspector for the state of California. Of the 162 workplace inspections I conducted during three years ending in 1985, about 40 resulted in citations for one or more serious violations. Ten of the narratives included here concern these employers. I have chosen these narratives because they illustrate the problems of enforcement and the challenges OSHA faces in meeting its goals.

After reading this book, one might well conclude that OSHA has failed in changing the attitudes of the thousands of employers across

America for whom workplace safety is clearly a low priority. But although many companies do not comply with OSHA's requirements, many do. In many of these companies, the requirements for safety and health surpass those of the government. I have conducted inspections that resulted in no citations or in citations for only minor infractions. I have inspected many companies—large and small—that maintain a high level of compliance and commitment to their employees' well-being. Many of these companies have comprehensive safety and health programs and correct problems as they arise. One of the narratives in this book is about such a company. To run a business, particularly a small business, with the aim of maintaining the well-being of one's employees takes courage, good sense, and hard work. Such employers deserve everyone's respect and the rewards they earn for their financial risk.

Dangerous Premises was written with the hope that, by revealing what happens during and as a result of an inspection, readers will be able to make informed judgments about the need for OSHA and how OSHA could better realize its goals.

The identities of the companies and individuals in the narratives have been changed to maintain their privacy. Any similarity to real people, living or dead, is coincidental.

ACKNOWLEDGMENTS

I would like to express my appreciation to several people who helped me prepare the manuscript for this book: Eric Tabb for his careful review of several chapters and for his criticism of sample material; John Geppert, Jim Burt, and a reviewer who wishes to remain anonymous for their helpful comments and criticisms on the conclusion; and Chuck Lange for his review of the introduction. I retain final responsibility for the opinions and conclusions expressed.

Thanks to my wife, Martha, for surviving the hours of my being there but not.

Finally, I would like to extend my gratitude to the staff of ILR Press and their reviewers. I would particularly like to thank Erica Fox for her interest and hard work on this project.

I. INTRODUCTION

The Occupational Safety and Health Act (OSH Act) was enacted into federal law in 1970 "to assure safe and healthful working conditions for working men and women."[1] The act provides for the Occupational Safety and Health Administration (OSHA) to set and enforce regulations for workplace safety and health through a graduated system of civil penalties; for a separate agency, the Occupational Safety and Health Review Commission, to hear appeals concerning citations, including those resulting from errors made by inspectors, and to check the power of the enforcement branch; and for the National Institute of Occupational Safety and Health to conduct research and promote safety and health through education and information dissemination.

In addition to the right to a place of employment "free from recognized hazards," the OSH Act grants employees the right to be notified by their employer if they are being overexposed to toxic materials or harmful physical agents; the right to file a confidential complaint with OSHA regarding unsafe conditions; and the right not to be discriminated against by the employer for exercising any rights granted by the act. Employees also have the right to have representatives participate in an OSHA inspection.

Employer rights include the following: the right to an opening conference and to accompany an inspector on an inspection; the right to seek a variance from a standard if another equal or better protective method of control is found; and the right to appeal any citations and fines that may be issued as a result of an inspection.[2]

One of the aims in formulating the OSH Act was to assign responsibility for occupational safety and health to the one entity that has the power to effect physical or personnel changes in the workplace—the employer. Congress's hope was that most employers would comply voluntarily by referring to pertinent standards and texts and by seeking public or private help when necessary. The law was structured, however, so that compliance could be enforced through the use of penalties.

The 1970 OSH Act allows states to establish their own OSHA programs, modeled on the original act. Federal OSHA has the power to approve and if necessary repeal state programs and is required to monitor the activities of state plans on a continuing basis. Differences exist among individual programs, but states that have their own agencies are required to set up compliance programs and to enforce standards that are "at least as effective" as or identical to the federal program. Federal and state enforcement procedures are basically the same.

Within certain limits, enforcement policies for federal and state programs may differ. For the most part, however, the differences between federal and state programs are no greater than those that may occur within federal OSHA under different presidential administrations or among regional offices of federal OSHA.

How an OSHA Inspection Is Conducted

OSHA inspections are initiated in response to an employee complaint about unsafe working conditions or an accident or as a follow-up of an earlier inspection. An employer may also be selected for an inspection from an OSHA list of companies in high-hazard industries. Except under limited circumstances, employers are not given advance notice of inspections.

Upon arrival at a work site for an inspection, the inspector will contact an appropriate employer representative, most often a plant manager, site superintendent, or owner. After explaining the purpose of the visit and showing identification, the inspector will generally describe the three phases of the inspection: the opening conference, the walkaround, and the closing conference. Employer and employee representatives have the right to be included in all three phases.

The opening conference is held with management and the employee representative, if one is available. The inspector discusses the OSHA program, employer and employee rights and responsibilities under the OSH Act, and the procedures for conducting the inspection. The inspector will examine pertinent records, including those for illnesses and injuries, and obtain an overview of the business. He or she will also review components of the company's safety and health program, if there is one.

The next phase of the inspection is the walkaround of the plant or job site. Both the employer and employee representatives have the right to accompany the inspector on this "tour." The walkaround is intended to enable the inspector to observe firsthand the hazards employees face and to determine whether the business is complying with required safety and health regulations. Evaluations are expected to be objective and professional, and throughout the walkaround, the inspector points out unhealthful and unsafe conditions to the employer.

The inspector notes whether machines are properly guarded, personal protective equipment is being used, ventilation appears adequate, and any other necessary items for controlling hazards are present or absent. The inspector usually conducts employee interviews, in private, to learn more about potential hazards and the company's safety and health program. Should noise or airborne contaminants need to be measured, arrangements for testing are made, often for a few days later.

Once the walkaround and necessary tests have been conducted, the inspector holds a closing conference with the employer representative and employee representative, if available. Depending on the complexity of the inspection, the closing conference may be held on the same day as the opening conference or several weeks later.

During the closing conference, the inspector formally reports his or her findings concerning the company's safety and health program. If there are no violations, the inspection usually ends with an encouraging remark from the inspector. If a citation is issued, the employer is given a description of those items in violation of OSHA standards and is informed whether any of the violations are of a serious or otherwise penalizable nature. Alternatively, citations may be mailed to the employer soon after the inspection.

When penalties are imposed, they are determined based on the gravity of the hazard and on the employer's history and safety awareness. Maximum amounts for each first-instance serious violation range from $1,000 to $5,000 depending on the OSHA program. Higher penalties may be assessed for repeated violations, willful conduct, or failure to abate a previously identified hazard.

The inspector also establishes dates by which the violations must be corrected, in consultation with the employer, and suggests ways to eliminate the hazard or sources of assistance. Procedures for receiving extensions of abatement dates and the rights of appeal are also explained. The employer is required to post a copy of a citation at or near where the violation occurred for three days or until the violation is abated, whichever is longer.

Cited employers may appeal a citation, the penalty, and/or the abatement date. The employer has fifteen working days from the time the citation is received to file the appeal. Most OSHA programs have a method for reviewing a citation with an employer before the formal appeal is filed. Adjustments in the penalty and a settlement are often the outcome of these conferences.

In the absence of a settlement, a formal appeal is held before an administrative law judge. The burden of proof is on OSHA. Either party may contest the decision of the administrative law judge, first to the managing appeals commission or board and then through the judicial system, up through to the Supreme Court.

Employees may not appeal a violation, but they may appeal a decision by OSHA *not* to issue a violation. They may also contest the time an employer is allowed to abate a hazard or request an informal conference with OSHA to discuss any aspect of a citation. They are also allowed to participate in appeal hearings.

Industrial Hygiene

The hazards discussed in this book primarily affect workers' health rather than their safety. Health hazards in an occupational setting include those that may cause harm through exposure to chemicals, noise, or microwave radiation. Examples include hearing loss as a result of noise, a fatal respiratory disease caused by inhaling minerals such as asbestos or silica, or a debilitating injury to the nervous system as a result of contact with a chemical that can penetrate the skin. In contrast, safety hazards include those that can cause death or injury by burial or fall or as a result of physical contact with machinery or electricity.

Health hazards generally are investigated by compliance health officers, called industrial hygienists, who are trained to recognize, evaluate, and help control health hazards in an industrial setting. Because of the complexities of evaluating and documenting hazards, the administators of the OSH Act and equivalent state acts have separated matters of safety and health so that there are two categories of inspectors: safety inspectors and industrial hygiene inspectors. Small companies in the private sector may have one person who oversees both safety and health, whereas many large companies have specialists, as in OSHA.

One of the primary concerns of the industrial hygienist is evaluating the amount of contaminant or physical agent to which a person has been exposed and which can enter or otherwise affect his or her body. Equally important is whether the amount of exposure is sufficient to cause physical harm. Much of his or her time an industrial hygienist is concerned with airborne contaminants, which have to be sampled with special instruments and equipment to determine the exposure level. The sampled level is then compared with legal and recommended limits.

The exposure levels of a contaminant in the air are usually expressed in parts of X contaminant per million parts of air or in milligrams of X contaminant per cubic meter of air. For example, visualize for a moment 999,999 white marbles in a given space and one red marble buried among the white marbles. It can be said that there is one part red marble per 1 million parts "contaminated" white marbles, abbreviated 1 ppm. Similarly, 1,000 parts hydrogen cyanide gas to 1 million parts of contaminated air (1,000 ppm) can be generated in a plating shop as a result of a salt solution of copper cyanide being accidentally mixed with an acid solution. At levels above 300 ppm, equivalent to 0.03 percent, hydrogen cyanide is immediately lethal, although it is only a small fraction of the air.

As another example, one milligram of titanium dioxide dust per cubic meter of air (1 mg/m^3) is thrown up during light sanding of a metal part for a jet airplane. This level is equivalent to a speck of metal being dispersed throughout small particles of dust, smaller than the human eye can discern, and distributed evenly in about a three-foot-by-three-foot cube. This concentration of titanium dioxide is one-tenth the exposure limit and poses no risk for most people who inhale it every day. Exposure limits for airborne contaminants are provided with a time factor for exposure. This follows from a principle of toxicology that, besides the concentration level, the amount of toxicant that can safely be taken into the body depends on the length of time of the exposure. Most limits are for an eight-hour workday, calculated as an eight-hour time-weighted average (8 hr TWA). What this means is that excessive levels may be experienced during the workday but the average exposure must be equal to or less than the established limit. For most of the working population *but not all*, day-in and day-out exposure at or below a limit during a forty-hour week is believed not to cause ill health even over a working lifetime.[3]

Not all chemical exposure limits are based on eight-hour exposure. Some chemicals can cause harm in a shorter time if the level is high enough. For instance, spraying an enamel paint containing toluene in a room with minimal ventilation could cause the painters to experience serious symptoms, even if they were painting for only an hour. To prevent the fast-acting effects of toluene, OSHA adopted a short-term exposure limit of 150 ppm, averaged over any fifteen-minute period.

Scope of the Book

The inspections described in this book are typical of OSHA health inspections in which there is serious noncompliance. The hazards represented—absestos, solvents, lead, noise, carbon monoxide, and formaldehyde—are some of the most prevalent occupational health risks in the nation. Over time, tens of thousands of workers throughout the work force, a few here and a dozen there, in hundreds of thousands of workplaces across America, are affected. Some are at immediate risk; others will suffer at some time in the future.

The inspection narratives are grouped by hazard. Each chapter begins with a discussion of the health effects of the hazard to help the reader understand the reason for regulation and the risk workers face. Several of the discussions also include background on how the chemical benefits society. Chronicled throughout are the hard-won battles OSHA and other groups have waged to pass today's regulations.

2. ASBESTOS

A sbestos is a fibrous mineral with unique physical properties. It does not conduct electricity, is resistant to fire, and is an outstanding insulation against heat and cold. It is nearly indestructible and can be powderized and mixed with cement, spun and woven into textiles, or pressed to form a paper.

As a result of these and other unique properties, asbestos has found its way into thousands of products since it was produced commercially around the turn of the century. For many years, it was used to make a sprayed-on insulation for acoustical ceilings and steel girders. Much of this insulation is still in place, "decorating" ceilings or protecting steel girders from buckling in the event of a fire. Asbestos was also used as an insulation for electrical wires, steam pipes, and boilers until substitutes were found. Thousands of tons of asbestos fibers strengthen products such as cement pipe, outdoor siding, and shingles, while thousands of tons of products made from asbestos cement enclose buildings or transport storm water and sewage. Asbestos has also been widely used as an insulating and reinforcing agent in the manufacture of roofing tar paper and vinyl floor tiles and in certain fire-resistant paper products and textiles. The mineral was even used at one time in welding blankets and in fire fighters' and foundry workers' fire- and heat-resistant protective clothing. Its outstanding insulating properties still favor its use in brake shoes and clutch discs. These and other asbestos-containing products sold well, and asbestos is now all around us—in the cars we drive, the machines we work with, and the buildings we work in.[1]

But, despite its usefulness, asbestos has caused some serious health effects. Tens of thousands of once-unsuspecting workers and consumers have already been affected, and many more will be in the future. What has been learned, tragically, is that the penalty for unsafe use of the mineral and its products can be death. Chronic exposure beginning at the age of eighteen can result in death by the age of forty and in some cases sooner.

Death from asbestos exposure can take several forms, including asbestosis, lung cancer, mesothelioma, and other cancers. Asbestosis is a lung disease caused by exposure to high levels of asbestos dust. A noncancerous yet disabling and deadly disease, asbestosis occurs as a result of indestructible microscopic asbestos fibers lodging deep in the lungs and, in time, causing a buildup of scar tissue. The fibers both scar and stiffen the lungs, inhibiting their ability to expand and reducing the volume of air that can be inspired, progressing to partial or full manifestation of the disease.

The first symptom, usually shortness of breath with exercise, is often not noticed until nearly a decade after the victim's first exposure to asbestos. Symptoms may then progress to shortness of breath even while at rest, coughing, noises from the lungs called "rales," a bluish or purplish color to the mucous membranes and skin, loss of weight, for some a feeling of pain and tightness in the chest, and eventually, in the most severe cases, death. The victim slowly, incrementally, suffocates. Some victims in the latter stages of the disease must carry a bottle of oxygen with them just to stay alive. Death can occur from pulmonary hypertension or attendant lung infections or from cardiac failure because of the destruction of the lungs.

Exposure to asbestos can also cause cancer. Some heavily exposed groups have suffered an incidence rate of more than 50 percent. Cancer of the lung poses the greatest threat and is often fatal. Lung cancer from asbestos exposure usually has a long latency period, some twenty or more years after exposure has begun. Smoking increases the risk of the disease, so that smokers who are chronically exposed to asbestos have a ninety-two times greater chance of getting lung cancer than the general population of nonsmokers.

Another disease caused by asbestos exposure, called mesothelioma, is a cancer of the tissue membranes that surround the lung cavity and abdominal organs. It has a latency period of thirty to forty years, spreads rapidly from its place of origin to other areas, and is usually fatal. It is extremely rare among people who have not been exposed to asbestos but accounts for 10 to 18 percent of asbestos-induced cancer. Other forms of cancer have also been observed at higher rates among asbestos workers than among the general population, though with less frequency than lung cancer or mesothelioma.

The adverse effects of asbestos exposure were known as far back as two thousand years ago in ancient Rome, where slaves were required to work with the mineral. And it is now known that between the 1930s and 1960s—the "boom" years for asbestos—much of the asbestos industry in the United States was aware of its adverse effects but hid and then denied the hazards.[2] In the meantime, hundreds of thousands of workers making or using asbestos products were exposed, and many died as a result.

The regulatory history of asbestos in the workplace (i.e., enforceable national standards) starts with the 1970 OSH Act, some forty years after American workers first began seeking compensation for diseases resulting from exposure. Earlier enforceable regulations were weak and limited in scope and, for most workers, nonexistent before 1970. The OSH Act promised mandatory risk reduction for workers across the nation, with the opportunity for further risk reduction as the need could be proven or political opposition overcome.

The earliest voluntary standard for asbestos in the United States, set in 1938, recommended a limit equivalent to thirty fibers per cubic centimeter of air (30 f/cc).[3] By contrast, the first OSHA-determined asbestos exposure level, adopted in May 1971, was 12 f/cc as an eight-hour time-weighted average. This level was presumed to be one workers could be exposed to for a lifetime "without undue risk"—a chilling thought by current standards.

At the time OSHA adopted the mandatory 12 f/cc standard in 1971, many health scientists thought this level was too high. The Industrial Union Department of the AFL-CIO acted on this concern and that same year petitioned federal OSHA to adopt a lower standard. As a result of this effort, an emergency standard of 5 f/cc was adopted in December 1971 and affirmed six months later. Included in the standard was a statement that the level would be dropped to 2 f/cc in 1976. In setting the new standard, OSHA indicated that the risk of cancer from asbestos exposure had not been fully considered and that both the 5 and 2 f/cc limits had been set to prevent asbestosis.

In October 1975, at the insistence of the AFL-CIO, OSHA proposed that the level be lowered to 0.5 f/cc.[4] It was OSHA's stated attempt to regulate asbestos as a human carcinogen at what was thought at the time to be the lowest level that could be achieved by industry and be measurable. The proposal was put on hold and its supporting documentation was later shot down by the courts in a decision over the standard for the carcinogen benzene, during which OSHA's method of risk assessment was rebuked. This loss was mildly atoned for in July 1976, however, when the enforceable standard was automatically lowered to 2 f/cc.

The issue did not die, though. The National Institute of Occupational Safety and Health (NIOSH), the research branch of OSHA, in December 1976 recommended that the standard be lowered to 0.1 f/cc. At the time, thousands of workers were breathing in asbestos at levels far above this limit. Surveys of some plants revealed exposures in the range of 0.3 to 22 f/cc, requiring the use of respirators in many operations.[5] One study in 1975 showed surprisingly high exposures (9.9 to 26.2 f/cc) among workers who wore asbestos fire- and heat-proof protective clothing.

In November 1983, OSHA again attempted to lower the limit to 0.5 f/cc through the issuance of an emergency temporary standard. The asbestos industry immediately challenged the lower standard through a group unabashedly called the Asbestos Industry Association. The association won, and the emergency standard was stayed by the courts and thrown out in March 1984 as invalid.

OSHA countered a month later with another proposal in which it recommended a new exposure limit and a comprehensive set of rules for asbestos control. This proposal also applied to the construction industry, which previous proposals, directed instead at fixed industries, had ignored. The proposal, however, was stalled.

Finally, two years later, in July 1986, a comprehensive standard was passed that included an exposure limit of 0.2 f/cc. This standard sets forth rules on how the limit and other protective measures are to be met and applies to all industries, including construction. A court challenge by a business group called the Asbestos Information Association, made up of fifty or so companies involved in the mining of asbestos or the manufacture of asbestos-containing products, failed to alter the standard significantly.

OSHA maintained that the 0.2 f/cc limit was necessary to reduce the risk of cancer and asbestosis to a minimal yet feasible level. Feasible was defined as capable of being measured in the air and complied with by the affected industries without prohibiting use. (Banning of substances is in the purview of other agencies, such as the Environmental Protection Agency.) Over a fifteen-year period, the mandatory exposure limit for asbestos had been reduced from 12 f/cc to 0.2 f/cc—*a sixtyfold drop.*

Years of unregulated use of asbestos have left much human data regarding the potency of asbestos exposure. Much of this information was included in the documentation OSHA used to support the 1986 standard. Consider the following risk assessments, for example:

- For every thousand workers exposed to asbestos time-weighted averages of 0.2 f/cc for forty hours a week for a working lifetime (forty-five years), seven will die from an asbestos-induced cancer and five will suffer from asbestosis. (Note that the standard does not prevent all cancer; it only reduces the risk.)

- At the previous exposure limit of 2.0 f/cc, the risk was such that sixty-four people would die from asbestos cancer and fifty would contract the disabling asbestosis for every thousand exposed workers.

- Occupational exposure for one year to 0.1 f/cc, a value that can currently be exceeded at many workplaces using or manufacturing asbestos or at construction sites involved in demolition, results in about 15 deaths out of 100,000 so exposed, and one year of work exposure to 10 f/cc, which is near and above the level to which thousands of temporary employees have undoubtedly been exposed and just a shade under OSHA's first-ever exposure limit of 12 f/cc, results in about 1,271 cancer deaths per 100,000 workers.[6]

The risk is greater, of course, at higher levels of exposure and for longer periods of time, which is why epidemiological studies have found that groups of workers who were highly exposed to asbestos often suffered death rates of more than 50 percent. OSHA admits that a significant risk still exists at the 0.2 f/cc level but that the current exposure limit is based "on a determination that this level is the lowest level that can feasibly be attained in operations in workplaces in both general industry and construction."[7]

There is currently a background level of asbestos to which we are all exposed, estimated to be 0.003 to 0.0000003 f/cc in outdoor air, depending on whether we live in an urban or rural area. One risk assessment by the National Research Council estimated that the cancer risk for the urban public exposed to ambient levels of asbestos for twenty-four hours a day for a lifetime is 1 to 7 out of 100,000 exposed.[8] (The current lifetime risk of death from cancer from all causes, including smoking, is about 25 percent or 25,000 out of 100,000.)

Many products are still made from asbestos, including certain papers, textiles, cement pipes and sheets, tiles, felts, and friction products such as brake shoes. Other products and uses have been banned over the years. In the 1970s, for example, the Environmental Protection Agency (EPA) banned the application of sprayed-on asbestos in buildings and of asbestos-containing pipe lagging, and the Consumer Products Safety Commission banned the use of asbestos in consumer patching compounds and artificial fire logs. In 1986, the EPA proposed a ban on the manufacture, importation, and processing of asbestos cement pipe and fittings, roofing felts, flooring felts, vinyl asbestos floor tile, and asbestos clothing. Included in the proposal was a plan to phase out other products containing asbestos, such as brake shoes and clutch discs, as substitutes become available.[9]

Regardless of future action by the EPA on the manufacture and importation of asbestos-containing products, asbestos will be with us in products and structures for many years, along with the opportunity for significant exposure and risk from its unsafe use, particularly during the demolition of asbestos-containing materials (asbestos in a contained form and without physical action to release fibers poses no risk). The 1986 comprehensive OSHA standard for control of exposure to asbestos, if enforced and complied with, will help considerably in preventing deaths from occupational exposure to the still widely used materials containing asbestos.

The Asbestos Wonderland

I had made inspections of asbestos rip-outs before, but the demolition of a former Johns-Manville plant was of a different magnitude.

"How soon can you get out there?" Dave, my boss and district manager, asked as he gave me the assignment. A subcontractor had filed a complaint, alleging that the main demolition contractor was being too carefree with asbestos.

From the tone in his voice, I sensed it was going to be a difficult inspection. "In about an hour," I replied.

I went to our file cabinets and looked at the Johns-Manville file. There had been several inspections at the plant over the years. Results from air monitoring, both the company's and ours, had indicated that the levels for the manufacturing operations were below the two-fiber limit then enforced. But there had been no recent inspections. No one had mentioned to me that a Johns-Manville plant even existed in the state, presumably because the plant had been closed down for some time. The file also showed that the company had received a "serious/repeat" citation almost seven years before for an asbestos "spill" when dust containing asbestos had been spilled and not cleaned up. Johns-Manville had appealed the citation, which carried a fine of $260, lost the appeal in a decision a year later, and appealed again to the next level. The company had lost that appeal too, but, more interesting, the decision had inexplicably come seven years after the citation was originally issued and while the plant was in the midst of being demolished. The file had confirmed the obvious: the plant had definitely made asbestos-containing products.

Later that day, a safety inspector and I were heading out for the plant. Approaching our turnoff, we looked for the plant but could not find it among the refinery towers and other buildings in the rundown industrial area. About halfway along the road, three buildings with gray corrugated walls and roofs, rising thirty to forty feet, loomed ahead. Nearing the end of the road, we passed by the plant's empty parking lot: weeds grew tall through the cracks in the asphalt. As we turned to park, the six-foot-high block letters on a side of one of the buildings stood out as if they were written in bright red rather than the now-fading black: JOHNS-MANVILLE.

We got out of the car and walked toward the former administrative building, where we were met by Jim Levy, the site superintendent for the demolition contractor, Malbuc.

After the formalities of the opening conference, Levy briefly explained that his dad, who owned part of Malbuc Construction as well as his own construction company, had given Levy the demolition project to run. His dad and his partners had bought the remaining equipment and structures from Johns-Manville through a bid and planned to resell all salable equipment and scrap any remaining metal for money. Johns-Manville still owned the land, he explained, and was trying to sell it.

Levy further explained that the job had been started about three months earlier and that he was using a fourteen-man crew to salvage the steel and other parts that could be scrapped. Subcontractors had bid and paid cash for the right to scrap certain parts, such as the electrical wire, motors, cranes, lights, and even some of the buildings that could be dismantled, moved, and rebuilt.

We told Levy that we needed to tour the site, interview workers, and possibly take some samples. Levy offered no resistance and led us out of the office.

We headed toward the east end of the building where asbestos cement pipe had been manufactured. The pipe was made of Portland cement, sand, and asbestos and was used extensively for water mains, sewer pipes, storm drains, and utility ducts. About 200,000 miles of the pipe had been used in the United States alone. Some of the pipes were large enough for an adult to stand in or for thousands of gallons of water to flow through each minute.

Inside the building, the roof and walls were mostly intact. There were man-sized holes at various spots in the roof where someone had apparently knocked out portions to retrieve something salvageable. The holes seemed to be where the ceiling lights had been. Most of the inside of the building had already been gutted, and the contractor had set up a cleared area for forklifts and heavy tractors.

A little farther west, the process equipment was still bolted into the cement floor, but in other places, all that was left was duct work hanging from the ceiling. Off to the side, two cutters worked their acetylene and oxygen torches over a doomed piece of equipment, showering orange sparks onto the cement floor. The floor was marred and pocked and littered with dirt, oil, plastic remnants of wire, nuts, bolts, and other miscellaneous rejections of a salvage crew that had time only for what it could sell.

In the center of the building stood rows of long giant autoclaves that I later learned had been used to cure the newly formed pipes. Toward the front of one of the autoclaves, the encasing wire and black covering had been removed, along with white insulation, which formed a sizable pile on the floor. A large bare spot of steel showed through. Someone had stripped the insulation to check the autoclaves for their worth in steel.

"Did any of your crew strip the insulation?" I asked Levy.

"No, I don't think so."

I stepped into the area and picked up a small piece of the insulation so that I could have it analyzed for asbestos, placed it in a plastic bag, and marked where it had come from. I snapped several photographs. We continued with the tour of the building.

Over in the far west corner was another large pile of insulation on the floor. Directly above was a steam pipe with insulation missing. I took a sample and pictures.

In this portion of the building, large production equipment remained that had not yet been sold or salvaged. Climbing onto a platform, I could see where the asbestos cement slurry once flowed on its way to being formed into the shape of a cylinder. I chipped off a piece of the dried cement from the process bed for analysis.

We next stepped outside. The baghouses used for air pollution control were still connected by several large metal ducts to the pipe-manufacturing building. The baghouses had been installed to recover the dust generated from the mixing and machining operations and to filter out the dust so that mostly clean air was returned to the environment. The steel, boxlike baghouses were on stilts, so that their tops rose at least twenty-five feet. I climbed to the first level and found a small hatch. A yellow plate near the hatch warned of an asbestos hazard:

Caution
Asbestos
Avoid Creating Dust
Breathing Dust May Cause Serious Body Harm

I cracked the door and took a sample of a gray flufflike mineral substance.

Back on the ground, I called over two workers and spoke with them privately. Both of them appeared to be in their early twenties. I explained that I was an OSHA inspector, checking out whether the workers handling asbestos at the site were being protected.

"Did you guys get any training or information on an asbestos hazard here?"

"No."

"Did either of you have to go inside the baghouse?"

"Yeah, I did," one of the workers replied.

"What did you do in there?"

"I was told to go in and check out how it might be demolished, how much metal might be inside."

"Did you know that there might be asbestos in there?"

"I thought there might be. Shouldn't we be wearing masks or something?"

"If there is asbestos in there, yes; you should have been protected." The poor guy had probably gotten a lifetime of asbestos exposure working in the baghouse, I thought. "There are probably other areas around here where you might be exposed."

"I knew this job was full of shit. The stuff we have to do. I knew that things weren't right. I don't need to get cancer. These guys here are full of shit."

He went on for a few more minutes about the place and concluded by saying, "I'm not going to work here anymore." I told him I would issue citations to the contractor if safety violations were being committed, but that did not seem to convince him to continue working for Levy. I thanked them and let them go back to work, or home.

From the baghouse, we cut across the center yard toward another manufacturing building. On the way, we came upon a pile of steam pipes that had been stripped of their insulation. Patches of white, caulky, fibrous material were scattered over a fifteen-by-thirty-foot area.

"Who worked on these pipes?" I asked Levy.

"Oh, I guess some of our cutters. I'm not sure. It could have been left by Johns-Manville people." His credibility was slowly sinking.

I took pictures and some samples of the insulation. It would have to be cleaned up promptly if it contained asbestos.

We continued over to the other manufacturing building, where most of the demolition was going on. Outside, on the far western end of the building, a large barren concrete pad showed evidence of having been the site of processing equipment. Off to the side of the pad sat several pieces of six-foot-high semicircles of steel plate. Two cutters slowly burned through the inch-thick steel, breaking what probably was a process tower into smaller sections that could be more easily loaded and stored on a truck bed for transportation to the harbor.

"Hey, can I talk with you?" I yelled to one of the cutters, staying out of reach of the sparks. The cutter shut off his torch and lifted up his goggles.

I walked over to him and introduced myself. I learned that he had been at the site since the job started and was aware that there was asbestos around.

"What areas have you been working in?" I asked.

"Oh, the yard, and both these buildings."

"Do you know who stripped the insulation off the autoclaves or the steam pipes?"

"Yeah, I did. We had to get a look at the metal."

"Did you remove it dry?"

"No, we wetted it down with a hose first."

"Did you wear any respirators or clothing or take any other precautions?"

"No. It doesn't matter. I'm too old to get cancer from this stuff."

"How old are you?"

"Sixty-one."

"Yeah, you probably won't get cancer from this job, but I'm worried about the younger guys who have more years ahead of them."

The cutter nodded. I thanked him for his time.

Levy and I walked into the west end of the building and found six cutters working over a steel frame that must have held additional processing equipment and now supported only a second level, which would itself be scrapped for iron. Levy explained that they were just about done with this building. The processing equipment in the center, as well as the building itself, might be sold, he said.

I talked with several of the cutters and learned that they had just recently been hired and that they had not stripped any asbestos. I found no problems in this section, so we continued our walkaround of the building.

We soon met up with another one of Levy's partners and, to my surprise, the former Johns-Manville plant manager. I held a quick opening conference with both of them. Levy then excused himself and left his partner to complete the inspection.

Levy's partner appeared nice enough on the surface, but I could sense through our initial small talk that he was concerned with the problems I might pose for him.

I asked the plant manager several questions about the site and its former production activities.

He explained that the building we were in was where asbestos brick insulation, called Thermo-12, was made, but that the company had switched about five years earlier to a nonasbestos product made from lime and silica. He pointed to some asbestoslike material on the ground and some bricks of white friable insulation in a drying box off to the side. He said that the material was the nonasbestos product they made before the plant was closed. (Later that day I took a sample of the material to be analyzed; by this time I did not trust anyone.)

We talked about the other areas at the site where there might have been asbestos. In response to a question about whether Johns-Manville might have left any asbestos debris on the floors or strewn about outside, the plant manager replied that the company had cleaned the manufacturing areas during the closing, leaving the floors and outside yards clean. "We cleaned the building—washed the equipment, even the walls."

"Oh, yeah," added Levy's partner, "the floors were so clean, you could eat off them." I wrote that comment down verbatim.

We continued with the walkaround, leaving the brick-insulation manufacturing building and passing by some now-dry waste ponds on the far north end of the site.

"There shouldn't be much asbestos in those ponds," the plant manager replied to a question about contamination.

Farther along, we passed a small storage shed. Inside were some curious-looking barrels against a wall. A closer look revealed that the labels on the fifty-five-gallon barrels read "ASBESTOS."

"What's the percentage?" I asked.

"One hundred percent."

It was pretty late in the afternoon, so we made the boiler room our last stop. It was located in the building where the pipes had been lined with vinyl chloride polymer and was full of insulated pipe.

"Asbestos?" I asked, pointing to the insulated pipe.

"Yes," the plant manager said.

On the half-mile walk back to the office, the plant manager and I fell back so we could talk privately. In a confidential tone, he said that the contractor had been "messing up" by exposing his employees to asbestos and not following the regulations and that the contractor, not Johns-Mansville, was responsible for all the asbestos debris. He added that he was glad to see OSHA inspecting. He explained that Johns-Manville had sold the demolition job to the "lowest bidder," but he had soon found out that the company doing the job knew nothing about asbestos. He said he had tried to change their ways but had been unable to.

I asked him if the contract called for complying with California OSHA regulations.

"Yes, it did," he replied.

"Why didn't you shut the job down, or give us a call? Johns-Manville even has its own industrial hygienists. Why didn't they come out here and help?" I asked somewhat accusingly. With that, the conversation ended.

Arriving at the row of administrative buildings, we stepped into the contractor's makeshift office, which appeared to be the remains of an executive's office. It had been redecorated with the plant's future in mind: nothing on the walls, a desk littered with empty beer cans, and a floor that was used as a wastebasket. I held a conference here with Levy, his partner, their foreman, the Johns-Manville plant manager, and the OSHA safety engineer.

I first reviewed what I had observed and explained that I would be submitting all the samples I had taken to the laboratory for asbestos analysis. I warned them that there was undoubtedly plenty of asbestos at the site and that I thought their handling procedures were not up to OSHA standards. I asked them not to do any more work with suspected asbestos-containing materials until I got back to them the next day. They agreed but acknowledged that they would have to work with it in the future and took issue with my saying they had not been handling the asbestos correctly.

"Couldn't we clean it off our clothes with an air hose?" Levy asked. The OSHA safety engineer looked at me and rolled his eyes.

"No, that's one of the worst things you could do. It would just put it into the air for you to breathe," I explained.

Levy asked for a copy of the asbestos regulation. Their foreman followed up by asking whether asbestos was known to cause cancer.

"I would like to take you to a hospital with some shipyard workers, who could best answer that question," I replied. "Many people have already died from asbestos-induced cancer."

Their ignorance and irresponsibility made me sad. The contractor may have been naive as far as bidding on the demolition job and not considering what was involved, but that did not absolve him of the need to comply with safety and health laws. I could not figure out whether the contractor had simply made a bad business decision or, rather, whether Malbuc had consciously decided to take on the job and work around any problems a regulatory agency might pose. Someone at Johns-Manville should have known better.

At the close of the meeting, I told the contractors that we would be back the next day with the laboratory results.

Before I could enforce any corrective steps on what appeared to be a bona fide asbestos disaster, we first had to get the samples analyzed. Legally, OSHA could not take steps or issue a violation without documentation that asbestos was present.

We left the site with six samples. I had used all the sample bags I had brought and could have filled a dozen more.

I returned to the site the next afternoon and spent a couple of hours exploring other areas of the operation that I had missed the first day. The day two tour was presented by the Johns-Manville plant manager and Levy's partner. The additional walkaround proved fruitful. I found a well-dusted ball mill, some other baghouses, and another set of insulated autoclaves away from the manufacturing building. I took additional samples to identify contaminated areas that needed cleaning up and possible asbestos in structures that were still intact.

The main discovery on day two was two waste ponds on the south end of the site. The drains and waste from the pipe-manufacturing building had been poured into these ponds over the years. It was an ugly site, more so since I knew the ponds were full of asbestos. One pond was dry; the other still had water in it. The dry pond was the larger of the two, measuring about three hundred feet long and one hundred feet wide. The surface was cracked and crumbly, like a miniature Death Valley. The smaller pond was partly filled with water and about half the size of its neighbor. The ponds had once been a necessary part of the manufacturing process, but now they were all liability.

Later that afternoon, I asked the demolition partner about his crew's asbestos-handling practices. He finally admitted that his employees had been stripping off asbestos insulation and crawling around much of the contaminated equipment. He contradicted what had been said the day before, that the crew consistently used wet methods to contain the dust, had respirators, and even used disposable protective suits. When I asked him to show me the protective equipment, he replied, after a cursory look, that "they must have been stolen." It was time to give the office a call for the lab results.

I called the office and talked with my supervisor, who had the results. Five out of the six samples had contained asbestos, he said, up to 70 percent by weight. The contractor's work was now linked to samples positive for asbestos, in hazardous concentrations. Employees had been exposed without any warning on the hazards of asbestos and without training in safe handling practices. Additionally, large areas of the site had been contaminated.

"Well, Dave, I think I'm going to have to shut them down," I told my supervisor over the phone.[10]

"Do what you have to. Let them know about their right to hold an informal conference. I'll set aside Monday morning."

An informal conference is a right provided to employers issued a shutdown order so they can discuss or challenge the order with OSHA officials.

I hung up the phone and looked around the room. There was silence for about a minute. The faces of the demolition partners and the foreman turned from disbelief into anger. I was surprised to see the Johns-Manville manager so surprised, even hurt. He spoke first.

"Isn't that a little drastic?"

"No. There is no compliance out here. Too much asbestos debris is scattered about, and the workers haven't been trained for the hazards. There's just too much asbestos and uncontrolled demolition. We have to have an abatement plan before work can continue," I replied.

"You can't shut us down," Levy jumped in. "We have crews working; we'll lose money. It's just not that bad. The guys aren't getting into asbestos now. You can't shut us down when we're only cutting steel."

"They have to be kept out of the asbestos areas until they know where they are and the mess has been cleaned up by a protected crew," I countered.

"There's no asbestos in the brick-insulation building where we're cutting now. Let us work in there until this thing gets straightened out, and then we won't have to lay off any of the crew. They don't have that easy a time finding work. We may have about three to four more days to do in there with the entire crew cutting."

Levy had a point. Although there was overwhelming evidence of disregard for the asbestos regulations, I was hard pressed to come up with a legal rationalization for keeping them from cutting steel in an area where there was no hazard.

"Okay. I'll tag-out all areas other than the west end of the brick-insulation building, where you can cut steel. I want it explained to your crew about the tag-out and the asbestos hazard at the site."

The OSHA safety engineer and I went out and hung tags on stands and equipment in the restricted area, which encompassed more than two-thirds of the sixty-acre site. When we had finished hanging the tags, I asked the demolition foreman to get his workers together so I could talk with them.

"I'm an industrial hygiene inspector with OSHA, and I have been conducting an inspection about the possible asbestos hazard at this site. There is a lot of asbestos here, and you guys will need to get training in how to protect yourselves, and the company will have to put together a control program. Asbestos is a known carcinogen and can cause lung disease. I have shut down most of the site except the west end of the brick-insulation building. You won't get into asbestos if you stay in that area and cut. We'll lift the shutdown after the mess is cleaned up and the company is complying with the state's OSHA standard. Any questions?"

"Yeah. Will we get showers and suits to wear?" one cutter asked.

"Maybe. It will depend on what you'll be doing. The guys actually working with asbestos will need to be protected. The rest of you will just need to know where it is and stay away from it. Any more questions? If anyone works in the restricted area, the company could get fined $1,000 and someone could be charged with a misde-meanor."

As the crew broke to go home, some workers grumbled. The older cutters gave me cold stares. They knew they would be cutting for only a few more days and then would be laid off.

Before leaving the site, I talked to the contractors about the need for compliance with the asbestos standard and the requirement for an abatement plan to clean up the existing mess and deal with the rest of the demolition properly. I urged them to hire an outside consultant, since handling asbestos was more than they should have had to deal with themselves. My suggestion for professional help got no response, though if ever professional help was needed on a demolition job, it was at a plant that had manufactured and used asbestos-containing materials on as grand a scale as this one did.

I asked the Johns-Manville manager to get some support from his office by getting a corporate industrial hygienist involved. Johns-Manville should have done this from day one, and especially once they had selected a contractor with no experience with asbestos demolition. The plant manager remained silent.

Levy promised he would work on a written abatement plan over the upcoming weekend and bring it to the informal conference planned for the following Monday.

I was grateful to get out of the place. It was my first shutdown, and it had taken some gritting of my teeth to tell Levy and his partners that they were temporarily out of business. I looked over my shoulder more than once while walking back to my car.

As the safety engineer and I drove out, I stopped by the guard shack and asked the teenage guard whether he had done any asbestos removal at the site.

"No. My dad won't let me work in there with all that asbestos. I'm just to watch the gate."

"Good for your dad."

When I asked him who his dad was, it turned out to be one of Levy's partners. The partner had enough doubts about the job to prevent his son from working there.

The Monday after the shutdown, Levy came into the OSHA office and sat down to discuss his abatement plan. He presented his plan, stiffly joking that he had not done so much writing since high school. It did not take us long to review the two pages he handed us. The plan looked as though it had been developed by someone who knew very little about asbestos control.

The OSHA regional supervisor, who also attended the conference, rejected the plan and allowed the shutdown to continue. After tactfully explaining the inadequacies of the plan, we gave Levy a copy of an asbestos abatement program another contractor had developed. We told Levy that the plan would help him rewrite his own. We also gave him a publication from the National Institute of Occupational Safety and Health that contained background material for setting up an asbestos control program and training for his crew. We tried to impress upon him the magnitude and difficulty of the project he had taken on and urged him to seek the advice of a consultant.

Levy took the material but refused our suggestion to seek outside help, saying he could do it himself. There was no law forbidding this. The California OSHA regulation at the time allowed anybody to do asbestos work, as long as they followed the standards requiring that asbestos be cleaned up promptly, dust suppression methods used, and the workers protected. The burden was on OSHA to prove wrongdoing. Unfortunately, given the delay in deciding appeals and the amount of proof necessary to obtain a temporary restraining order from the superior court, "bad actors" could contaminate an area and be long gone, escaping justice.

The abatement plan Levy was asked to prepare would at least force him to think about the asbestos hazard and what constituted proper work practices, although it was not required by any standard. Given the magnitude of the hazard at the site, we felt comfortable in asserting our authority beyond its usual bounds.

We were on firmer ground for the shutdown, however, and flatly told Levy that his crew could not do asbestos work until the workers were trained and an asbestos control program was in place. We further informed him that someone from our office would attend his worker training. We concluded the conference by saying that citations for the earlier violations would be issued at a later date. Levy argued over the demands but lost. Though his eyes were shaded by dark glasses, it was easy to sense his rage. He left quietly, promising to drop off the revised plan as soon as he could.

Several days later, Levy submitted a revised plan. It was nearly identical to the sample we had given him. He also told us the date he planned to train his crew in asbestos handling.

The required training session was given to about twelve crew members and three OSHA officials, including myself, my boss, and his boss, the regional supervisor. Surprisingly, the training, which was given by Levy's foreman, was well done. I later learned that the foreman had read the entire NIOSH document we had given to Levy and had taken everything to heart.

Besides classroom training, members of the crew were taken on a tour to help them identify asbestos-containing materials. The foreman pointed at different areas of asbestos contamination and explained that a separate cleanup crew would be designated and that those workers selected would be required to wear respirators and disposable suits, to use wet removal procedures, and to bag the asbestos material as they went.

At the conclusion of the employee-training program, the cleanup crews were permitted to go to work, and the tagged-out areas were progressively lifted as the asbestos was cleaned up. We started to have hope for the project.

I monitored the cleanup crew on its first assignment by placing samplers on workers who were assigned to bag asbestos insulation waste from the pipe-manufacturing building. The crews wore approved paper respirators and disposable protective clothing. I also took several area samples in the building and outdoors, particularly by the waste ponds. The latter samples were taken in an effort to see whether the location was contaminated enough to produce high background levels of asbestos even outside.

The laboratory reported the results of my sampling within a week. A high value of 0.02 f/cc was reported for the breathing-zone samples of the workers and values of less than 0.01 f/cc for the areas outdoors, including those downwind of the dry asbestos pond. All values were strikingly below the action level of 0.10 f/cc and the ceiling level of 10 f/cc, at which protective clothing would have been required according to the standard then in effect. It was ironic, and demonstrated a weakness in the standard, that members of the cleanup crew were wallowing in asbestos up to their ankles, yet protective clothing technically was not required because the levels in the air were low. What might happen if the workers took their clothes home with them and the asbestos dried out in the meantime? The standard then in effect did not deal with this question as well as it could have. The inspector could call the clothes contaminated waste and require the worker to dispose of them at the end of the shift only if it could be documented that the worker would otherwise be exposed above the action level of 0.10 f/cc over an eight-hour period.

The low levels of asbestos in the air were surprising, but less so given that most of the work was completed in wide-open areas. Also, the members of the cleanup crew used their hands and a shovel to pick up the asbestos, which barely disturbed the material. And they used water—lots of it.

Now that the contractor was complying with the law, surpassing it in some instances, I met with Levy to close out the report.

Although the contractor was now in compliance, there were still about five pages of citations with fines. My explanation that the citations were all for "past sins" did not mollify the obviously upset Levy. The citations and fines may even have been on the light side, since the contract with Johns-Manville had called for compliance with California OSHA standards and there was a basis for citing Levy for willful neglect.

I went over each violation. The company received a serious citation for having uncontrolled asbestos spills in four locations, a serious citation for failure to inform and train the crew regarding the asbestos hazard, and an automatic $500 fine and citation for failure to notify our office before beginning the demolition job.

This latter requirement and its mandatory not-to-be-reduced fine were unique to California at the time. The state legislature had developed this useful requirement in an attempt to initiate greater motivation for compliance from day one of an asbestos job. The reasoning was that those who reported would in most cases comply better with the standards if they knew that they could be subject to an inspection. Those who did not wish to comply faced a nonnegotiable $500 penalty if caught. My experience had been that the result was greater compliance and fewer disasters. But there were exceptions.

Levy took the citations, complaining about unnecessary regulations and unjust fines. The fine totaled $1,775. I warned Levy that further fines could be imposed if there were more violations.

Levy called me back as I was leaving and demonstrated a coin-operated video game he had installed for his workers. I watched as he shot down invading spaceships on the screen, scoring several thousand points in less than a minute. He paused just long enough to say that the object of the game was to see how many times you could shoot down OSHA.

"See you on the follow-up," I said.

Within the fifteen-day time limit, Levy filed an appeal, contesting the violations as well as the amount of the penalties.

By the time of the follow-up, a Republican governor was in office and had replaced the entire top management of the California OSHA system with his own appointees. The previous management of the state OSHA system, appointed by a Democratic governor, had professed a belief in strong enforcement and in issuing tough regulations. The former executives made sure none of the field people were shy about issuing fines and frequently got involved in the bigger cases. (The OSH Act leaves some room for different enforcement policies, though not as much as many administrators and field supervisors, on both state and federal levels and on both political sides, exercise at times.) Now, with a new governor in office, there was some apprehension that policies and enforcement styles would be more relaxed, and there was some indication that the new deputy chief of OSHA expected more cooperation with the business community that came under OSHA sanction. In a recent memo to OSHA staff, he had lambasted a staff member for an error. Going beyond constructive criticism, the deputy chief had used the opportunity to set a tone of conciliation toward cited businesses. Through such memos and examples of "wrongdoing" by staff, changes in policy can be subtly and progressively effected, and in a manner that produces change without the strong criticism that surely would be generated in a press conference that outlined the new administration's goals.

As the new deputy chief accompanied me and my supervisor and my supervisor's boss, the regional manager, to the demolition site for the follow-up inspection, I could sense their uneasiness about how to handle Malbuc, the demolition contractor. Should they ease off and let the contractor "get the job done"? Field supervisors, like my boss, would be the first to face any change in the wind and would be the most susceptible to pressure, including possible transfers to undesirable locations.

The tour with the deputy chief included all of the carcinogenic attractions at the site: the asbestos ponds, the manufacturing buildings, and the asbestos burial sites. We even watched asbestos removal in progress.

Stopping in front of the boiler room, where the front wall had been removed, the tour group watched a rip-out job. One hundred feet away, a crew stripped insulation from numerous steam pipes. I was a little amused when, on leaving the area, the deputy chief walked right through a contaminated area, placing his shiny black shoes on patches of asbestos insulation.

After the tour, the deputy chief acknowledged the high potential for asbestos exposure. He gave little indication, at least to me, of his expectations for enforcement at the site.

The follow-up ended without any violations being observed.

About a month later, I initiated a second follow-up. Our office intended to keep a close eye on the project, or as best we could without being accused of harassing the contractor. We had grounds for being suspicious. Our suspicions, unfortunately, proved justified.

On walking the site with Levy, I found more uncontrolled spills than I had during the inspection that had led to the shutdown. There was asbestos-containing debris on the roadway, a busted barrel of 100 percent asbestos fibers with the gray fluffy material spilled out on the ground, and steam pipe insulation on the floor of one of the buildings. There was one other notable pile. In the concrete pit where the autoclaves in the pipe-manufacturing building once stood was a mound of stripped asbestos insulation, a volume estimated to be *160 cubic yards*!

More than interested, I asked Levy to explain what had happened. He related that the crew first began stripping the autoclaves by hand, using four workers suited up in protective equipment, but that he had found it was taking too long and costing more money than he wanted to spend. With so many autoclaves to strip, each nearly a hundred feet long and ten or more feet in diameter, they had tried something else. He explained that they had found that using a front-end loader with a large tractor bucket was far more efficient. They had simply cut loose an autoclave from its support brackets with torches, hooked a cable to it, and dragged it out of the pit with the front-end loader. The loader was then used to strip the insulation by running the cutting edge of its bucket along the top surface of the steel tube, breaking the metal retaining bands and stripping free the bricks of insulation. The asbestos bricks were then pushed into the rectangular autoclave pit, where the debris piled up. To control the dust, they applied water with a fire hose during the stripping. With the stripping now done, he hoped to leave the asbestos in the pit or to dump it all into Johns-Manville's waste pond. The massive steel autoclaves were thus cleansed of asbestos, one at a time.

Standing back from the pile of debris, I could see the last autoclave from the pit being cut into transportable pieces. The front-end loader used in the stripping was parked next to Levy's newly formed hazardous waste site. The loader showed evidence of its dirty work. Chunks of asbestos hung on the lower portions of its frame, and there were patches of white on the tires, as if they had driven through snow.

I asked Levy to wash the debris from the tractor into the pit before using it again.

"Oh, yeah. We plan to do that," he replied.

I was not very concerned about his particular removal method since it probably produced the least amount of exposure. Rather than having a crew of four labor directly with the material for weeks, he had one man in a tractor do it in a couple of days. It was a better method from a business standpoint and for worker protection. Levy was innovative, if not concerned about asbestos health hazards. Nonetheless, the remaining mess had to be cleaned up. He was supposed to have bagged or placed the debris in a plastic-lined dumpster while it was being stripped. The regulation was clear about that, and having been cited on this item, he knew it. The alternative—dumping the waste into the asbestos ponds—was not acceptable to Johns-Manville since the mess in the ponds also had to be removed sometime later.

During the walkaround, one of the workers caught up with me when I was alone. Requesting confidentiality, he said that the contractors had been talking about hauling the voluminous asbestos waste out at night and dumping it somewhere free of cost, illegally. The aim was to save money by not having to contain the asbestos or hire a licensed hauler to carry it away.

"You really think they would do it?" I asked.

"Yes. You don't know these people. I believe they would. They've been lying to you, doing as they please out here."

I asked him to keep me posted.

Concluding my walkaround for the second follow-up, I then held an exit conference with Levy and again explained that the asbestos waste was supposed to be cleaned up as crews worked or at the end of the day. I added that he would probably receive more citations and a fine.

Levy stood in front of me, a wild look on his face and a suspicious white stain on his cowboy boots. "I don't want to hear about any more fines," he said. "We've been trying our hardest out here. We're just trying to finish this job and be done with it. I hate this place, and I hate asbestos. Last night I dreamed that my kid was eating the stuff." Levy continued on about how he had not counted on the expense of the asbestos. He concluded our conference by saying that he might subcontract out much of the remaining work because his crews were "not efficient enough."

It did come down to efficiency or, what he actually meant, money. If he tried to handle the asbestos by protecting his workers and carefully controlling the cleanup to prevent the least amount of contamination and uncontrolled waste, Levy would surely go bankrupt and lose the sizable bond Johns-Manville required for the job. If he tried to comply minimally with the current California OSHA regulation, he might not go bankrupt, but the profit he had counted on before starting the job would be significantly reduced.

A few days later, the laboratory reported that all eight samples I had collected during the follow-up inspection were in fact positive for asbestos. The samples varied in concentration from a low of 4 percent to a high of more than 50 percent. The high values were for samples taken from the remains of the autoclaves. Once the laboratory reported the values, citations were drafted.

Before issuing the citations, it was decided that the regional manager, my supervisor, and I would tour the area again. The closing conference would then be held and the citations issued.

During our tour we found another "surprise." Walking around a large building, little more than a steel frame soon to be scrapped, we discovered hills of dirt grown over with weeds.

"That's where we buried cement pipe that was flawed or unusable," the plant manager said, pointing to the hills of dirt on the acre or more of land that formed the western end of the site. He added that they had broken the rejected asbestos-containing pipe into small pieces for more compact burying.

Based on the size of the area, it was going to be quite a job to remove it, should the material ever have to be removed. I wondered who would buy the site with asbestos debris buried under the ground.

In front of the mounds covering the broken pipe, and of more immediate interest, were a couple of twenty-foot-high piles of mixed unsalvageable debris, most of it broken panels of asbestos cement siding. The contractor had used an unsafe shortcut method to remove the outside wall panels.

"I'm going to require these piles to be cleaned up and disposed of as asbestos waste, like the rest of the asbestos spills we've seen today," I said.

"But this material is not friable. It's not posing a hazard," replied the plant manager.

"When it's broken up like this, it's spreading around asbestos; it's friable," countered the regional supervisor.

The argument continued for about five minutes over what was friable asbestos (i.e., whether or not the material was in a form that could release hazardous amounts of asbestos fibers into the air or on the ground to be later resuspended). Steam pipe insulation is clearly friable; it crumbles in your hand and, when so disturbed, can release harmful levels of asbestos fibers. But asbestos bound in cured cement, as in the sections of wall material in the piles, is not truly friable; it does not crumble and release fibers easily unless it receives harsh physical treatment, such as hitting with a sledge hammer or smashing with a bulldozer, as apparently had happened.

The contractor jumped into the argument as it heated up, raising his voice in support of the plant manager, who said that the material posed no problem. The contractor had a vested interest, in that handling the material as hazardous waste would take money out of his pocket. As one of Malbuc's partners had earlier lamented to me, asbestos disposal and gentle handling were not part of their bid. They had not figured the cost of dealing with so much asbestos-containing material.

The debate reached its boiling point.

"That's it, you're on my property, and I want you all out of here," the contractor said. "You're trespassing. I'm getting tired of you guys telling us what to do. I want you off our property, NOW!"

The contractor meant business, and without a warrant, we were obliged to leave.

"Okay, fine. We'll mail the citations to you," replied the regional supervisor.

My boss did not want to be so accommodating. On the half-mile hike back to the entrance gate, he said, with an anger I had never seen before, "You got any tags?" referring to the yellow tags used to shut down an operation. By now, he had heard all the "good faith" he could stand.

"Maybe you should reconsider shutting them down. We don't really have any high air levels of asbestos recorded," I said to my boss.

"I DIDN'T ASK WHETHER WE SHOULD SHUT THEM DOWN. I ASKED IF YOU HAD ANY TAGS!"

"Uh, . . . yeah, Dave, I have the tags, wire, order to prohibit use, and a pen, all you need," I replied.

In a meeting between the three of us at the parking area, cooler, but not necessarily wiser, heads prevailed. A decision was made to issue a serious citation as quickly as possible through the mail, ordering prompt cleanup of the mess we had seen that day. At the same time, we would get our legal staff to obtain a warrant as fast as possible so we could check on compliance with the citations and take air samples as needed.

At this point, with the constraints of the law, we could only shake our heads, issue the citations and a $2,000 fine, and get the warrant so we could not be thrown off the site again.

The warrant was soon drafted and prepared to be taken to the superior court for the signature of a judge. Our attorney had put in a fine effort in providing the rationale for why OSHA should have access to the demolition site to inspect for safety and health violations. Included with the warrant were copies of past citations, as well as my observations regarding the problems at the site. The attorney had even included one of the contractor's comments I had recorded, that before Malbuc had taken over the site, Johns-Manville had left the floors so clean "you could eat off them." No more.

Before we had the time to get the warrant signed and served, Levy's father called and notified us that there had been a misunderstanding. The partner who had thrown us out was not in charge, he assured us. "We don't do business that way," he said.

"Welcomed" back, the regional manager, my boss, and I held a meeting with the younger Levy. We met at the site and discussed the recent citations. Levy partly defended himself and partly admitted to wrongdoing. He had to admit to some wrongdoing; the evidence was overwhelming. To deny everything would have caused a complete loss of credibility and squelched the desperate hope we had that the situation could get better. It was part of Levy's strategy to play on the hope that is part of human nature. He also promised to do better. He had a plan, he said, repeating his earlier statement that he was going to subcontract out the work to more efficient crews.

No one was being exposed to the contaminated areas, Levy argued, and he could rope off the areas to prevent access. He would just as soon make one grand cleanup rather than take time to clean up individual piles. He planned to bring in some dumpsters at a later date.

I countered with a review of his past history and the argument that all the existing waste needed to be cleaned up right away. To leave it would set a precedent at odds with the standard and allow Levy to contaminate areas his crew worked. I was already having a hard time keeping an account of Levy's demolition derby. It would become impossible if he was allowed to make asbestos piles as he went and to clean them up "at a later date," which could mean never. The potential for spreading the contamination was too great, and, besides, how was he going to keep the piles wet and the workers out of them?

The regional manager, who in earlier controversies had impressed me as a tough enforcer, ruled in favor of Levy, commenting that "they have to be able to get this job done." He ruled that the current piles in the buildings and in the autoclave pit could remain but that they would have to be cleaned up later. He rationalized that the contractor had a big job to do and that for the demolition to proceed, it was necessary to allow the uncontained asbestos to be stockpiled.

I felt certain that this concession, in light of Levy's poor practices and bad faith, was an attempt to toe the line of the new administration, particularly since Levy had accused OSHA of causing him financial loss and interfering with his right to conduct business. It would have been difficult for the regional manager to come down hard on the contractor when the new OSHA executives, appointed by the newly elected governor, were beginning to send out messages that they were loosening their policies. Perhaps the manager thought it was not a good time to push too hard. After all, his work location and work pressure were sensitive to the whims of upper management.

Soon after the meeting with Levy, subcontractors were brought in, as Levy had said. My hopes for improvement were completely dashed, however, when I found out that the subcontractor was a cousin of Levy's.

Within the first two weeks after I heard this news, I initiated an inspection of the demolition site. The foreman at the site was pleasant, and I had renewed hope for cooperation. But the hope lasted less than an hour. I soon learned that, although the foreman would be running the job, Levy's cousin was expected to be going to jail soon; his sentencing was the following week. Also, I soon discovered that the cousin had hired illegal aliens from Mexico, whom he was paying lower-than-average wages.

I closed my inspection by saying that the cousin was following the minimum requirements of the standard. My sampling showed that the air levels for the outdoor work and wet-work practices were again low, at least while I was there. But even this minimal level of compliance did not last long.

In a follow-up inspection about three months later, the cousin's company was issued two serious citations with a $2,000 fine for improper cleanup and disposal. "I didn't know it was asbestos," complained the foreman during the closing conference. It was a poor excuse for leaving asbestos pipe insulation and an asbestos-containing gray dust over the entire work area. The pipe insulation was obviously vintage asbestos, and what should have been equally apparent was that the gray dust also contained asbestos. The same gray material abundantly coated the insides of the duct work the crew was demolishing, and given that the duct work was once part of the asbestos pipe-manufacturing process, it should not have been difficult to surmise that the dust would contain asbestos. Unfortunately, the cutters were required to work unprotected in the midst of the dust without any concern by the foreman.

Levy's cousin reacted angrily to the citations, but his attitude soon turned to one of indifference. As soon as this job was done, he and his crew would vanish. By this time, it was clear that the threat of fines meant little to Levy or his relatives. By this time, I was also beginning to wonder whether the OSHA penalty structure and its administrative process were adequate for this job. Part of the problem was that appeals are scheduled nine to twelve months after a citation date. With such long delays, a temporary job can be completed and a contractor have a new name and address long before action can be taken. And, while the citation is under appeal, the contractor is not liable for repeat citations, which carry higher penalties. Furthermore, in this case, the state agency responsible for collecting unpaid fines may have been less than eager to do its job well, given the desires of the governor's office to maintain a cooperative relationship with the business community. The setting and issuance of fines, the appeals process, and the collection process must all occur within a reasonable amount of time and with surety for enforcement to be effective. It is a large task to ask of the present system.

In the meantime, an out-of-state construction company had been hired to remove the nonasbestos-brick manufacturing building, piece by piece. The building was to be reconstructed at another site.

Because the work was some distance from their homes and the job would last several months, the crew members brought their entire families. Many of the families were related since the company was owned and operated by two brothers who freely hired their relatives and in-laws. On their arrival, they all drove in and parked their campers and trailers on the Johns-Manville site, next to the building they would be working on. Soon after setting up camp, their children were playing in areas probably contaminated with asbestos. A county health inspector paid a visit and gave the brothers twenty-four hours to get their families out. Although I was unsuccessful in explaining to the bewildered brothers that it was best not to have their families living in an area with such a high potential for incidental asbestos exposure, they were taken aback and hurt by what they felt was the strong-arm approach of the county in ordering their families off the job site.

Once the families had gotten off the site and the company was into its work, I initiated an inspection. Unfortunately for the already "government-terrorized" brothers, I found that their crews were working unknowingly on a fine layer of asbestos-containing dust, which covered the entire cement floor of the building they were working in. The workers, in removing the building's steel frame and taking off the wall panels, had knocked down asbestos dust left from the previous manufacturing operation, contaminating the floor and undoubtedly their lungs. I found one worker dry-sweeping the dust. I had warned the brothers before they began the job that there was possibly asbestos residue on the steel frames and walls. When I handed them the citation requiring prompt cleanup, work practices that would prevent further contamination, and a $1,000 fine, they did not understand the regulatory action and were very upset. One of the brothers cried. They were very religious, good, honest people, and the amount of work they were doing was a quantum leap beyond what Levy's crews had done. Unfortunately, asbestos-induced diseases do not take into account a person's morals or values. The brothers complied with the citations, however, and managed to dismantle the building without further trouble.

After four months of inspecting and issuing repeat citations in a near-vain attempt to control the cleanup, time-out was called. One fine summer day, officials from the city arrived at the site, and, backed by armed representatives of the police department, shut down the operation. The contractor had not taken out a city building permit, they said. But of course it was more than that.

Earlier in the demolition, city officials had become curious about the project and had made inquiries with the OSHA office and the local air pollution agency. Their concern had grown with each telephone conversation and meeting. In one meeting, I had flatly admitted that I expected Malbuc to make another mess and be issued another round of citations. "Can't you stop them?" a city official asked my supervisor and me.

As best we could, we had explained the limitations of the state OSHA law, which provided authority for shutdowns only when there were imminent serious hazards. The problem was whether asbestos exposure could legally be considered an imminent hazard. In that the risk increases with length of exposure, and the possible injury is a delayed one, occurring ten to forty years after initial exposure, the risk was not by definition "imminent." OSHA has disregarded this distinction when the asbestos exposure is high and the exposure is completely uncontrolled, as was the case during my very first inspection of the site. Under such severe circumstances, OSHA believes it can defend its actions in court. The only other method we could have pursued but did not because it would have posed a greater legal challenge was to seek a temporary injunction.

City officials had also contacted the local air pollution agency. Levy had not paid much attention to the agency's regulations either, they were told.

Once the city officials learned that both OSHA and the local air pollution agency were issuing repeat citations and that Johns-Manville and Malbuc had done little to no advanced planning to control the asbestos at the site, the city took action, shutting down the operation. LIABILITY was written all over the few remaining walls at the site. The city had communities downwind, and anyone who bought the land might get upset about the asbestos and file a whopper of a lawsuit. Understandably, the city officials did not want to be sued or to have their council members or themselves appear as "guests" on "60 Minutes."

The city was also sincerely impressed by the danger the asbestos presented and by its duty to the community. Adding to that impression were strong recommendations by a consulting firm the city had hired. The consultants made sure that the city was aware of all the asbestos dangers, including the importance of the consultants' services. The consultants were architects and engineers and, more recently, experts in the increasing asbestos abatement business. Their $20,000-plus bill for a report warning of the terrible liability the city faced, and which justified their services, was later billed by the city to Johns-Manville.

The OSHA office participated in all the meetings the city held in its attempt to organize an orderly demolition of the site. The city had contacted nearly everyone who would have an interest in the demolition, including city officials, the county sheriff, the local air pollution agency, OSHA, the county building and safety agency, the county fire department, the state hazardous waste department, and the county health department. The meetings were a little crowded but proved useful in coordinating the agencies.

Not to be left out, Levy and representatives from Johns-Manville were invited to some of the meetings, which were held in a face-the-agencies format at a table filled with accusing bureaucrats. From the contractors' point of view, it probably looked as though the agencies were ganging up on them, as, in a sense, they were.

In one meeting, Levy and his defenders were asked to explain how they were going to clean up the contaminated areas and conduct their demolition in the future. The discussion was heated and accusatory, and, not surprisingly, Levy complained about the numerous regulatory bodies he had to deal with to complete the demolition.

I was unsympathetic. It was time for Levy and company, as part of their punishment for creating the asbestos disaster, to satisfy fully the agencies that had been played the fool once too often.

In response to the bold demands made by the agencies at the meetings, and to the city's shutdown, Levy and his attorney put together a well-devised demolition plan that made old promises look new. They urged agency representatives to tour the site and to discuss with them exactly where the problems were. They placed the blame for their troubles not on the people running the project but on the inefficient work crews they had hired. Writing in the abatement plan, Levy's attorney stated that "[the contractor, Malbuc] has terminated fifteen members of its previous crew, leaving only one continuing employee. Said employees were terminated for failure to follow company and/or OSHA rules and regulations. [Malbuc] intends to impress upon all new employees the importance of complying with the regulations."

A month later, the city was ready to allow Malbuc to go back to work. Levy had completed a lengthy environmental impact statement for the city, something he should have done before starting any demolition project of this magnitude, and had again detailed his work practices and employee protection plan for OSHA and the air pollution control agency. He had also obtained permits and appropriate variances from the Department of Hazardous Waste. The plan called for a cleanup of all existing asbestos piles before any further demolition could take place and then cleanup as work progressed, as was required by the state OSHA standard. I was not optimistic that this was the end of the violations.

The one obvious solution was to force Malbuc off the job and require Johns-Manville to bring in a firm that could handle the asbestos. But no agency had the legal authority to require this. Malbuc had its legal rights and much money invested in the deal; the company had paid Johns-Manville $465,000 for salvage rights to existing equipment and structures, a bid that had been calculated to earn profits for Malbuc. Malbuc had also posted a $400,000 performance bond, which it could lose if it did not complete the job successfully. The stakes were high on both sides. The only thing preventing further disaster was enforcement of the then-existing regulatory laws, which, although less than adequate, were far better than no laws at all.

The demolition and cleanup proceeded for a couple of months with some problems but none significant enough to cause a shutdown.

Then, on a Monday during an inspection of the site, an OSHA industrial hygienist, accompanied by an air pollution inspector, noticed that the giant outdoor autoclaves were gone, after recalling that they had been there the previous week. Like the indoor autoclaves, they had been wrapped with asbestos insulation. On closer examination, the inspectors found white-gray insulation scattered about where the autoclaves had been. There was a lot of insulation, but just a fraction of the amount that would have wrapped the autoclaves. Some of the debris was suspiciously forming two curving lines with a constant distance between them, about the width of a car, or, more accurately, of the bucket on Levy's front-end loader. The path, outlined with chunks of asbestos, curved away from the autoclave site and down the road. The inspectors followed. The path led right to the far western end of the dry asbestos pond. On the dirt near the pond's edge were the track marks of the front-end loader and, at the end of the path, a large pile of asbestos insulation partly covered with dirt. The OSHA inspector took pictures and samples, as did the air pollution inspector. An interview with some of Levy's people pointed the finger at Malbuc.

The reaction could not have been worse when the news got back to the inspectors' offices and the city. Our office prepared serious/repeat/willful violations with $20,000 of fines proposed and then tagged-out the whole site. The city issued a stop-work order, and the air pollution agency went to court and obtained a temporary restraining order. Malbuc and any remaining friends were "locked out." Malbuc deserved it all, or at least most of it. Not only had Malbuc dumped the stuff in the pond, but, more important, the crew had left considerable amounts of asbestos debris scattered over the site.

Levy fought back, not just with lawyerly rhetoric, but with more experienced finesse—Levy, Sr.

Levy, Sr., was not new to the project or to its problems. From the beginning, he had been involved in the demolition. Although Levy, Jr., had made the day-to-day decisions, Levy, Sr., periodically stopped by to visit and help his son.

Now, with the additional help of Levy, Sr., another written proposal was prepared challenging OSHA's authority even more boldly. The proposal set out conditions by which a different contractor would clean up the existing asbestos and proceed with a planned and orderly demolition. The new contractor would be helped by a "third-party consultant knowledgeable in the handling and disposal of toxic waste" and by a Johns-Mansville representative, assigned to supervise the new contractor. The plan went into great detail, noting who would supervise each step to ensure compliance with all regulations. But those named did not sound very knowledgeable. The third-party consultant turned out to be not an asbestos demolition expert, or even an environmental or industrial hygiene consultant, but the owner of the containers Levy, Jr., had used to haul out some of the waste. But the real insult was the identity of the new contractor. In a portion of the written proposal challenging OSHA and the air pollution agency's actions was the following statement: "Rather than litigate these issues on the merits, [Malbuc] is willing to pull off the job in favor of a contractor of its choosing. After consulting with the bond company and meeting with the representatives of Johns-Manville, [Malbuc] has elected to retain the services of [R. J. Levy, Sr. Construction Company, Inc.] to complete its contractual requirements." Levy, Sr., was the "new" contractor! Since the first shutdown eight months earlier, he had had the authority to change the course of the demolition at any time. Could the agencies expect anything different now?

By now, the power had changed hands. The agencies took their time in deciding the fate of the demolition project and of Malbuc. They now had enough evidence of bad faith to hold up under court challenge and political pressure from within their own agencies. Regulatory agencies can be slow to act, particularly if they have a grudge. So word by word Levy's twenty-four-page proposal was joyously criticized. The inspectors could finally release their pent-up frustrations. The beneficiary of this arduous process was the bank account of Levy's attorney.

The agencies asked for and rejected several redrafts of the proposal. As a result, the project remained at a standstill for more than a year until Johns-Manville, eager to complete the demolition and sell the land, stepped in and consented to hire a new contractor to finish the project, with the help of a recognized and qualified consultant.

Conveniently, Levy and company had dropped from the scene. A Johns-Manville investigator was assigned to the case and attempted to find Levy and his relatives. The investigator mentioned one day at the OSHA office that he suspected that Johns-Manville's corporate agent and Malbuc were involved in a kickback scheme since much of the demolition had proceeded at a much lower cost than it would have been had a qualified asbestos demolition company done the work from day one.

In retrospect, the agencies did their jobs as well as could have been expected, given the limitations of the laws they were empowered to enforce. At times there was some loss of backbone, and there were some bad judgments. But the multiple inspections did prevent a major disaster at the site, which would have left a monstrous bill for the taxpayers and exposed the workers to even more hazardous levels of asbestos.

Laws with known penalties are supposed to provide the motivation necessary to prevent problems. And, in cases when companies fail to comply, issuing citations, setting abatement dates, and imposing monetary fines for serious infractions are supposed to ensure that the immediate problems are corrected and future compliance assured. For those who repeatedly or willfully fail to comply, higher fines are supposed to make it prohibitively expensive not to comply.

In this case, the laws, or more appropriately their administration, did not prevent Malbuc from consistently trampling on the agencies' rules. Citations could be appealed, delaying the issuance of repeat citations and higher penalties for almost a year. Payment of penalties could be delayed or reduced through negotiation with OSHA or by presenting a well-devised case to an administrative law judge in the appeal. Fly-by-night companies, which have proven to be the worst violators of OSHA regulations, may never have to pay, even after losing appeals. They can avoid the weak state collection agency by changing the names of their businesses and by refusing mail from the state. Unfortunately, the tenacity of many government agencies, other than perhaps the Internal Revenue Service, can be minimal to nonexistent in taking on the really bad offenders, who know how to fight the system. But, in spite of the problems with the agencies and their appeal and penalty collection processes, beneficial enforcement can still be effected.

This case would have had a different outcome had current regulations for asbestos been in effect. The new regulations are more comprehensive and are based on a much lower exposure limit. The requirements and complexity of the asbestos standard and the degree of protection specified essentially mandate that a specialty contractor perform major asbestos demolition work. The probable result in this case would have been the awarding of a subcontract for asbestos removal and cleanup to a competent asbestos abatement contractor, either before the start of the job or right after the first shutdown.

3. SOLVENTS

L ike oil, many industrial solvents are "organic," meaning they are in a class of chemicals based on carbon atoms. Such solvents have physical characteristics similar to oil, so that they hold true to the chemical law "like dissolves like" and are capable of dissolving and mixing with oil. Not surprisingly, many industrial solvents are themselves derived from carbon-rich petroleum or coal tar, a distillate of burning bituminous coal.

The synthetic organic solvents, preferred over the natural organic solvents for many industrial uses, are also capable of dissolving oil-like compounds. Synthetic solvents mimic the chemistry of the petroleum and coal tar solvents through the substitution of other atoms, usually chlorine and fluorine, for the hydrogen atoms on the backbone of the carbon. In most cases the use of chlorine and fluorine atoms makes the synthetic solvents noncombustible, an important advantage for many industrial processes.

Both the natural and synthetic solvents are used in large quantities to help make the numerous consumer products derived from oil and coal tar. The manufacturing processes for these products rely extensively on the solvating properties of industrial solvents. Paints, resins, inks, and glues use great quantities of solvents as carriers and diluents for the active ingredients. Solid plastics are shaped and molded into desired forms by solvents, which soften and dissolve and are later removed by drying. The synthetic chemicals used in consumer and industrial products from drugs to fabrics are manufactured using solvents that help bring together diverse chemicals into a single solution so that they may react and unite. In many applications the solvents are purposely consumed in a reaction; single molecules function as building blocks for larger chemicals or polymerize into the long-chain polymers prevalent in so many useful products. Solvents also make outstanding cleaning agents for removing paint, other oil-based products, and grease and grime. Solvents are used to clean a range of items, from fabrics to the outsides of jet aircraft.

All industrial solvents have the potential to cause harm. Most have the ability to extract the skin's natural oils, causing a dryness and roughness that can cause dermatitis if there is chronic exposure. A few solvents are more destructive and can actually destroy the skin on initial contact. Still others can pass through the skin and be absorbed into the bloodstream, causing systemic toxicity.

The vapors of the solvents can also be harmful. The type and extent of the toxicity depends on the chemical structure of the particular solvent and on how much is inhaled. Almost all industrial solvents have an effect on the nervous system, similar to that of narcotic drugs, when the vapors are inhaled in excessive concentrations.

Because of their ability to dull the senses, some of the more volatile solvents were used as surgical anesthetics in the mid- and late nineteenth century. One such solvent was carbon disulfide. The side effects were found to be so serious, however, that its use as an anesthetic was discontinued. Later, in the early part of the twentieth century, the solvent was popular in industry, but it earned disfavor again when it was found to cause poisoning among exposed workers, one effect of which was insanity. More recently, carbon disulfide has been used in the manufacture of viscose rayon, though not without some problems. Until improvements in the control of the vapors were made, overexposure caused workers to suffer serious neurological and cardiovascular effects. The limit for worker exposure to carbon disulfide is now set at a level far below that needed to prevent acute effects and is designed principally to protect workers who are chronically exposed from cardiovascular disease or reproductive dangers.

The vapors of the solvent carbon tetrachloride were also used in the nineteenth century as an anesthetic, but, like carbon disulfide, it produced serious health effects. More surprising, the solvent had a popular use at that time as a waterless shampoo. Carbon tetrachloride was used in this century in coin-operated dry-cleaning machines until many consumers who cleaned their sleeping bags hit the sack for the last time, inhaling fatal doses. The solvent was also used in fire extinguishers during the 1950s until one too many fire fighters inhaled the very toxic chemical that results when the solvent is burned.

The solvent was also popular as a general cleaning solution in the 1950s and 1960s in both homes and factories. Because of its toxicity and the availability of safer solvents, carbon tetrachloride is now rarely used in industry or in the home. In addition to its narcotic properties and toxic effects on the liver and kidneys, more recently it has been found to cause cancer in animals.

Two other solvents that contain chlorine—tetrachloroethane and chloroform—have been rejected as cleaning agents but were once used widely in industry. Tetrachloroethane, used in the aircraft industry between World War I and World War II, was responsible for many poisonings. This once-popular solvent is now extinct.

Chloroform also has some negative history. It was one of the first anesthetics used in the nineteenth century and was used up to about the time of World War II. When safer anesthetics became available, it was discontinued because it caused death from liver toxicity in some patients. Its use in pharmaceutical preparations was banned in 1977 by the Food and Drug Administration.

Chloroform also had wide use as an industrial solvent years ago, resulting in liver damage in overexposed workers. Modern science has found both chloroform and tetrachloroethane to be reproductive hazards, and chloroform is further suspected of being a carcinogen. A controversy still rages over the presence of trace amounts of chloroform in chlorinated drinking water and over its alleged carcinogenic risk to the public.

Benzene, a coal tar- or petroleum-based solvent, was used before World War II as a fuel-octane booster for automobiles. The chemical is now found in gasoline in far lower concentrations (less than 5 percent of the fuel). Benzene was used as a solvent in airplane dopes during World War I and in paint and varnish remover, but its ability to cause leukemia and debilitating blood diseases among those who repeatedly inhale small amounts of the vapor, or absorb the liquid through the skin, has increasingly limited its use. The chemical is now used principally as a building block for industrial and consumer chemicals that require its unique structure of six carbon atoms in a nearly flat ring. The aromatic solvent, so described because it was originally obtained from a smelly distillate fraction of coal tar, is still used in fantastic tonnages each year. Benzene is currently produced from oil by the petroleum industry, and, not surprisingly, this industry has challenged OSHA's attempts to lower the exposure limits for the chemical.

OSHA's first exposure limit for benzene was established in 1971 at 10 parts per million (ppm) for an eight-hour workday. Although the limit offered workers some protection, health researchers at the time believed it was not low enough to prevent many cases of blood disease. In 1977, OSHA sought to lower the exposure limit to 1.0 ppm as a temporary emergency measure, but a lawsuit by the American Petroleum Institute and other groups successfully stayed the standard. OSHA attempted to lower the standard permanently to 1.0 ppm in 1978 but was again challenged by industry groups. The case eventually reached the Supreme Court, which ruled that OSHA had not provided sufficient documentation that workers were truly at risk. The lower limit was thrown out. Finally, in 1987, in a belated reaction to a petition by unions and interest groups in 1983, OSHA successfully adopted a more protective comprehensive standard. The exposure limit for benzene is now 1.0 ppm for an eight-hour workday.

Other petroleum-based solvents, such as hexane and n-butyl ketone, were used as specialty solvents for many years, with concern only for their narcotic properties, until they were discovered to produce neurological disorders. The discovery of more serious toxicity eventually resulted in the substitution of other solvents.

The current popular industrial solvents include toluene, the xylenes, methyl ethyl ketone, naphtha, the mineral spirits, methylene chloride, perchloroethylene (dry cleaners' solvent), methyl chloroform, the acetates, the glycol ethers, and the fluorinated hydrocarbons, which include the "freons." For the most part, these modern-day solvents are much less toxic than their forebears. Nonetheless, overexposure can cause varying degrees of respiratory irritation and narcotic effects and, with greater exposure, fatal or disease-producing damage to the heart, lungs, liver, and brain. Recent evidence indicates that long-term subacute exposure can result in permanent damage to the nervous system, including a decrease in emotional reactivity and impaired memory and psychological performance.[1] In addition, a few of the glycol ethers were recently found to be associated with risks to the reproductive system, and methylene chloride was recently found to cause cancer in animals.[2]

In many industrial settings, however, the solvents are used without harmful effects, and, unlike the earlier solvents, those used today need to be inhaled in much larger doses for severe *acute* effects to occur.

There are no guarantees that scientists will not find more toxic effects associated with the solvents in use today. But science has come a long way since the early testing of anesthetics in the nineteenth century. Industry has also come a long way in controlling hazardous exposure, though there is room for improvement.

Out-of-Position Work,
in Position for Danger

Bill Landers had worked at Century, a company that built large jet aircraft, for more than ten years when he was assigned to work as a tank mechanic in building M-4. His job required him to get inside the fuel tanks in the wings and test the seams and rivets for leaks.

Landers and his co-workers would first pressurize the tank to determine if there were any leaks. If the tank lost pressure over a set period of time, then the leaks were located and repaired. Finding a leak required two mechanics—one on the outside of the wing applying pressure over the area to be tested, and another inside the tank applying a, soap solution. The presence of bubbles indicated the location of a leak. The mechanics were also required to clean the tanks with a specially formulated solvent that removed the soap residue left from the test procedure and any grease or excess glue left from other tank-assembly operations. Later, other mechanics would coat the insides of the tanks with a protective paint.

Landers and some of the other mechanics had been testing wing tanks in building M-4 for the past six months because production had outpaced the regularly scheduled testing and assembly. Tank work was normally completed in the adjacent building, M-2, where the wing was worked on before it was connected to the fuselage, but with the high production and economic demands on the company, some wings were bypassing M-2, thus requiring testing and assembly to be completed in M-4. The rescheduling of work meant that the aircraft could advance along the assembly line without any unecessary delays, especially when a test could be done or a part added at another point in the process. Such "out-of-position" work was not unusual.

With the increase in production and out-of-position work, the mechanics were putting in more overtime, including weekends. Landers began an overtime shift early one Saturday morning. There were not many production people around as he checked in with his supervisor and went over what he had to do. He then went over to his work area and began gathering his equipment. One of his co-workers, Edwards, stopped by and asked Landers if he needed any help. No, Landers said, he had only a minor job: to check one area in plane 2788, and maybe clean up a small spot. Edwards replied "okay" and told Landers that he was going to the other building for coffee.

Landers climbed the stairs and entered the fuselage. Inside, he found it as it had been the afternoon before: a hollow, aluminum-skinned skeleton with no seats, no overhead compartments, and no floor. A temporary wooden platform stretched over the lower frame of the fuselage, partly covering the bundles and bundles of plastic-coated wire underneath. Landers walked to the midsection of the fuselage and, kneeling over the center fuel tank, loosened one of the two hatches. He had occasionally worn an uncomfortable half-mask chemical cartridge respirator for such jobs, but he decided this job would take only a minute and he proceeded without one.

Landers removed the hatch and stepped through the small elliptical opening into the tank. It was a tight fit. Mechanics with large waists or long bodies were not selected for this work. Before ducking down, he grabbed his rags and a bottle of a solvent that was widely used throughout the plant for removing grease.

Landers crawled on his knees to an opening in the spar of the first wing. The wing spars divided the center tank, which had a volume of several hundred cubic feet, into six smaller sections. Each spar had a pair of holes that allowed the fuel to pass between sections. The larger hole in the spar was just big enough for a tank mechanic to pass through. Landers crawled through the larger hole and, twisting his body, moved into the next section. This was the area he had been concerned about the day before. He cleaned the area with a squirt of solvent on his rag. Satisfied with the way it looked, he was turning to crawl back out when he noticed another area that was quite dirty. He decided to clean that area also. Later he would recall that he had used about a cup of the solvent. As he wiped and cleaned, the solvent rapidly evaporated.

Within seconds, Landers began to feel dizzy. The air in the small tank was quickly becoming contaminated, and, with each inspiration, Landers was taking in more and more of the vapor. The chemical passed through his lungs, poisoning the tissues, into his bloodstream, and then throughout his body. The solvent has a pronounced effect on the more sensitive nerve cells of the brain and Landers passed out. He would not remember the seconds between the time when he began to feel dizzy and when his head fell to the bottom of the fuel tank.

The percentage of oxygen left in the contaminated air near the bottom of the tank was not enough to support Landers for more than a few minutes. Even if he was rescued before his heart or brain gave out, his lungs, which were becoming increasingly poisoned, would probably release so much fluid that he would literally drown. It was only a matter of minutes. Landers's body lay cramped between two wing spars, inside a small fuel tank, inside a hollow fuselage, and no one was around.

Edwards, back from a thirty-minute coffee break, looked for Landers around the north end of the building. He climbed up the stairs of plane 2788, looked in the fuselage, and saw one hatch open. He walked over to the hatch and kneeled down; the odor of the solvent hit him. He peered into the tank. He did not need to see more. Edwards ran out of the fuselage, down the stairs to the nearest phone, and called an emergency number.

The local paramedics had planned in advance for accidents inside wing tanks. The quickest and most direct method to rescue someone would be to cut through the unfinished wing and tank wall with a saw and pull the victim out. Cutting up tens of thousands of dollars' worth of a jet aircraft did not appeal to the company, however, so this plan had been rejected. An alternative plan was used to save Landers. A paramedic entered the tank, wearing a respirator and carrying a bottle of oxygen equipped with a mask. The paramedic then attached the oxygen mask to Landers and attempted to revive him. Fortunately, Landers recovered enough of his senses to help with his rescue. Without this help, the removal would have been much more difficult. Once out of the tank, Landers was rushed to the hospital.

Bill Landers recovered, but he was out of work for several weeks as his lungs healed. And when he returned to work, he still did not feel normal. In addition to some physical symptoms, he felt guilty about the accident. Some of his co-workers did not help; he felt their stares and heard them say it was his own fault: "Why didn't he use common sense? Any time a tank is entered, ventilation must be added."

Landers also heard that, right after his accident, the tank mechanics had been required to go to a class in safe tank entry. He learned that the procedures in place for tank operations in other buildings had been adopted for tank work in building M-4. If the accident was his fault, Landers wondered, why had Century adopted more stringent procedures?

I was well into my investigation when Landers returned to work. My assignment was to investigate the accident. I received the assignment after my office was notified of the near fatality by way of an accident report from Century. The report stated that three days earlier a mechanic named Bill Landers had been found unconscious in a tank after using a cleaning solvent. My plan was to open the inspection that afternoon and to determine first whether the circumstances that led to the accident still existed and then whether there had been any safety and health violations.

Before I left for Century, the other inspectors in my office recited their complaints. They did not think much of the company's commitment to safety, and they thought it would be a difficult inspection since they usually had been given a lot of canned statements whenever they inspected the company. Adding to the difficulty, the union officers, I was told, had long before grown weary of shaking their heads in disgust over what they saw as mistreatment of union members. A bitter strike had just ended that had further contributed to their poor attitude. I also learned that the union did not expect much from OSHA.

Attesting to the company's poor safety record was the "C" drawer in our office's file cabinet. Half the drawer contained reports on Century, initiated either as a result of accidents or employee complaints. The reports contained more than enough serious citations to give the company a poor history ranking.

Later that afternoon, I was met at one of Century's guarded gates by the company's senior industrial hygienist, Fred Slater, who escorted me to the safety department office. I was introduced to the safety and health staff—three other industrial hygienists and three of the first-shift safety engineers, who happened to be in the office that afternoon—and to the director of the safety department. The director then called up the union safety steward and requested that he come over.

I asked the director of safety for some specifics on the accident. It had caught the safety department off guard, he said, since his staff was not aware that work requiring the use of solvents in fuel tanks was being done in building M-4. He had since found out that the company had recently instituted out-of-position work there. I was given the impression that out-of-position work was rare. The director explained that Bill Landers had been using the company-designated solvent, PMM-40, a mixture of isopropanol and methylene chloride.

When I asked the director about the company's written procedures for safe tank entry, he said that his department had well-designed procedures for tank work in other buildings.

When the union steward arrived I briefed him on the inspection I planned to conduct. He was already aware of the accident. He did not know the victim personally but was familiar with what a tank mechanic did.

The safety director assigned his senior safety engineer, "Doc" Cipiano, to escort me and the union steward to the area of the accident. Two of the company's industrial hygienists accompanied us as well.

Arriving at the north end of the massive M-4 building, I was ushered through a small door and instantly dwarfed by a row of partly assembled jet planes lined up one behind another. The line of planes stretched for as far as I could see. The building was wide enough for two of the giant planes to be placed side by side and tall enough for the jets' rising tails.

My entourage and I met first with the second-shift foreman for the tank mechanics. I learned that several of his staff worked inside wing tanks and center tanks, installing parts, removing excess sealant, and cleaning the insides before the tanks were painted.

When I asked him about safety procedures and the ventilation they used when cleaning the tanks, he replied that it was up to the mechanics; they could use whatever they felt was needed. He said they had two fans, which they could place in each of the wing tanks to blow air toward the center tank. The painters usually wore air-supplied respirators, he explained, and some of the mechanics wore chemical cartridge respirators.

"Do you have any written safety procedures?" I asked.

"No."

"Have the mechanics been given any training on safety procedures for tank entry?"

Not that he knew about, the foreman replied.

"Have you ever tested the air in the tanks?"

"No, . . . ah, maybe several months ago."

"Are you doing anything different since the accident?"

"No, not really," he replied, adding that Landers should have used the fans or his respirator as the other mechanics usually did.

"Will mechanics be entering the tanks tonight or tomorrow?" I inquired.

"Yes, I think so."

"How long have you been doing tank work here?"

"Oh, about six months. Out-of-position work happens now and then."

We went over to a plane in the out-of-position area for tank work and found two fans resting on the floor. They were not the usual type used to control chemical exposure but more like house fans.

I asked to see the solvent used in the tanks. I was shown a pint-sized plastic squirt bottle, a good choice for use in a small space. The nozzle was the type used on bottles of shampoo or pancake syrup. In this case, it would slow the rate of vaporization from the bottle and prevent excessive spillage and loss if the bottle was laid on its side or accidentally knocked over. The mechanics could squirt just the amount of solvent they needed, thus keeping to a minimum the amount that could volatize into the tank. Because small spaces such as wing tanks can rapidly accumulate dangerous concentrations of solvent, the squirt bottle was a simple and important feature. As the safety director had said, the solvent was a volatile mixture of mostly methylene chloride with a smaller amount of isopropanol.

I asked one of the industrial hygienists why the tank mechanics did not use a less volatile solvent. He explained that the solvent had been picked because it was volatile and would evaporate without leaving a residue. Plus, it cut through grease and glue well. I was informed that selecting a solvent was not an easy task. Besides needing something that wasn't highly toxic and cleaned well enough to pass muster with the company's quality-control personnel, the solvent also had to pass Federal Aviation Administration standards. The FAA was involved with the construction and maintenance of aircraft fuel tanks and was concerned whether the solvent would leave behind residue that could foul up the fuel system—a potential disaster if the plane was airborne. The government agency had to be consulted on any change in procedures, I was told. To switch solvents could take months.

We next climbed the stairs to the plane's fuselage. Carefully stepping around workers transforming the hollow shell into the modern interior of a jet aircraft, we came upon the center fuel tank. The foreman opened one of the hatches, and I looked in. I could see only a small section of the tank; a wing spar on either side blocked my view. I looked at the opening to the hatch and thought that if I sucked in my stomach, I could fit through. But even if I could get inside, I would be unable to put my six-foot-plus frame through the necessary contortions to crawl between the spars.

The tank was a classic example of the industrial hygiene term *confined space*, for which special standards usually apply. Confined spaces have accounted for more acute industrial health fatalities than any other cause except, perhaps, carbon monoxide poisoning. About three hundred workers lose their lives annually in confined spaces, and, even more tragic, roughly half of those who die are would-be rescuers. There are documented cases of rescuers, one after another, entering a toxic atmosphere in a confined space to save "Joe, who must have had a heart attack," and needlessly dying as Joe did.

It was obvious that a well-designed system was needed to ventilate the areas between the spars. Well-designed entry procedures were also needed, or the tank could turn into a mechanic's coffin, as it nearly had.

Still bothered by the foreman's statement that the entry procedures had not been changed since the accident, I proceeded with my inspection and requested to speak with some of the tank mechanics. I was introduced to one of them. Before beginning my interview, I notified the company safety engineer, Cipiano, that I wanted the interview to be in private. He did not restrain his irritation over my request that he leave. The union steward joined us when the mechanic said it was all right.

On questioning, the mechanic related that whenever he used the solvent, he would place the fans over the hatches and wear his respirator. If the job was minor, he would use only the respirator. The equipment was handed out, he explained, and they used it as they saw fit. He had not been given any training in chemical hazards or on safe procedures for entering the tanks and therefore did not know the hazards of the solvent. Nor had he received any training in the use of the respirator. He said he knew it worked because he no longer smelled the solvent when he used it.

The next mechanic I interviewed had not been given any safety instructions either. He had heard about a class the company had in safe tank entry, because his foreman had said several months ago that he and the other mechanics should go to it. But he added, "We just can't get up and go over to the training class on our own. Our supervisor has to send us over." When I asked him if he had ever had any problems while using the solvent, he replied that just the week before he had passed out when he stuck his head inside the tank to ask a co-worker a question. He remembered smelling a strong odor when he put his head through the hatch and then passed out. The other mechanic was using a respirator, he said, but there was no added ventilation.

I asked him if any changes had been made since Landers's accident. "No."

I thanked him and let him get back to work.

After the interview, one of the company's industrial hygienists approached me and said that he had recently completed an investigation of an incident involving the mechanic I had just interviewed. The industrial hygienist said that, although it was possible that he had suffered overexposure to the solvent, the mechanic thought that the problem was the chicken soup he had had for lunch. The industrial hygienist had included this in his report, he said, as one of the probable causes of the incident—drinking a cup of vending machine chicken soup on an empty stomach.

The union steward smiled at me. The mechanic had apparently invented the chicken soup story so as not to cause trouble.

It appeared that the company's industrial hygienist had misled himself, perhaps in an unconscious attempt to make his job easier. If there was no health hazard, he did not have to risk being accused of causing extra costs and production delays by requiring additional safety procedures. He certainly was not the type to cover up an accident.

Next, I interviewed two mechanics who painted the insides of the tanks. They reported that they used a special paint that was exceptionally useful in protecting the metal fuel tank. In its uncured state before application, the paint contained a flammable solvent, a potentially carcinogenic form of chrome, and a strong lung irritant called diphenylmethane isocyanate.

I was relieved to hear that the company had sound measures for the tank-painting operation. The painters would hook up a special dedicated ventilation system that I found a few feet away from the plane. The system was mounted on a mobile platform, which could be moved to wherever it was needed. The fan was located on the platform and was equipped with flexible ducts that could be placed into several hatches to provide ventilation. The painters would then wear full-body covering with hoods and air-supplied full-face respirators to protect themselves from any paint mists and vapors that the ventilation system did not completely dilute out to a safe level. The respirators provided a continuous supply of fresh air and did not rely on a cartridge to purify the contaminants. Nor was the respirator prone to leak on inspiration, for the continuous flow of fresh air, if used at the air pressures required by the manufacturer, would plug small breaks in the seal around the face. It was the Cadillac of respirators.

Unless the painters used such protective measures, the highly flammable and immediately dangerous toxins in their paint could destroy the strongest lungs in seconds. Though it was pleasing to learn that these protective methods were being used, it was apparent that the company, or certain managers, were not consistently following a safety program.

Next, I was shown, at my request, the area in the adjacent building where tanks were normally tested and assembled. A wing containing the partly constructed tanks stretched the width of this enormous room.

I climbed up the stairs leading to the top of the wing and walked lightly over the aluminum surface to the midsection, where a couple of tank mechanics were working. I introduced myself and asked them about their work and the safety procedures they followed. The mechanics knew the hazards of their job and described how they placed ventilation ducts into the hatches whenever they cleaned the insides of a tank. I also learned that their well-designed ventilation system had been installed several years before. The mechanics in this area had also been provided with both chemical cartridge and air-supplied respirators.

I asked one of the mechanics what he thought had caused the accident in building M-4. He replied that the injured mechanic should have known better than to go into the tank without ventilation, adding that he would never enter a tank to do cleaning without first setting up a ventilation system. It was not surprising that the mechanics in this building would be so judgmental. They had all been through the company's class in safe tank-entry procedures.

They were unaware that the mechanics in M-4 had not had the same training.

Back at the company's safety office, I met again with the head of the safety department. After reviewing all the problems I had found, I asked him what steps were being taken to remedy the situation in M-4. He said his department was embarrassed at what I had found, but he assured me that his office had communicated months before with the foremen in M-4 about the need to follow safe procedures. He said that a safety engineer would be stationed in M-4 whenever the mechanics did tank cleaning and that the mechanics would promptly be signed up for training.

I replied that I trusted his sincerity but was not sure about the production manager's. I told him I wanted assurances from someone in charge of production in M-4 that the unsafe situation would be taken care of and added that I wanted to meet with this person. He then picked up the phone and, to my surprise, called the production manager in charge of M-4. A meeting was immediately set up. Fred Slater, the senior industrial hygienist, was assigned to accompany us, along with Cipiano, the senior safety engineer.

On our drive over to the production manager's office, I apologized to the union steward for keeping him far beyond his leave time. He said it was quite all right; he would not miss this for anything.

Cipiano introduced me to the production manager, whom I thanked for his valuable time. A bit intimidated, I described the safety problems and probable violations I had uncovered, emphasizing the danger to the mechanics. Cipiano and Slater looked a little peaked when I explained the fines for serious and willful violations and the possibility of prosecution for work-related fatalities, but their color improved when I added that the safety department was able and willing to help. All that was needed was for the production foremen to allow the safety department to help and to follow the department's recommendations.

I wound up my "presentation" by saying, "If nothing is immediately done to correct the current situation, I will have to shut down the tank-cleaning operation." I then added, "But this would be ridiculous since Century has the resources to take care of the problem. You can issue instructions to stop tank cleaning until the proper procedures can be followed."

The production manager could have called my bluff right then simply by raising his voice and telling me to get out, for I was not sure about my justification, legally, for shutting down part of his operation. Instead he politely replied that he had already instructed his foremen to ensure that all tank mechanics were trained before any more work was done inside the fuel tanks. His subdued tone indicated that he was not confident about what he had ordered or, perhaps, whether he had even issued an order.

Cipiano interrupted by saying that he would immediately work on obtaining better ventilation units for the operation.

Not completely assured by the production manager's response, I asked, "Did you issue a memo to your foremen saying that the mechanics were to be trained before doing any more tank entries?"

"No," he replied, "I told them this afternoon."

"Are you sure they all got the word?"

"Yes."

"Good," I said, and, after thanking the production manager, we left his office.

Just out the door, on an impulse, I told Cipiano that I wanted to make sure everything in the M-4 tank area was in line. By now, the inspection had extended far into the second shift.

When we got to the area, Cipiano located the second-shift foreman for me.

"Do any of the tank mechanics have to enter the fuel tanks tonight?" I asked the foreman.

"Yes," he replied.

Surprised by his answer, I asked, "Have the mechanics been through the class in safe tank entry?" I knew they could not possibly have attended training in such a short time.

"No, I don't think so."

"Did you get any memo or verbal instructions from the production manager about the tank-cleaning operation?"

"No."

I looked at the union steward, who shook his head and smiled tightly. I turned to Slater and asked him what was going on. He shook his head.

"Look," I said to Slater, "either you shut down this operation or I will." By this time Slater had had enough, and he dispatched his assistant to get the tags needed for a shutdown.

With this sudden turn of events, Cipiano panicked and ran off, saying he was going to find some better fans. It was his intention to improvise a system that would allow the mechanics to enter that night.

When the assistant returned, Slater filled out the tags that warned of the danger and prohibited entry into the tanks.

I requested a photocopy of the tags for my report. Slater was not pleased with the request; he understood what it meant. The senior industrial hygienist was in a "squeeze." Professionally, he had to act to prevent any more accidents. But by hanging the tags, he was in effect admitting that Century had not followed proper safety procedures. Though he looked as if he had second thoughts, he did not hesitate any further. Slater made a photocopy of the tags for me and then, to his credit, boarded the plane and hung the tags on each of the hatches of the fuel tank. His assistant turned to me and said it was the first time the safety office had actually shut down a production operation. It was clear that the production managers had long ruled in matters of safety.

Soon after the tags were hung, Cipiano showed up with two squirrel cage–type fans. His herculean attempt to set up an on-the-spot ventilation system was cut short, however, when he could not locate the ducts to carry fresh air from the fans to the hatches. Tired from the day's events, he assented to the tag-out.

I was also worn out and asked to be escorted out. The safety staff was glad to oblige.

The next day I returned to Century to make sure that the production people in building M-4 were adhering to the shutdown. They were, and several of the mechanics were attending the class in safe tank entry.

While at the site, I conducted more interviews and requested a copy of Century's tank-entry procedures. Although I had the legal right to these materials, the director of training told me that they were confidential and did not want to give them to me. After minutes of polite argument and an explanation of my right to review the document, I grew impatient. "Either you give me a copy or I'll consider your delay a refusal and obtain a warrant," I complained.

The director grew red in the face and angrily said he would contact the company's lawyers. If he decided to give me a copy, he said, he would send it over to the safety office, where I could pick it up before I left. A copy was available for me when I left late that evening.

I ran into a worse runaround trying to obtain records on the company's monitoring of exposure to methylene chloride, one of the solvents used to clean the tanks. The company had conducted extensive monitoring of tank-cleaning operations at two sites after it had been issued an OSHA citation some time earlier. I thought the data would be helpful in determining whether excessive exposures routinely occurred in the fuel tanks and, if so, the control methods that would be needed. Also, I could verify compliance with the earlier citation.

"You don't need that data," the director of the safety department said in response to my first request.

"Yes, I do," I replied unhesitatingly. I knew I had the authority to review the data. The right of access to exposure records and company documents relating to employee exposure to hazardous chemicals is provided to exposed employees, their union, and OSHA inspectors by an important OSHA standard. I reminded the safety director of the regulation, but he still refused to turn over the records.

I obtained some of the data later after a meeting with the safety department in which I made it clear that the department was in willful violation of OSHA regulations. About a month after my initial request, Cipiano and Slater came to the OSHA office with part of the data and pleaded with me not to mention to Century's attorneys that they had turned over the material. They still refused to give up some material, they said, because it had been obtained by a consultant who considered the data "confidential." Was the safety department, or more likely the company's attorney, hiding the results for some reason? To further debunk the claim that the material was confidential, another industrial hygienist in my office later recalled seeing the data presented by the consultant at an industrial hygiene association meeting.

Fortunately, other material was easier to obtain. An unsolicited copy of a memo from the safety department to production managers detailing proper safety procedures and the requirements for training mechanics for tank entry was given to me surreptitiously. The memo had been lifted from the tank mechanic foremen's log on their desk in building M-4. Along with the memo was a photocopy of air-testing records showing that the foremen had routinely conducted tests for oxygen sufficiency in the tanks before workers entered them but that the tests had been discontinued about three months earlier, before the accident. On a subsequent visit to Century I casually asked to look at the foremen's log and confirmed the presence of the memo and the record of oxygen testing.

From the facts I had on the accident, I had to hold the foremen partly culpable. They were responsible for taking the actions necessary to ensure that the workers were trained and took precautions, particularly since the company's safety department had warned of the dangers of tank work and had procedures for safe tank entry. At the least, the foremen had been negligent in not informing upper management that the department was unable to maintain safe practices because of production demands.

A couple of the foremen I interviewed softened me a bit by giving me some insight into their problems. I learned that maintaining the high production demanded by upper management, scheduling the numerous assembly tasks, and solving the never-ending problems that can lead to unacceptable delays was an exceptionally stressful and complex job. Nonetheless, it was stimulating for some of them. As one foreman said, "I love every minute of it." Another foreman dryly commented that retired foremen did not live long enough to receive their first retirement check.

After these discussions, I started placing more blame on upper management for the recent safety infractions. What could a foreman do if safety concerns could not be used as a valid reason for minor delays? If upper management looked the other way when a safety problem arose, or failed to discipline a foreman who violated company safety rules, the message was that production was of primary importance and safety secondary.

I interviewed Bill Landers before closing the report and was saddened to hear that he was taking most of the blame for the accident. I tried to console him by pointing out that by practicing safe work procedures in building M-4 and enhancing safety awareness, another serious, perhaps fatal, accident might be prevented.

The director of safety, the safety engineer, two staff industrial hygienists, and the union steward all attended the closing conference. It had taken more than two months to obtain everything I needed, including a memo from the OSHA medical unit confirming that

Landers suffered serious effects and would have died had his co-worker not found him as soon as he did.

Before I began the conference, I noted to the safety director that the production manager for building M-4, whom I had asked to attend, was absent. The safety director apologized, saying the production manager's secretary had called and said he would be out of town. I had hoped to make it clear to him that if proper safety procedures were not followed and there was a fatality, the company could be charged with criminal negligence.

All were silent as I passed out copies of the citation and read off the violations: WILLFUL/SERIOUS/REPEAT for failure to ensure the use of proper ventilation when employees entered the fuel tanks for cleaning; WILLFUL/SERIOUS/REPEAT for failure to provide training to the mechanics on safe tank-entry and work practices; and SERIOUS/REPEAT for failure to provide training on the hazards of the solvents and paints used by the tank mechanics. The willful characterizations were partly based on the company's history of near misses in wing tanks.

The safety staff did not offer any argument. Everyone knew there was no point in debating the violations now. The policy of the company was to appeal all violations anyway.

Cipiano interrupted me right before the discussion of the fines. He said it was the policy of the company to exclude union representatives from this portion of the conference. I was surprised and told him that the information was not confidential but that I would hold a separate conference with the union steward if he preferred.

Cipiano jerked his head back, protesting that the company considered the amounts confidential.

"I don't," I said.

He quickly wrote a note on his pad of paper, apparently recording my "disobedience." There was no law or regulation that made this portion of the conference confidential; employee representatives have the right to participate in closing conferences in which citations and penalties are discussed.

I asked the union representative to step out of the room for a moment while I held a "confidential" discussion about the fines with the company representatives. I would hold a separate meeting with him later, I explained. The company and the union may have separate closing conferences if the employer requests them.

Facing the now-resentful Cipiano, I pulled out my penalty calculation sheet, described the poor history ranking and the level of fines for each violation, and pointed to the total fine of $22,125. It was the largest fine I had ever issued. Cipiano had no comment.

The union steward was readmitted to the room and Cipiano and his staff left.

After I had explained the fines to the union steward, we discussed what had happened since the accident and what could be expected in the future. The safety department had made an intensive effort in the fuel-tank area of building M-4 since the shutdown. Between the time of my first inspection and the closing conference, a new ventilation system had been set up that could be moved around for the out-of-position work. Sampling conducted by the company's industrial hygienists had verified that the ventilation system was controlling the level of exposure to solvent. Further, the safety department had reactivated an old policy of considering all fuel-tank work as occurring in "confined spaces." Finally, a safety engineer would be stationed at each tank operation to conduct air tests prior to entry and to ensure that proper procedures were followed. In spite of these changes, the union steward was not encouraged. He said he had been around a long time and was pessimistic that any of the changes would be permanent.

My investigation and the citations had given the safety department more courage to challenge production. The department could point to the citations and the tremendous fine that would result if another hapless mechanic was hurt while working in a tank full of solvent vapor or that lacked oxygen.

Century appealed all the citations related to Bill Landers's accident. A date for an appeal hearing was set for twelve months after the closing date of the inspection. Several weeks before, the company's attorney requested a continuance. The hearing was reset for six months later. But before the hearing was held, the attorney requested another continuance because he would be on vacation. The hearing date was reset again for two months later. But before this date, another request for a continuance was made and granted because some of the company's safety staff were involved in an audit. The hearing was rescheduled again for a date just short of *two years* after the citations had been issued. During this time, a follow-up inspection could not be conducted, and, by law, the company did not have to comply with the requirements of the citation, although in this case it probably did comply. While the case was under appeal, the company's attorney proposed various deals to the OSHA attorney handling the appeal. The proposals were rejected; the company's history and the documentation gathered made the case solid. Also, several of the workers, backed by a strong union, were willing to testify at the hearing.

Finally, Century made an offer that could not be refused. The company offered to drop its contest of the amount of the penalty and the citations and agreed to pay the $22,125 fine in full. In addition, the company offered on its own to drop several other pending appeals over unrelated safety violations. It was an unprecedented offer from a company that appealed and fought every citation. In return, OSHA agreed to drop a willful characterization. (Another willful characterization was removed by the OSHA attorney because he believed the documentation was too weak, leaving the citation as a serious/repeat.)

Flammable Attitudes

One thing some owners and managers detest more than being inspected is being inspected as a result of a complaint from an employee at a neighboring company. Generally, OSHA has little power to force one business to make changes to protect a neighboring business's employees. OSHA's jurisdiction, except in some contracting relationships, is limited to the employer of the employees who are at risk. In this case, my assigned inspection was generated by a boatyard worker who claimed that harmful solvent vapors were being released from a spray booth owned and operated by a boat builder on an adjoining lot.

I located the complainant's employer's office and introduced myself to the manager, who was quite friendly. I soon confirmed that the spray booth alleged to be causing the trouble was on the adjoining boatyard, which is how I found myself standing in front of another manager who, weighing about 250 pounds and standing over six feet tall, cursed me, OSHA, and other regulatory agencies.

After conducting the opening conference with the manager, I listened patiently as the diatribe continued. He described how the last company he had managed had spent thousands of dollars needlessly on an overhead crane as a result of an OSHA inspection. The inspector, he added, had not known anything about the business. Such complaints are sometimes valid. Some inspectors are poorly trained and supervised and end up requiring companies to spend dollars needlessly, but, more often than not, such complaints come from employers who have been forced to comply with a well-devised regulation.

The manager also complained about being inspected when he had a perfect safety record—no accidents in the past ten years. He had no basic safety program that I could discern from my questions during the opening conference, but he was insistent that what he did have was effective.

This was also a common complaint but overall a wrong supposition. Would it take a serious accident, an amputation, or a loss of life to prove that the business needed a basic safety program? Many companies are accident-free for years, and some never have a serious accident. But some do. It is therefore reasonable, for the purpose of reducing the overall rate of tragedies, to require all businesses to have accident prevention programs.

The manager finally began to tire of his tirade over regulatory agencies and my intrusion into his affairs, and I asked to tour his facilities.

"Do I have the right to kick you off the site?" the manager asked in a tone indicating he knew the answer.

"Yes," I replied.

"Okay. Just wanted to make sure. You didn't bother to mention that," he said, raising his voice. "Let's take the tour now," he snapped.

We spent about half an hour walking through the parts department, the shop, and around the boat-building area until we reached the spray booth under question. The booth was located in a thirty-to-forty-year-old single-story warehouse. The frame and walls were all ripely aged very dry wood—perfect for kindling a fire.

The spray booth was at least ten feet wide by fifty feet long, long enough to hold the masts and other parts painted in it. At the far end of the rectangular booth was a fan that sucked air from the opening of the booth, blowing it into the yard of the neighboring boat builder. In answer to a question, the manager explained that the business used paints composed of flammable solvents, as well as some that contained isocyanates, a lung irritant.

The idea that paint containing a lung irritant and solvent was being blown into another business's work area bothered me, but not as much as the lighting system inside the spray booth. It posed a more immediate problem.

The lighting system consisted of bare lamps and exposed electrical parts that hung over and were attached to the sides of the spraying area. The booth was an accident waiting for the right conditions—in this case, flammable solvent vapor drifting near one of the lights and being ignited by a spark from the electrical system. A painter could be spraying a mast and, with an inadvertent twist of the wrist or compromised ventilation, or just because he was spraying more paint than usual, suddenly find himself in a ball of fire. Victims who survive such accidents suffer from massive, torturous skin burns and are usually disfigured for life.

His options according to OSHA standards were to enclose the lights to prevent concentrations of flammable solvents from reaching the electrical apparatus or to disconnect them and purchase lights that were sealed and thus "explosion-proof." The only other solution was to paint outside.

I informed the manager of the fire hazard in the booth and of his options.

He quickly exploded, rejecting my suggestions of enclosing the lights or painting outside. He complained that it was too dusty to paint outside and that the company could not afford to do all the necessary electrical upgrades. He did not want to add explosion-proof lights, he said, because the city would consider it a building improvement and make him bring the whole warehouse into compliance with city building codes.

"We considered buying a new spray booth, but one hundred thousand dollars is too much for the company right now. If you require me to add noncombustible walls and a new lighting system, I'll have to stop painting and lay off ten to twelve employees, and December is a bad time to be laying off so many people. You got to think about those families and jobs."

Was he trying to intimidate me into overlooking the violation? It didn't matter. The booth was a clear and immediate danger. One or more people could be killed or badly burned because of the safety deficiencies. He made me consider, though, whether it is ever right for a company to place other priorities above a danger and continue in business, risking the lives of employees.

It is rare for a business to fail because it cannot afford to operate safely. In this case, the company should have decided years before, when it was formed, either to build a safe spray booth or to contract out the painting until a safe booth could be built.

According to the manager, the choices were to continue painting in the "relatively safe" booth or to have twelve workers laid off in December. I had no choice but to issue a citation. If I overlooked the hazard and there was an accident, the state and I would be liable. I remembered what an inspector had once coldly said to me, that should I fail in my job and the accident occur, "you can go and explain it to the worker's widow and family why you didn't write the company up."

I issued a serious violation with a fine to the manager in a closing conference a few days after the inspection. Though I was troubled by his threat of a layoff, I believed the threat was a bluff. He said he would stop painting altogether and send the work to one of his competitors, who, he added sarcastically, did not have an approved spray booth either. The manager refused to name the competitor.

I explained that if he continued to use the booth as it was and someone was hurt, he could be criminally liable and probably would be prosecuted.

About a month after closing the inspection and issuing the citation, the manager returned an OSHA form on which he was required to describe how the company was complying with the regulations in violation. The manager wrote that his workers were no longer spray-painting in the booth.

Included with the form was a letter in which the manager complained about how unreasonable regulatory agencies were, particularly those that went after employers that had had no accidents at their sites. He stated that as a result of my actions, he had had to lay off twelve employees just days before Christmas. He concluded by saying that he hoped OSHA was happy that it had caused these layoffs. Enclosed was a copy of the layoff notice he allegedly sent to the employees, which explained that OSHA was responsible for their losing their jobs.

My supervisor wanted to bury the letter. If there was any truth to it, he certainly did not want it landing on the desks of his superiors or, equally dangerous, the press. If it did get to the media, any attempt at an explanation on our part could be quickly squelched by the emotionality of the claims. A story about twelve people out of work at Christmastime could easily be written to appear much worse than a report on one or two workers spray-painting in a booth that "had not blown up even once." It would be easy to explain to the general public, and easy for the public to understand, the pain of being out of work during the holiday season. It would be less easy to explain the dangers of working day in and day out in an ill-equipped spray booth.

A month later I conducted an unannounced follow-up visit, as required by law. The inspection was done with the help of one of our safety inspectors who specialized in electrical problems. We found that the company had stopped painting in the illegal spray booth, as required. Some of the painting was being done outdoors, away from any spark-producing equipment.

I interviewed one part-time employee, who said his job was to paint masts. I asked if there had been any layoffs. "Not any that I know about," he replied.

After determining that the risk of fire and explosion had been abated simply by not using the spray booth and that the present location posed no hazard, I closed the inspection by asking the manager how many employees he had had to lay off.

"Oh, one or two."

"Not twelve?"

He did not reply.

It was doubtful that anyone had been laid off, and, fortunately, it was now unlikely that anyone would be laid to rest while working in the booth.

More than a Headache

Industrial Microcircuits and Electronics Incorporated. The name sounded familiar.

The accident report on my desk stated that an employee had been overcome by solvent fumes and taken to the hospital. The report, submitted by paramedics, noted that the accident had been caused by "faulty ventilation."

I had the vague feeling I had been to Industrial Microcircuits, and when I looked up the company's name in our files, as required before inspecting, I found that I had, about two years before. Another industrial hygienist in my office had been assigned to inspect the company, and I had accompanied him as part of my field training. I could not remember what citations, if any, he had issued.

From a review of the file, I surmised that at the time of the first inspection the company had not had a written program for workers who used air-supplied respirators during the handling of toxic arsine gas. There was no record that a citation had been issued, but a copy of a program, dated three months after the date of the opening inspection and about a week before the closing conference, was in the file. The inspector must have gotten the company to comply with the regulation without writing a citation, producing the desired result and little paperwork for him. The report indicated that few workers had been interviewed. On the front page of the standardized inspection form, under the "attitude" section, I noted that the inspector had given the company a "good-faith" rating.

After reviewing the company's file, I drove out to the site, where I met with the quality control manager, who also acted as the safety manager. I learned that the worker who had been sent to the hospital had been released but that her doctor had advised her not to return to work yet. She had developed a lung irritation, the manager said. He did not know exactly what her problem was. The company doctor had reviewed her medical report, he explained, and had concluded that there was no relationship between her symptoms and exposure to the chemical. I deduced that under the current circumstances the woman's problems were being considered personal. Her medical bills would not be paid by workers' compensation, and she would have to deduct her days off from sick leave or vacation time. Considering the information I had so far, it was possible that the woman's symptoms and the as-yet-undefined level of exposure were coincidental.

I explained to the manager that I would have to conduct my own investigation and asked him to describe the incident. He explained that the woman had been using chloroform to clean electrical parts. He admitted that the workers in the department where she worked had thought that there was a strong odor on the morning before the incident. He blamed the odor on a dirty exhaust screen in the ventilation system. If any solvent had been released, it was not in dangerous amounts, he said, adding that there had never been any health problems in the department.

I was curious why the company used chloroform as a solvent; other cleaning solvents had much less toxicity. Chloroform is quite volatile, and since research had disclosed its carcinogenicity and adverse effects on the female reproductive system, many companies had switched to less toxic solvents.

I asked the manager why the company used chloroform and not some other less toxic alternative. He explained that the microelectronic chips and transistors the company made went through a complex process and were highly sensitive to changes in procedures or in the environment. He was reluctant to substitute another solvent and risk having the quality of their product suffer, adding that the microelectronics business was highly competitive. I suggested that it would be worth trying a different solvent on a limited number of parts, but he did not respond.

After discussing the company's overall safety program, which I noted lacked training in chemical hazards, we left his office for a tour of the microchip department, where the incident under investigation had occurred. The manager introduced me to the department supervisor, who showed me the suspect spray-cleaning unit.

The unit, which was sitting atop a workbench, consisted of a small box, about the size of a ten-gallon aquarium, and a quart-sized bottle of chloroform. The box had a removable face plate made of clear plastic. The face plate had a square hole on the right-hand side through which a worker slipped a part to be cleaned. In front of the face plate was a bottle of chloroform capped with a spray nozzle that fit through a round hole in the face plate. The nozzle was attached with a wire and a pressurized hose that ran off to the side of the workbench. The quality control manager explained that the chloroform was drawn from the bottle using an inert gas and was then passed through a heating element in the spray nozzle.

The department supervisor demonstrated how the unit worked. She put on a protective glove, and, holding a pair of tweezers in her gloved right hand, she picked up a small tray of electrical parts. She then placed the tray in front of the spray nozzle. Using her ungloved left hand, she pressed a button on the bottle, releasing warm chloroform vapor. An exhaust port in the bottom of the box appeared to collect the vapors. The manager explained that the exhaust port was ducted to a fan and then up to the roof, where the vapors were released.

At first glance, the operation did not look menacing. At the same time, it does not take much chloroform in the air to poison someone.

The exposure limit for chloroform has been progressively lowered over the years because of the danger of chronic toxicity. California's eight-hour limit was 10 ppm at the time of the inspection, in contrast to the federal ceiling limit of 50 ppm, set in 1971. The National Institute of Occupational Safety and Health had recommended in 1977 that the limit be lowered to 2 ppm, measured over any one-hour work period. Federal OSHA reacted in January 1989 by setting a new limit of 2 ppm as an eight-hour average, effective March 1, 1989. The new level was set in an effort to prevent birth defects and problems conceiving and to reduce the risk of cancer and liver toxicity. Workers exposed to chloroform above the 2 ppm level on a chronic basis are at increased risk for one or more of these effects. At levels of 100 ppm or higher, the risks are more immediate and include headaches, nausea, dizziness, and drowsiness. At higher levels, the risks include unconsciousness, irritation of lung tissue, cardiovascular depression, ventricular fibrillation, coma, respiratory paralysis, and, finally, death from failure of one or more affected organs.

After the demonstration of the spray unit, I informed the quality control manager that I wanted to conduct some interviews in private. I began by interviewing the supervisor in the microchip department. When I asked what had happened on the day the worker got sick, she recalled that the spray unit had been emitting a stronger-than-usual odor, but she had not thought it was a problem. She explained that the operator had become ill all of a sudden, blaming it on the solvent. After the paramedics had taken the operator away, the supervisor discovered that the metal screen covering the exhaust port in the unit was dirty and needed cleaning. She noted that maintenance of the screen was done periodically, though not according to a schedule. Before the unit was used again, she added, someone from maintenance had cleaned the screen. When I asked her whether other workers had had any complaints about the unit, she answered, "Not really."

Another operator had more to say. When I asked her the same question, she replied that when she had to spray all day, as she had in the past, she would get headaches, feel sleepy, and get "a feeling in the chest."

"You don't spray all day anymore?" I asked.

No, she said, because of the problems she was having, she and another operator split the shift so that she sprayed only half the day. As a result, she said, she no longer had any symptoms. She added that another woman in the microchip department had been taken off the operation because of the physical problems she was experiencing.

When I asked my interviewee to show me how she operated the spray unit, she first removed the face plate and set it aside. She explained that being left-handed, she needed to use her left hand to hold the tray of parts to be cleaned. She said she did not think it mattered whether the face plate was on the unit or not. Within seconds, however, I smelled chloroform coming from the box and asked her to stop the demonstration.

"Did you receive any training or instruction in how to operate the unit's ventilation system and keep your exposure low?" I asked.

"No."

"Did you receive any information on the possible health effects of chloroform?"

"No. Why, is it very bad?"

Earlier, her supervisor had expressed similar ignorance and curiosity about chloroform. In that one of their co-workers had been taken out on a stretcher, it was not surprising that the department's employees had become much more curious about whether chloroform was dangerous.

After completing the interviews, I called over the quality control manager and asked to see the spray units in the process board department. The manager directed me to a small room that contained two units similar to the ones in the microchip department. The room also contained a "degreaser," used to clean parts with solvent.

As I looked at the degreaser and spray units, it struck me that I had seen the operation during my training inspection two years before. I recalled passing by the room with the other inspector, and then, at my request, going back for another look. I remembered commenting to him that the spray units in the room appeared to be poorly designed. They had no face plates, and, although there was an exhaust port on the floor of the units, it appeared that the pressurized chloroform vapor could bounce out of the box and into the face of the operator. The other inspector had said that it was not a problem since only a small amount of chloroform was being released and there was a ventilation system. He did not think it was worth sampling the vapors, and my concern was not expressed to the company.

I felt now that I should have persisted. In any situation in which there is even a small chance of overexposure, the investigating industrial hygienist must conduct the proper tests to determine if workers are being subjected to harmful exposure.

While I was studying the unit, one of the operators came into the room. After introducing myself, I motioned to the quality control manager that I wanted to interview the operator privately. I began by asking her if she had ever had any problems while using the unit. She replied that whenever she used it for most of the day, which she did more than two times a week, she would get headaches and feel nauseous. She had been cleaning parts for almost three months, she explained. No one had provided her with any instructions other than in how to clean the parts, and, not surprisingly, she did not know that the solvent was hazardous. The woman replaced several months before had also had physical complaints, she said.

She continued by saying that she had started feeling symptoms during her first week on the job. She had reported the problems to her supervisor, she said, who had told her to leave the room for a while whenever she felt sick. "Two days after I first complained, I was given a respirator," she said. She described the respirator, which was made of white paper with a single rubber strap that went around the neck. "The respirator didn't work that well," she said.

I shook my head and told her that the single-strap paper respirator she had been issued was useless for vapors, and even for dust, for which it was supposedly designed. As an industrial hygienist friend of mine once said, it provides as much protection as a coffee filter fastened to the face with a rubber band.

She showed me the respirator she now used. It was a rubber half-mask-style respirator that fit over the nose and chin but not the eyes. It had a "chemical cartridge" on it for absorbing organic chemicals. It was adequate for some chemicals but not for chloroform. The problem was that the wearer had no way of knowing when the cartridge was used up; by the time the operator smelled an odor, she had been overexposed for some time. With few exceptions, such respirators should be used only for protection from chemicals that provide a warning, such as a harmless odor, taste, or irritation, indicating that the cartridge is spent. It is an often overlooked rule.

Next, I interviewed the supervisor who had given the operator the useless paper respirator. When I asked him why the operators were using unapproved respirators, he became uncooperative and began answering in the shortest sentences possible. I asked him if he knew whether chloroform was hazardous or not. He replied that he didn't know.

"Did you tell your supervisor that your operator was having problems with the solvent, so that someone could check into it?"

"I didn't think it was a problem."

After the interview I pulled the quality control manager aside and asked him why the operator had been given the cartridge respirator. He said he had issued it several weeks before, after learning that the operator was complaining about the odor of the solvent.

"Did you consider monitoring the exposure to find out if there was a problem?" I asked.

"Well, I considered it," he said, "but I wasn't sure where to pick up the badges for monitoring." He also acknowledged that he had not given the operator a test to determine whether the cartridge respirator fit well enough to prevent leakage.

I gritted my teeth. I was fairly certain that several of the operators were being or had been overexposed to chloroform on a chronic basis. I was even more certain that all of the operators were ignorant of the health hazards of the chemical they were using. To make matters worse, the quality control manager and on-line supervisors had apparently failed to find out about the dangers of the chemical, in spite of the operators' symptoms.

At my office the next day, I called the home of the operator who had been taken to the hospital. I learned that she had not yet returned to work. She was still upset about what she was certain was overexposure to the solvent and complained that the company was talking about contesting her claim that the accident was work-related. Her time off would be charged against her sick leave and vacation time, she said.

I asked her to relate the events of the day when she got sick. She had felt fine on the morning of the incident, she explained, and had been assigned to clean several trays of electrical parts, as she had been doing off and on since she had started working for the company. The odor from the solvent had bothered her before, she said, but whenever she had complained, her supervisor had thought nothing of it. That particular morning, the odor had been stronger than usual, but her complaints had again gone unheeded.

Later that morning, she continued, she had begun feeling dizzy and sick to the point that she thought she would pass out. She called for help. Her co-workers recognized her distress, and soon paramedics were taking her to the hospital. She was in the hospital for several days because she developed a lung irritation. Her doctor was certain that it was related to exposure to the solvent, she said. She added that she had never received any information about whether chloroform was hazardous and that she knew of another woman in the department who had had so many problems that she could no longer operate the spray unit.

I also spoke with the paramedic who had filed the woman's accident report with my office. He recalled that the woman had felt faint when the paramedics arrived and that some of her co-workers had told him that the woman was exposed to the solvent because of a ventilation problem. Based on the woman's condition and the possibility of chemical exposure, the paramedics had rushed her to the hospital. The paramedic also related that one employee had approached him and asked whether the solvent was dangerous. She had had problems with it the week before.

I returned to the company two days later to monitor the operators for chloroform. I was equipped with two different devices. One of the devices, called a badge monitor, is about the size of a small cookie. It conveniently clips to a shirt lapel. The badge contains a wafer of charcoal covered by a membrane permeable to air and vapors. Once the badge is unwrapped and exposed to the air, certain chemicals stick to the charcoal. The more chemical is in the air, or the longer the exposure, the more chemical vapor sticks to the charcoal. After several hours of exposure, the badge is removed, covered, and taken to a laboratory for analysis. The average concentration of the chemicals is then calculated using a formula supplied by the manufacturer of the badge. The concentration of the chemicals can then be compared to established exposure limits. This is an extraordinarily easy method for monitoring vapors. The alternative, still necessary for some chemicals, is to have the worker wear a cumbersome pump that draws contaminated air through a small glass tube packed with charcoal.

I also brought along a halide meter, which provides instantaneous readings of the levels of chloroform and other chlorinated solvents in the air. The device consists of a small metal box containing a pump that draws air through a sampling tube into a chamber that, using ultraviolet light, stimulates the chlorine atoms in chloroform. The chlorine atoms emit another type of light, which in turn is quantitated by a light meter, also in the metal box, that is sensitive to the emitted light. The more chloroform vapor is in the sampled air, the more the needle on the meter moves to the right.

I arrived at Industrial Microcircuits, Inc., at the beginning of the first shift and proceeded to place the monitoring badges on one operator in the microchip department and one in the process board department. Once both operators were set up, I warmed up the halide meter so that I could get some immediate readings on the levels of chloroform. I first used the meter in the process board department. Before long, the meter was indicating chloroform levels of 30 to 150 ppm in the breathing area of the operator. At these concentrations, it would not take long for an operator's exposure level to exceed by several-fold the eight-hour average limit of 10 ppm. The defect in the design of the box was obvious. Now that I had proved that there was overexposure, I could require the company to alter the unit. As I had suspected more than two years before, because there was no face plate, the vapors could bounce out of the box into the operator's face. The large opening in the front of the box made the ventilation system ineffective.

The quality control manager stopped by while I was using the halide meter. Pointing out the high reading, I explained the defect in the unit. The manager stopped the operation immediately and assigned the worker another task to do. The manager then found the operator's supervisor and told him that the cleaning operation would have to stop.

While I waited outside the room, the manager went over to the maintenance shop and brought back a shop employee. He measured the front of the box and left. I could guess what was happening.

Before leaving for the day, I returned to the process board department and found a newly constructed face plate in place. I learned that within two hours after the unit had been shut down, a piece of clear plastic, with the appropriate holes for the operator's hand and the nozzle of the spray bottle, had been installed. Cleaning, however, had not been resumed.

I returned again several days later and monitored the modified spray box in the process board department to gather data on the success of the new face plate. The halide meter showed a much reduced exposure. I also sampled the operator's exposure level using a sampling device that more accurately measures exposure averaged over time.

Several weeks later, I received the laboratory report on all the samples. The results showed that the modified unit had generated exposure readings at just below the 10-ppm limit. The new face plate had done the trick.

The badge sample taken before the new face plate was installed verified that the exposure level had been five or more times the 10-ppm limit on the day the operation was shut down. More than likely, operators had been overexposed by several-fold several times a week for the years the unit had been in use.

What did it take to motivate this company to change? Not years of overexposure resulting in adverse health risks, including reproductive effects and cancer. Not persistent complaints from employees. Not acute exposure resulting in hospitalization. Rather, it took an OSHA inspection as a result of a serious incident of toxicity. A more responsible attitude could have been expected; indeed, the law required it. A quick look in a reference book or a call to an occupational health physician, to OSHA's consultation service, or to one of many private consultants would have validated the workers' complaints and resulted in a recommendation for prompt and appropriate control.

Sampling done in the microchip department, where the accident occurred, indicated that when the ventilation system was operating properly, the levels of chloroform were just below the limit. The operators had recently been required to use the face plate, and, following the accident, the exhaust screen had been cleaned. Also, the operators worked no more than four hours each on the unit, per shift, reducing their exposure by half.

As my investigation revealed, before my inspection, the operators in the microchip department had most likely suffered overexposure daily in that they routinely cleaned parts for a whole day. On the day of the accident, the exhaust port had been dirty and the ventilation system compromised, so overexposure had undoubtedly occurred.

I held the closing conference with the quality control manager about four weeks after I had started the inspection. During the conference, I discussed how the company could act more responsibly in the future regarding the safety and health of its employees. It was an oblique way to say that the quality control manager and the supervisors had acted irresponsibly in the past. I told the manager that there was some evidence to support issuing a willful citation, but I did not tell him that the operators had said that their complaints had gone unheeded. There was no need to generate additional mistrust and bad feelings between the workers and the managers and risk having the operators victimized again. The operators presumably still wanted their jobs, and some might even have had hopes of promotions.

The circumstances did not quite meet those demanded by administrative law judges for a willful violation, so I issued the company a serious violation for the overexposure to chloroform in the process board department. Control could be attained by providing face plates that enclosed the units, thereby letting less vapor escape. Though I was certain that overexposure had occurred chronically in the microchip department, culminating in the accident, I could not document it without more hard evidence, such as earlier monitoring data.

I also issued a serious violation for failure to provide training in the hazards of chloroform, the symptoms of overexposure, and safe work practices. If training had been provided years earlier, the employees might have been more persistent with their complaints. At the very least, having knowledge of the risks they faced, they could have filed a complaint with OSHA or sought other employment. And, had the work force been better informed, the quality control manager and first-line supervisors might have been more responsive.

Training would inform everyone about the need to use the face plates on the spray units and to have at least two operators for every eight-hour shift, though the latter "administrative control" was less preferable than providing better ventilation and enclosures. The quality control manager would, I hoped, learn something from setting up the training program or sitting in on one provided by a consultant. As safety manager, it was his responsibility to be aware of the hazards workers faced and to ensure that the hazards were controlled.

Additional violations, "general" or nonserious, were noted: improper use of chemical cartridge respirators for protection against chloroform; failure to inspect the ventilation system periodically; failure to monitor exposure levels; and, unrelated to the use of chloroform, improper ventilation of a flammable-liquid storage room attached to the main building.

Industrial Microcircuits was issued a penalty of $655, a little less than what a private consultant would have charged to monitor the level of chloroform, make recommendations, and provide a training session. The threat of a higher fine probably would have brought the manager's regard for safety and health to a higher level and forced the company to act more responsibly long before my inspection.

A short time after the closing conference, I received a phone call from a man who introduced himself as the corporate attorney for Industrial Microcircuits. For at least thirty minutes he talked pleasantly about the merits of the citations I had issued. But then he began to question my method of monitoring chloroform exposure levels and whether overexposure was really dangerous. "Getting a headache isn't all that serious. Just how do you determine if a violation is serious?" He read from a book that described the acute effects of chloroform as being like those of an anesthesia and asked how I could claim that this sleep inducer, which had hardly caused any harm to the employees at the plant, was a serious problem.

When I asked him what book he was reading, he gave me the title and edition. I asked him to wait a moment as I checked my office's library. The book he was using had been published ten years earlier. I told him that science had progressed in ten years and that severe chronic toxicity (i.e., harm that is not done immediately but that may be suffered some time in the future) is a risk of low-level exposure to chloroform, as was occurring at the plant.

He went on to say that OSHA should have conducted a medical study to determine whether the workers were having ill effects. I explained that such studies are time-consuming and costly, requiring researchers and medical doctors, and are usually inconclusive for small populations. Even if such a study is conducted, problems in conceiving, deformities in newborns, or increases in the number of miscarriages, cancers, or other illnesses can be difficult to relate to workplace exposure unless the incidence rate is significantly above background levels. Further, some of the effects develop far into the future, making assessments possible only after the damaging exposure has occurred.

He was not convinced, and, although he remained polite, he continued, unrelentingly, to rephrase his argument.

I grew weary and offered to send him copies of my reference materials and of the California OSHA policy and procedures on methods for monitoring solvents and for determining the gravity of citations. I also gave him the phone numbers of the regional manager and the medical unit. I concluded by giving him my thoughts on what a responsible company would have done when workers complained of symptoms of overexposure to a solvent such as chloroform.

He acted surprised to hear that complaints had gone unheeded and that band aid-type solutions had been used. Apparently the quality control manager had not bothered to give the attorney much background on the problems.

I must have made my point with the corporate attorney, for the company did not appeal and the fine was paid.

On a follow-up inspection, I found that the company was complying with the requirements of the citations. The spray units were being used correctly, so that the exposure levels were below the limit; the operators had been given a training program on chloroform, as confirmed by interviews; and the maintenance department had established a schedule for periodic inspections of the spray units. At my recommendation, the quality control manager had purchased an air flow meter so that he could periodically check the effectiveness of the exhaust systems on the spray units. And, most important, the company seemed to have given safety and health matters higher priority.

4. NOISE

Everyone has experienced excessive noise at some time. Sometimes the noise can be so intense that it is painful, such as a jet engine warming up, speakers blaring from a stereo, or someone shouting in your ear. Though too loud for some may be just right for others, many would agree that jet engines, loudspeakers, motorcycles, and jackhammers produce unpleasant, sometimes painful, noise.

Many exposed to loud sounds may recognize a temporary loss of hearing. For a period of time after the intense noise has ended, they may notice that they have to turn the television volume up to the point where others complain or ask others to repeat themselves during conversation. Too many such episodes of excessive noise can permanently damage the sensors in the ear.

Thousands and thousands of people have permanently lost their hearing because of excessive noise at their workplace, and thousands and thousands more are at risk. The amount of damage that results is dependent on the level of loudness, the years of exposure, and differences among individuals. Only the latter cannot yet be controlled. The damage is temporary and permanent. It is temporary in that after a day's exposure at work, hearing may be affected to the point of being noticeably reduced but regained soon thereafter without any perceived loss; it is permanent in that the nerve cells are imperceptibly damaged, so that some of their ability to respond to sound is irreversibly lost. Repetitive overexposure takes a permanent toll. Gradually, hearing is lost, beginning with the inability to hear the flute or high notes of a violin during a concert and increasing to the frustrating and socially isolating experience of being unable to carry on a conversation. Eventually, complete deafness may result.

The loss is usually not noticed until there is major, irreversible damage. But if the exposure is intense enough, serious damage can occur in a short time. Even without exposure to noise, old age brings with it some loss in hearing. Exposure to loud sounds compounds the loss caused by old age, however, causing a more severe loss than would have otherwise occurred. Clearly, that extraordinary listening device, the human ear, needs protection from the industrial world.

Special instruments are generally used to analyze and quantitate noise for the purposes of determining exposure and risk of hearing loss. The instruments measure noise with respect to frequency (low versus high pitch) and loudness. The sound level or loudness is reported in decibel (dB) units. While sampling, the instruments correct for the human ear's relative insensitivity to lower frequencies. The correction is called "A" weighting, and worker exposure is measured in units of dBA. A high dBA means that the sound being measured has a greater degree of loudness and potential for causing damage. The dBA unit is based on a "log scale" in relation to sound energy. Thus an increase in loudness or sound pressure of 3 dBA, for instance, from 90 dBA to 93 dBA, is a twofold increase in sound energy.

The first OSHA health standards, adopted in 1971, included a requirement for protection from continuous noise levels exceeding 90 dBA as an eight-hour time-weighted average. Exposure could be controlled through engineering or administrative means or, less preferably, through the use of hearing protectors. The standard also established feasibility as a criterion, still in effect, for determining whether a company would be required to solve its noise problem by installing enclosures or other sound-proofing controls or by having employees wear earplugs or muffs.

The exposure limit and method of monitoring noise established by the 1971 standard had been developed years before and was based on certain compromises that some researchers believe resulted in underestimation of the risk. For example, the method used until 1981 did not allow measurement of noise below 90 dBA. The assumption was that only levels above 90 dBA affected the ear significantly. Consequently, hundreds of thousands of exposed workers went unprotected.

In 1972, an attempt was made to strengthen the OSHA standard by adding an amendment requiring companies with noise above a certain level to have an "effective" hearing conservation program. Unfortunately, the standard did not define the components of such a program. The intent was to ensure that overexposed workers received periodic hearing tests.

Compliance with the amendment was poor and resulted in a proposal for a standard that required hearing conservation programs to include annual hearing tests and training in noise hazards. Notably, workers exposed to 85 dBA or more over a workday were to be included in the program. This more specific standard was proposed in 1974 but was not actually adopted until 1981. It is the standard currently in effect.

In introducing this standard, entitled the Hearing Conservation Amendment, OSHA cited evidence that the old standard was not preventing hearing loss satisfactorily and that exposure at 85 dBA, 5 dBA below the previous maximum, presented significant risk.[1] OSHA reasoned that the amendment would lead to a "more equitable distribution of the costs and benefits of industrial production" and, optimistically, that "most workers will no longer bear the cost of occupational hearing loss, while those who share the benefits of industrial production will share the costs of preventing the loss."[2] The cost of implementing the standard was calculated to be $50 to $60 per affected worker.

The number of workers affected was significant. In determining the new standard, OSHA estimated that greater than 5 million were affected by noise levels of 85 dBA or greater and that if even half the affected industries complied with the new standard, a sorrowful but perhaps optimistic estimate, several hundreds of thousands of workers would be prevented from "material impairment" of their hearing. Material impairment was defined as a specified minimum loss, which in practical terms translates into difficulty understanding normal conversation and, in extreme cases, total deafness.

In the rulemaking for the 1981 standard, OSHA presented estimates of risks for workers exposed to various levels of noise over a working lifetime.[3] Evidence indicates, for example, that 10 to 15 percent of unprotected workers exposed to an average noise level of 85 dBA for forty years will suffer the minimum or greater hearing impairment. The risk increases to 21 to 29 percent for those exposed to average noise levels of 90 dBA. The figures are even greater when one includes damage such as being unable to hear whispers or other low-level or high-pitch sounds. Exposure to higher dBAs but with fewer years of exposure also incurs high risk of impairment. Even at

80 dBA, there is some risk, affecting 0 to 5 percent. Other risks include tinnitus, or "ringing in the ears," especially disturbing when it is a chronic condition, and less quantifiable effects that can contribute to ulcers, heart disease, and other stress-related problems.

The OSHA record for the Hearing Conservation Amendment included the following testimony from an individual who suffered *minimal* material impairment:

> It has been a gradual loss of hearing for me, so gradual that I never realized it until a few years ago, when a relative asked me if I did not hear well. After that I started noticing that it was getting worse and that I was having to strain more to hear clearly. I became alarmed and consulted a specialist, only to be told that nothing could be done and that the hearing loss had been caused by high noise exposure. It is truly a sad, helpless feeling . . . when you have lost a significant part of your second most important sensor. As time passes, I have been embarrassed because I was not able to hear well enough to know what was going on. At times it has become so disturbing that I have actually sat down and cried. . . . Persons who do not suffer any loss of hearing can't possibly realize the humiliation those of us who have impaired hearing go through.[4]

And, as the following testimony illustrates, using a hearing aid is not a solution:

> In a situation where there is a high ambient noise level, such as parties, I might as well leave my hearing aid at home, and very often, I go home after a short while since the multitude of speakers and all the noise frequently make it impossible to follow conversations. In any situation where there is background noise, such as an air conditioner, I find that communication is difficult, with or without the hearing aid. . . . I submit to you that the people with my hearing loss are considerably more than just barely impaired.[5]

The current OSHA standard requires that workers exposed to an average daily noise level of 85 dBA or greater be provided with a choice of several types of protectors, as well as annual hearing tests and information on the risks of noise-induced damage and on the proper use of hearing protectors. The use of protectors is optional for exposures less than or equal to 90 dBA and mandatory for exposures higher than 90 dBA. A few states require mandatory protection at 85 dBA and above.

Hearing protectors are the least desirable option from the standpoint of preventing hearing damage, yet they are widely used because of their low cost. Most protectors on the market are supposed to be capable of providing an overall reduction in exposure of about 20 to 35 decibels, depending on the brand. But as hearing tests of workers taken right off assembly lines demonstrate, the actual reduction is far less, usually 10 to 15 decibels.[6] The reason is that the protectors leak noise if they are worn imperfectly or are damaged. And, unfortunately, many workers use hearing protectors inconsistently or improperly.

Having a selection of hearing protectors, as required by the standard, is important. Some workers find plugs uncomfortable or difficult to fit properly in the ear canal. Plug or insert protectors are also impractical in dirty or oily plants, and workers can end up transferring the grime or grease into their ears while inserting the plugs. Others find earmuffs uncomfortable, especially in warm weather.

Annual hearing tests are required in part because hearing protectors have such a high failure rate. The tests, or audiograms, are important in that they provide an early warning of hearing loss and a chance to secure protection before significant disability is incurred.

The training requirement in the OSHA standard is designed to ensure that workers exposed to high noise levels are aware of the risks and consequences of unprotected exposure. For example, knowing the risks may motivate exposed workers to wear protectors consistently. Training also ensures that workers know how to use the protectors properly for maximum noise reduction.

The OSHA standard requires that engineering controls be used where feasible so that noise levels can be reduced, one hopes, to a level where hearing protectors are not necessary. Engineering controls are the best solution for reducing noise but are not always feasible for technical or economic reasons. Nevertheless, many engineering controls are available. When engineering controls are used successfully, so that levels of exposure are reduced below 85 dBA, other provisions of the standard do not apply.

The engineering control requirement is weakly enforced because few inspectors have the training or resources available to evaluate and propose controls. Furthermore, inspectors are sometimes reluctant to force a company to spend the money required to engineer out a noise problem when 90 percent of its uninspected competitors are unwilling to do so.

When complied with by employers and employees, the OSHA Hearing Conservation Amendment will make good on its promise of reducing hearing loss among the work force, and compared with other aspects of running a business, compliance is simple. A training program takes only thirty to sixty minutes of a worker's time, and workers can be trained in groups. Hearing tests can be obtained from a contractor and involve only fifteen to thirty minutes of each affected employee's time once a year. The steps required by the standard are the minimum necessary to prevent hearing losses among overexposed workers. As many hearing-impaired workers will testify, not adhering to these minimal requirements will result in many more workers suffering hearing loss.

Wheels of Misfortune

W hen I arrived at Wheels Unlimited, I was met by the personnel manager, Hal Baker. He was obviously in a hurry and made sure I knew I was taking him away from more important matters. Yes, he was in charge of the safety program at the plant, Baker said, in addition to personnel. And, yes, the company was quite busy right now. He slowed down a bit to say proudly that the company had a contract with a major automobile manufacturer to produce customized wheels, as well as its own line.

He was about to tell me about another problem when he received a phone call, which he concluded by saying, "No, no, that would cost Mr. Joey an additional one hundred thousand dollars, and Mr. Joey can't afford that right now." He explained after putting down the phone: "The company may not be open tomorrow as a union is trying to organize the workers, and the employees may organize and strike to demand more pay."

I explained that I was conducting an inspection based on a referral from a safety inspector who had been to the plant about a year before. He had identified several workers who appeared to have inadequate noise protection. I added that I was aware that other safety inspectors had been to the plant in the past several years. This comment clearly irritated the manager. "I'm getting tired of OSHA coming in here," he said. His attitude was a little surprising considering that the previous safety inspectors had not imposed very stiff penalties. I was more curious than ever to see the plant. Experience has taught me that companies where management hates OSHA usually have problems. And problems I found.

Next, I asked to review the company's log of injuries and illnesses, OSHA's 200 form, required in all companies with eleven or more employees. The log for the previous ten months was more than seven pages long and included 138 entries, an unusually high number for a company that employed only about three hundred production workers.

One reason to maintain the log is so that a company can track injuries and, one hopes, take corrective action as necessary. Among the entries were fourteen for burns from splashes of molten aluminum. Workers had been burned on their legs, forearms, feet, and one on his back. What was the company's excuse? The 200 form also listed incidents of lacerations in the machining areas and of heat stress in the foundry. No one was identified as having suffered hearing loss, but, based on the referral report, I expected the noise levels to be high enough to cause hearing damage.

Hearing injuries are rarely listed on 200 forms because of the long period of exposure usually necessary before the worker notices the damage. In addition, an injured worker does not always attribute the loss to his present job or to a job he left years before. Injuries such as cuts, burns, and amputations are obviously easily recognized and recorded. But hearing loss and other chronic problems that occur over time are not usually recognized or acknowledged by the employer, let alone recorded.

In this case the 200 form provided clear evidence of a deficient safety program since most of the injuries had been preventable. After obtaining a copy of the forms, I asked to conduct the walkaround of the plant.

We started in the foundry, where metal ingots were melted and transformed into the shape of wheels. There was much activity in this hundred-foot-by-hundred-foot area. Among the fumes and smoke, the roar and heat of the furnace, and the reverberating noise from the air-operated chisels, more than twenty men labored through the production cycle, dipping their long ladles into pots of molten metal, carrying the full ladles to the molds, pouring the metal into the molds, breaking the molds open to remove the hot wheel, chipping away the excess casting, and finally stacking the newly made wheels on a pallet while co-workers began the process over again. There were at least eight casting stations, each with a crew of three to four, and four pots of molten metal. As I watched, the stacks of wheels slowly grew taller.

I asked the foreman the exact composition of the alloy being used. Knowing the composition would indicate what hazards there might be. He replied that the wheels were basically aluminum, and, pulling a piece of paper from his desk, he read off the trace metals in the alloy. The only metal that produced significant fumes was the aluminum, one of the least toxic metals. Considering the quantities of fumes being released and the relatively high exposure limit, I decided that overexposure to aluminum was unlikely.

If the levels of fumes were legally tolerable, the levels of noise were not. Few workers were wearing protectors, and, using a hand-held sound-level meter, I discovered that the furnaces were producing a low-frequency rumble that gave the whole foundry a constant background noise level of 90 dBA. The air-powered chisels used to hammer away the excess metal on the newly formed wheels added frequent jaw-rattling bursts of more than 100 dBA.

I asked Baker whether the company had ever monitored the noise levels, as required by the OSHA standard.

"No, we haven't. The insurance company has talked about it."

"Have you provided any hearing tests or noise hazard training?" I asked.

"No, we've been planning to." Wondering how long the company had been "planning to," I noted that I would have to conduct full-shift noise monitoring in the foundry.

Walking around the foundry, I examined the protective equipment the men were wearing in hopes of discovering why so many were receiving burns from the molten metal. The ladlers wore wrist-length gloves, which allowed them to carry a ladle of molten metal without being burned, and face shields, which protected their faces if molten metal splashed out. Fine, except that they were missing the protective aprons and safety shoes the previous safety inspector had required and that might have prevented some of the leg and foot burns. Three of the foundry workers shared a single protective foot spat. None had safety shoes, and many wore tennis shoes, which would prevent a burn from the molten metal for a second or less. The company's accident log also indicated that the ladlers were receiving many burns on their forearms. I found it more than curious that none of the workers had been issued gloves that went above the elbow or other protection specially made for the forearm. Were the men that replaceable?

Continuing with the walkaround, we followed the unfinished wheels to the next two production steps, located adjacent to the casting department. Here, the wheels were strengthened by heat in a large furnace and then cleaned in several tanks. The heating process involved few workers and was enclosed. After the heat treatment, depending on the style of the wheel, some went to blasting booths, where their rough outer surfaces were smoothed using a black abrasive silicate material. The blasting booths were small, basically metal boxes with glass windows. The men reached into the boxes through attached gloves that kept the enclosure entirely sealed from the outside. There was virtually no dust exposure until the operator opened the door to remove a wheel, and even then it was minimal. The noise levels were not overpowering, but the operation would need monitoring over a full shift.

Hal Baker next showed me to one of the two machining areas. There were two long rows of machines that acted as lathes. A wheel to be machined was first attached to the shaft of a lathe and then rotated at a tremendous number of revolutions per minute. A knife strong enough to cut through aluminum then automatically and precisely fell onto the spinning wheel, removing the dull cast aluminum and leaving a smooth, bright surface.

I watched several wheels being machined. From the cutting action of the knife, a continuous strip of aluminum was thrown off like rope. Rising several feet into the air, it then coiled to the floor. The operator wisely stood to the side until the machine had finished its cycle.

A lubricating and cooling solution was also thrown into the air in the form of an aerosol. The aerosol remained suspended, filling the high room with a gray-blue haze that had a slight odor. A later investigation revealed that the solution was a new synthetic chemical with no known health hazards and that it was not listed in any of the chemical exposure tables. Powered ventilation, rather than relying on fresh air through distant open doors, was recommended to the personnel manager.

The only clear health hazard in this area was the noise. The high-speed lathes produced a constant background noise that was intensified by the screeching sound of the aluminum being stripped from the wheels.

The second machining area was larger and was also noisy and hazy. There were rows of drilling machines and rows and rows of lathes where the wheels were further customized to meet the demands of Detroit and America's auto buyers. I noted the number of workers in each section and the machines and operations that would have to be monitored for noise.

One lathe caught my attention, and I stopped Baker to point it out to him. At the back of the machine, a large-diameter pulley whirred at thousands of revolutions per minute, pulling a V-belt around a smaller pulley near the floor. The cover for the pulley and belt was set off to the side. I expressed my concern that someone could receive a serious injury if he or she inadvertently got too close. A shirttail, an arm sleeve, a finger, or a hand could be grabbed and thrown into the pulley, resulting in a serious laceration. I told him that the unguarded pulley and belt constituted a violation and would have to be corrected. This and other instances of unguarded machinery provided further evidence of the company's poor safety program.

Adjacent to the second machining area was the painting department. Here, the nearly finished wheels were first hung on hooks attached to a motorized track and then passed through a series of cleaning solutions and a rinse. The wheels were then routed through a series of spray booths where they were given a bronze or frosty aluminum coloring, heat-dried, and readied for shipping. The noise levels, as measured by my meter, were borderline, which again necessitated full-shift monitoring.

Curious about worker exposure to the cleaning solutions, I asked to speak with the foreman. At first he was suspicious about my intent and vague about what solutions were used and what first aid was available in the event acid got splashed in someone's eyes. I explained that if there was appreciable exposure to corrosives, the company had to provide an emergency eyewash and shower station, as well as eye and face protection. He must have thought it over, for later he approached me and explained precisely how the company used the large quantities of acid, adding that only pint-sized squirt bottles of eyewash were available. Revealing a new interest in my inspection, he added that as one of the workers who poured and mixed the acid, he personally would receive the benefits of having proper emergency first aid facilities.

With the walkaround concluded, I informed Baker that I would return the following week to monitor noise in the foundry, the machining areas, and the painting operation. I also reviewed the serious safety violations I had observed. Baker went on to remind me that, in addition to the "problem" I posed, he was facing the possibility of a strike.

I called Baker later to find out whether the workers were on strike and was told that the crisis had passed, for now. The employees had decided against the union. I scheduled my monitoring for later that week.

The morning of my return visit, I and another industrial hygienist met the workers as they arrived at their work stations. I had brought along the other health inspector to help me with the noise monitoring. We picked several workers in each department and greeted them with a card written in Spanish and prepared by California OSHA that explained the monitoring we planned to do. The card included a statement that, by law, participating in the sampling would not threaten their jobs. We hooked the workers up with noise dosimeters and recorded the assigned numbers and the workers' names. We received mostly curious looks but a few appreciative smiles.

We kept watch over the dosimeters throughout the shift, making sure they were operating and that the microphones were positioned correctly. I also used a hand-held meter, as a check on the dosimeter readings. Infrequently, an enterprising person will stick the dosimeter microphone right into the heart of a noisy machine, dramatically raising the reading in hopes, presumably, of dramatically increasing whatever benefits may result.

We also studied the individual operations and noted the sources of noise. Sometimes making a simple mechanical alteration or using an enclosure can bring the levels below the 85-dBA action level. If the levels significantly exceeded 90 dBA, we would consider requiring engineering controls.

During the day-long monitoring, an OSHA safety inspector stopped by at my request, and we toured the departments together, conducting additional interviews. The safety inspector spoke Spanish and helped with the translations. We found that none of the employees had received any training in noise hazards or hearing tests or been told that protectors were mandatory. Further, the foundry employees had received no safety training regarding their exposure to the molten aluminum or in how to use the protective equipment issued to them. Nor had they been given any information on the hazards and prevention of heat stress.

The safety inspector found several violations, one of which demanded immediate attention. In one of the machine shops, a worker was operating a lathe right next to a pallet of wheels stacked ten feet high. The wheels on the top of the stack were teetering over the operator's head. A light bump from a forklift truck or removal of a wheel from an adjacent stack would have sent several twenty-five-pound wheels crashing down on the operator's head, with obvious severe consequences. Other wheels were stacked equally poorly.

We called over the foreman and pointed out the teetering wheels. "That's not my problem," he said. "The foundry does the stacking. You'll have to talk with the foundry foreman."

We called him over, and soon a loud argument erupted between the two foremen over who was at fault and who was going to correct the problem. After about five minutes of arguing, we interrupted by saying that if the problem was not corrected immediately, we would shut down the lathe operation and consider issuing a willful violation. Grounds for issuing a serious violation had already been established. Suddenly attentive, the foundry foreman promised to have the foundry workers stack the wheels more securely, and the machine shop foreman left to have the teetering stack corrected. We could only hope that the serious citation the company was to receive would be a reminder of its responsibility to prevent hazardous conditions in the future.

While on one of my periodic "rounds" to check the dosimeters, I noted who was wearing hearing protectors and who was not. I was not surprised to find that many more workers were wearing them than on my first visit, which had been unannounced, as required by law.

Unannounced inspections most accurately reflect day-to-day compliance and what may be expected in the future without enforcement. Observations made on the first day are duly recorded by the inspector. If controls are not being used and subsequent representative sampling documents overexposure, the company is subject to a citation.

On our second visit to Wheels Unlimited, we purposely monitored several foundry workers who were not wearing protectors, even though many more were wearing them than on the first day. Was I sandbagging the company or merely enforcing the law? Inspectors sometimes sandbag companies when they issue serious violations after observing one or two workers who are not wearing protectors among many more who are, and the company otherwise requires the use of protectors and has a good hearing conservation program. Such action can constitute an abuse of OSHA law. In this case, the company did not require workers to use protectors and had not given them any hearing tests or training in noise hazards. Given the widespread failure to use protectors evident from the first walkaround, it seemed clear that without some measure of enforcement, workers would continue to be harmfully exposed in the future.

Further evidence that the company had no noise protection program was revealed when the second shift came on. Preparing to leave for the day, I noticed that none of the second-shift foundry workers were wearing protectors. When I asked the foreman why, he responded, "Oh, we ran out of hearing protectors a week or so ago and haven't got any in yet, but I'll check." He soon returned with a box of plugs and, asking everyone to put them on, he handed them out. Some workers showed surprise as they were given the order. The supply of plugs had probably been purchased soon after my initial walkaround.

Monitoring with the dosimeters indicated that of the twenty workers sampled, all of them were being exposed to noise above the 85-dBA action level. The eight-hour time-weighted average values ranged from 86 dBA to 101 dBA. The loudest exposures were recorded in the foundry. Ten of the twenty workers there had levels that exceeded the 90-dBA mandatory protection limit (for exposures at or above 85 dBA but less than 90 dBA, hearing protectors are not required to be worn, but hearing tests, training, and access to protectors are required). Of the company's 300 workers, the now-pending enforcement affected the 150 workers who were exposed to levels above 85 dBA and were therefore covered by the hearing conservation standard.

At the closing conference, I told Mr. Baker the obvious: that he needed help managing his safety program. He acknowledged that he was having difficulty handling personnel problems on top of trying to prevent the high number of accident claims. He seemed to understand that a good safety and health program could reduce the number of compensation claims, reduce his insurance costs, and keep his workers healthy and on the job. But the company was learning this lesson the hard way, at the expense of many injured workers. Baker added in meek defense that the owner of the company was concerned about his employees' safety, though my inspection clearly showed that somebody in management was not.

I reviewed the noise violations first. Most of the workers in manufacturing would have to be included in a hearing conservation program, I told him, which included training, making protectors available, and providing annual hearing tests. In areas such as the foundry, where full-shift exposures exceeded 90 dBA, the use of protectors would be mandatory. I explained that the company would receive serious violations for not providing protection from overexposure and for not having a hearing conservation program that included hearing tests and training. Some of the noise and heat stress in the foundry could be reduced, I added, by better insulating the furnaces. I also suggested that the company install fans to introduce outside air into the foundry, but, as Baker rightly pointed out, they would provide little, if any, relief on the hottest days of summer.

Other serious violations included improper foot protection for foundry employees (a repeat violation); no forearm protection for the ladlers, who had a history of receiving burns on their forearms; improper stacking of the wheels on pallets; exposed electrical wires; unguarded machines; and no eye protection for one of the lathe operators (a repeat violation). The company also received a citation for not complying with an order issued by a previous inspector requiring the company to provide the ladlers with protective aprons. Earlier compliance might have prevented the recorded leg burns, and future compliance would at least prevent more such burns. Other nonserious violations were explained, including not having an emergency eyewash and shower for workers handling corrosives in the painting department, and the obvious, not having an accident prevention program. I was thankful that I could mandate changes; based on its past, the company would certainly not improve on its own.

A total of eight serious violations were issued, as well as nine general. After explaining how fines are calculated, I pointed to the figure at the bottom of the work sheet and read off the number: $7,600.

During the closing conference, Baker explained that he was to meet the next day with management and the company's owner to discuss the budget and that he planned to request additional funds for safety. With sufficient funds, Baker said he could hire someone part time to run the safety program. I suggested that he use the citations as justification to the owner that the company had to make greater efforts to improve safety, not just to offset the insurance and employee replacement costs, but also to avoid fines for repeated failure to comply with regulations. I added that serious and repeat violations can be expensive, even for hazards such as noise.

Perhaps if the previous safety inspector had issued higher fines, the need for a better safety program might have been recognized sooner and greater motivation induced. Not all companies with poor safety programs receive multiple inspections, and, as could have happened here, many companies get off lightly and never receive the additional inspections needed to bring about compliance.

About thirty days after the closing conference, before the due date, the company returned the OSHA form used for reporting compliance. The form, signed by Hal Baker, indicated partial compliance. I returned the form with a note saying that we would accept it as a progress report and that if more time was needed, it could be granted on request. I received no reply.

A few days later the company filed an appeal. I called Baker and learned that his main problem was the fines. He added that the company was making the required corrections.

I could only hope that the company was indeed changing its ways, for I was unable to conduct a follow-up to verify compliance during the appeal process. The hearing was scheduled just short of a year from the date of my first walkaround.

About two weeks before the day of the hearing, and long after the abatement date set for correction of the violations, OSHA's attorney settled with the company. The total penalty was reduced from $7,600 to $4,600, but our attorney felt it was still commensurate with the "crime." The fines for the serious repeat violations were reduced the most.

The inspection process had finally come to a long-overdue conclusion. In this case, the delays had been atrocious.

Because of understaffing in our office and a delay while the company appealed the previous safety inspector's citation, I could not conduct my inspection for about a year after the safety inspector first noted the problems. During this period, workers had been subject to noise damage and burns from splashed molten metal. Once my inspection was completed, it took almost another year before the company and OSHA settled. The process was scandalously slow because of the indifferent appeal system and partly because of understaffing of inspectors.

Ears, Nose, and Fingers

Without fear of a follow-up or convincing penalty, many companies do little to correct their problems, and attempts at enforcement turn into exercises in futility. Huntington Tables had already received three safety inspections and one health inspection, all more than a year and half before.

The health survey in our file indicated that the inspection had resulted in citations for failure to provide hearing protectors and training for employees in a punch press department exposed to high levels of noise. The inspector had also warned the company of the need to conduct hearing tests on all the workers exposed. Our file did not contain a copy of the employer's report of correction, however, only a note promising to return the report a few days late. The inspector had failed to keep track of whether the company had complied with the citations.

I recalled all of this as I waited in the lobby of Huntington Tables for the receptionist to locate the plant manager. A company-produced dinette set—well designed and well made—was on display. The set was made of glass, highly polished chrome, and solid oak. While I was thumbing through the company's catalog, which showed equally attractive and expensive dinette sets, a door flew open, interrupting my perusal of the company's products. Addressing me in a hurried manner, the plant manager asked me what I wanted. Once I introduced myself, his manner took on a more aggressive tone. He was quite familiar with OSHA, he said. Motioning for me to enter, he sarcastically added, "I hate OSHA inspectors."

The plant manager introduced himself as John Robles and led me to his office. I explained that I was there to inspect a possible problem in the machine shop, based on a complaint alleging harmful exposure to dust from the machines. I was vague about the scope of the inspection. After spending about thirty minutes discussing the company's overall safety program and reviewing its records, I asked to visit the shop.

It did not take long for me to determine that the claim was false. The small amounts of steel and other dusts from the work materials, grinders, and drills did not pose any health hazard. The complaint must have been from a disgruntled employee, or a former disgruntled employee. Had the inspection ended here, the company could understandably have been angry about receiving an unnecessary inspection based on a false allegation. At the worst, it would have wasted several hours of a couple of people's time.

Fortunately, however, the inspection did not end here, for, as I had just learned from Robles, nothing had been done about the noise in the punch press department. In fact, as Robles admitted, little had been done about noise in the whole plant. Further evidence of the apparent negligence was tucked away in a file Robles gave me that contained a report from the plant's insurance company detailing noise overexposure in the mills and the need for compliance with OSHA requirements.

After the inspection of the machine shop, I informed Robles that I needed to tour the rest of the plant. Robles unhappily obliged.

From the outside, the Huntington Tables plant did not look very big, but once we started on the walkaround, I found the total floor space to be incredibly large. Production had to be high to justify the several hundred employees and large space.

As we walked around, the plant engineer talked about himself. By his own account, Robles was invaluable to the company. He fixed all production problems and kept production flowing. He was a free-lance engineer, he said. I later learned that he owned a sizable chunk of the company. Regardless of his immodesty, he had a quick mind. I also believed at that point that he appreciated the purpose of the inspection, even if he had been aggressive earlier. Surprisingly, he said he had been a safety inspector with OSHA in its early years. He must have had some bad experiences.

At my request, a union shop steward joined us (employees have the right by OSHA law to have a representative participate in the walkaround). A thoughtful family man with a long history in the company, the shop steward had the important role of listening and informing the union members about the inspection. As it turned out, he also translated some of my interviews since most of the workers spoke only Spanish. Unfortunately, he did not say much, probably because he felt forced into an uncomfortable adversarial role with the company.

One of our first stops was the punch press department. Hundreds of metal frames and brackets sat in wooden bins, ready for stamping and shaping into what would become the legs and connectors of the dinette sets. The rows of punch presses reminded me of giant microscopes in which the "stage" portion held the die and metal piece to be stamped and the shaft for the hydraulic punch represented the "eyepiece."

As I watched the presses do their useful work, the stamping and punching actions resulted in short but exceptionally loud noises. With repetitive operation of the machines, the operators were undoubtedly being exposed to enough noise in a day to damage their unprotected ears.

During interviews, I learned that none of the press operators had ever had a hearing test or received any information on the risks of hearing loss or the methods of protection. The company had been cited in its last inspection for not providing training and had been warned of the due date for administering hearing tests. Most of the operators I interviewed had been with the company since at least then, so clearly the company had failed to comply with the violation or heed the warning.

In addition to the noise, I noted that a punch press in use was missing a guard designed to keep hands and fingers out of the "pinch-point" area. The tremendous energy released by the machine to punch a hole through steel can effortlessly take off a hand or finger. At some time in the history of safety, after many workers had lost parts of their limbs and hands, someone came up with the brilliant but simple idea of constructing a cage around the area where the punch meets the die. The cage is designed to allow the workpiece, but not any fingers, in the area of contact, preventing the operator from reaching in to grab a piece or to clean out debris while the punch is operating. Relying on the operators not to put their hands in the die area during the repetitive operation belies human nature and accident statistics.

Following California OSHA policy, punch press number 10766 was "tagged-out," prohibiting it from use until a guard was attached. To the front of the machine, I attached a yellow tag that declared in large letters in English and Spanish: "Danger. Use Prohibited." Such tag-outs can lawfully be used whenever a worker faces an imminent serious hazard. If a company wishes to appeal the tag-out order, the law provides for an immediate hearing with OSHA management to review the "just cause" for the sometimes costly shutdown.

Finishing with the press department, we moved toward the buffing department. As we approached the area, an acrid odor wafted toward us.

I was introduced to the department foreman, whose hobby was clearly weight lifting. I hoped I would not find much wrong in his department. As the foreman explained the operation, I watched as about fifteen workers each pressed long chromed tubes and angled frames against a buffing wheel with their hands, using one knee to position the piece and the force of their backs to apply pressure. The work was visibly tiring and dirty. Their faces and hair were covered with lint and dark buffing compound thrown from the wheels. I correctly guessed that it was the department that employed the company's newest employees.

I approached one of the wheels to get a closer look, turning my head several times to get relief from the now very acrid odor. I was forced to back off. When I asked the foreman about the smell, he brought over a partly consumed chunk of what looked like lard and, putting it nearer my nose than I wished, explained that it was an animal fat product used to polish the chair legs. The buffing process generated high enough heat to cause the fat to decompose and let loose the wrenching aroma.

Concluding the review of the department, I marked it for monitoring for both noise and dust, though both appeared marginally within OSHA limits. The odor was obnoxious, but there were no limits for the chemicals involved and, barring sickness among the buffers, the department could continue to stink, at least to the uninitiated. In one of the interviews, a buffer told me that he had gotten used to the smell and it no longer bothered him.

Next door to buffing was the plating department, where a thin layer of chrome was applied to nearly completed frames of chairs and tables. In an automated process, the frames passed through various tanks, suspended from an overhead rail, where they were washed and plated. The plated frames were then efficiently removed and transported to buffing and later to assembly.

The plating department was one of the cleanest plating shops I had ever seen, and, because of the automation, workers received little exposure to the chemicals. Some types of chrome plating generate high levels of chromic acid mist, which is known to eat away part of the septum of the nose and to present a significant cancer risk to those exposed. Thankfully, the chrome plating in use here was not this type. Also, the area was noticeably more quiet than the other departments.

Before leaving the plating department, Mr. Taylor, one of the owners, stopped us and, visibly irritated, wanted to know why a punch press had been removed from service. Before I had a chance to explain, the plant engineer, Robles, was explaining my action. The conversation turned into a shouting match between the two company officials, which Robles concluded by saying, "Do you want to take somebody's hand off using that machine without a guard?" Unconvinced of the danger, Mr. Taylor left in anger. As he walked out, I made the untactful but necessary comment that not having a guard was a serious violation and the tag-out legally binding. I added that he could appeal the action with my supervisor.

Facing down such challenges is one of the more unpleasant aspects of being an inspector, but the alternative is risky. The recent experience of another safety inspector had dramatically revealed the wisdom of requiring shutdowns in imminently hazardous situations. In that case, the inspector had accepted the owner's promise that the machine would not be used until a guard was installed. A few days later, our office received an accident report from the company—a press operator had lost part of his hand using the machine the owner had promised not to use. The main fault for the injury lay with the owner, who received a citation and penalty that fell short of the offense. The experience was difficult for the otherwise good inspector, but not nearly as difficult as it was for the amputee.

Our tour continued with the welding area, where welders fabricated the table and chair frames and legs. The welders were certainly taking enough iron oxide fumes into their lungs to show up eventually on x-rays, but the levels were below OSHA limits. The metal has not yet been proven to cause serious disease.

As we entered yet another large building that housed the assembly area, I wondered whether the plant would ever end. Here, workers upholstered and wove the different styles of seats and backs for the chairs and assembled the chairs and dinette tables. Robles explained the operation as we walked around, and I conducted a few interviews with the mostly female workers. The workers had no safety or health complaints. Ergonomic problems affecting the joints or muscles were possible, caused by the repetitive and awkward motions of the limbs that occur in some assembly operations, but without complaints from the work force, and particularly without any definite OSHA regulations addressing such problems, I pressed on.

The noise and wood dust were obvious as we passed through the doors into the next section of the plant. Robles identified the department as mill 1; mill 2 was down the block in a different building. He explained that the mills produced the oak tabletops and legs used for some of the dinette sets. The previous industrial hygiene report made no mention of the mills. For some reason the inspector had missed them. Viewing the numerous sanding machines, saws, and routers, I felt certain there was overexposure to noise, especially since some of the workers were not wearing hearing protectors.

Following Robles into the office, I was introduced to the foreman, who looked to be near retirement age. Answering my questions in a friendly manner, he said it was up to the employees whether they wore the protectors. It was also up to the workers whether they wore paper masks for protection from dust. In interviews with the workers, I learned that none had had hearing tests or been given training in the use of protectors or the hazards of noise or any warning about the dust. I found a similar situation in the other mill.

At mill 2, Robles asked another union steward who was more familiar with the mill to accompany us on the walkaround. He showed much concern for the workers and even pointed out some possible safety problems that I referred to an OSHA safety inspector. After briefing him in private about the inspection, I asked him whether the workers were required to wear hearing protectors. He said they were not required to wear them, though a few workers did. The company bought plastic earplugs, he said, but there had been none for some time, and several workers had complained to him about not being able to get any. They had had no hearing tests that he knew about or any training in noise hazards. When I expressed concern about the levels of wood dust, he asked curiously whether the dust could be harmful.

The foremen were all in the mill office when Robles, the steward, and I entered. Robles introduced me, then left to deal with a problem. The foremen confirmed the steward's comments: it was up to the workers whether they wore hearing protectors. I asked to see the earplugs they had on hand and, after some cursory looking, one foreman admitted to being out of them.

"Have any more been ordered?" I asked.

"I'm not sure," one foreman replied.

"Have the mill workers been given hearing tests?"

One foreman recalled that some of the workers had been tested, but he couldn't tell me how many.

Finally, I asked who was responsible for informing the workers about the noise hazard and use of protectors, purposely not asking whether *they* provided the training. Robles was responsible, they replied. During the opening conference Robles had said that training was the foremen's responsibility.

One of the foremen offered to take me and the steward on the required walkaround of the mill. As we slowly walked through the aisles, one automatic router particularly caught my eye. Although it was partly enclosed in a boxlike structure with an exhaust system attached, it emitted a tremendous amount of dust, right into the space where the worker operated the controls. The operator had attempted to compensate by wearing two unapproved single-strap respirators—doubly ineffective and doubly uncomfortable. The spinning blades moved precisely and automatically around a rectangular oak top. As it formed a grooved edge, it threw out dust and small pieces of wood. When the machine completed its cycle, I got closer and looked in the box to study the design of the exhaust system. The piles of dust inside indicated a lack of air movement.

On the front of the machine was a warning plate, apparently placed there by the manufacturer:

WARNING. FOR HEALTH AND SAFETY REASONS,
THIS MACHINE MUST ONLY BE OPERATED WITH A
COMBINED GUARD AND CHIP COLLECTION BOOTH
AS SPECIFIED BY MACHINE MANUFACTURER.

I was surprised to see the warning, having never seen one on woodworking equipment. The name plate indicated that the router had been manufactured in England, which probably accounted for the warning. Studies conducted many years earlier in the English furniture industry had found an association between some types of wood dust and cancer.

Engineering controls, such as dust-collection systems, are common in the furniture industry. The use of *effective* dust-collection systems, unfortunately, is not. It is not difficult to control dust levels through good ventilation and hood and duct work design, but it takes a commitment to adapt machines that do not come with well-engineered collection systems already installed. What usually happens is what happened in this company: the collection system is poorly designed or adapted; the exhaust fans are too small, resulting in too little air being exhausted; and the system is poorly maintained, so that it works at less than the original subpar level.

Later, I called the contractor who had installed the hood on the router and asked him why the hood was not working right. He hedged. I then suggested that perhaps the fan was not drawing enough air through the hood to capture and remove the dust properly. He admitted that the amount of air being exhausted was probably too low but added that, after he had installed the hood, he had expressed this concern to company personnel. They had indicated that they were satisfied with the way it was.

With completion of the walkaround of the second mill, I had finally concluded my initial survey of the plant. I caught up with Robles and explained that I still had to monitor the noise and dust to determine whether the exposure actually exceeded the eight-hour time-weighted average limits. Monitoring would probably take three days to complete, I told him. Robles, realizing that I was committed to a full inspection and perhaps believing that angering me could cost the company money, nodded warmly and smiled, showing not a trace of animosity.

In preparation for monitoring, I studied my notes and developed a sampling strategy. There were fifteen to fifty workers in each department from which I could select a few for representative monitoring. Though I had ten dosimeters and six pumps, monitoring would still take three full days.

I also prepared my sampling equipment, which included ten battered but functioning noise dosimeters, each consisting of a microphone connected with a long plastic-coated wire to a box about the size of a transistor radio. The size and design of the box made it possible to place the dosimeter in a worker's shirt pocket or fasten it to a waist belt. The microphone could be clipped on a worker's shirt, around the shoulder. The dosimeter recorded noise throughout the day—all the roars, whirrs, pings, and bangs—that exceeded 80 dBA. At the end of the day and with the touch of a button, the dosimeter would report the average dose of noise. The dose for the eight hours could then be compared with the eight-hour exposure limits.

I also carried dust monitors, which are bulkier than the dosimeters and consist of a battery-powered pump. The pump can be adjusted so that it draws air at about a liter per minute through a filter contained in a holder for the dust, called a cassette, which is connected to the pump by a piece of plastic tubing. A worker wears the pump on a belt and the cassette clipped to a shirt, on the shoulder or lapel. The plastic hose is generally draped over the worker's back. Similar sampling methods are used to sample fumes or other dusts and particulates.

After the sampling is completed, the cassette is returned to the laboratory for weighing. The laboratory reports the average concentration of dust in the air, which is then compared to legal exposure limits.

I planned to spend one day monitoring the noise and wood dust in mill 2 and another day monitoring mill 1 for both dust and noise and the punch press department for noise. I planned to spend the third day monitoring the buffing department for noise and the "nuisance dust" generated from the buffing compounds and the buffing wheels.

As I monitored in mill 2, the operators worked hard, as did their machines, cutting, shaping, and sanding. Much dust and noise were the by-products.

As the day wore on, I was certain there would be proof of overexposure to the wood dust. Though a few of the newer machines had factory-designed and -installed exhaust systems that reduced exposure, the exhaust systems on most of the machines were visibly ineffective.

All of the workers I sampled for dust were unprotected, including those who wore the unapproved single-strap respirators issued by the company. The wood dust, flying off the cutting blades and sanding paper, accumulated about the machines and on the operators. By the end of the shift, the mill operators could correctly be called "dustmen"; they were covered with sawdust. One "high-tech" shaper, which automatically routed out a pattern via its own computer, produced a large "low-tech" visible dust cloud that drifted over to a corner of the mill, exposing other workers. I pointed out some of the deficiencies in this and some of the other machines to the plant engineer, but he refused to recognize any problem or responded with statements such as "We're working on it."

The fine oak dust covering the workers' clothes was clear evidence that they were breathing in large amounts of the minute particles of wood. Exposure on a chronic basis is associated with an increased incidence of eye irritation, coughing, sneezing, throat irritation, sinusitis, frequent and prolonged colds and ear infections, and nose bleeds. Chronic exposure may be associated with increased risk of lung disease, Hodgkin's disease, and nasal cancer. Other species of wood are known to produce asthmalike symptoms on exposure. At the time of the inspection, California OSHA's standard for all wood dust was 5 mg/m^3.[7]

If overexposure to oak dust was not clear in mill 2, the high noise levels were. My noise monitoring showed unequivocally that the workers were at certain risk of hearing damage. Eleven, or about half the workers monitored, had full-shift average exposure levels of more than 90 dBA, and practically all the workers in both the mills and punch press department had levels above the action level of 85 dBA. Including the second-shift workers, who were not sampled but worked under similar conditions, more than fifty employees had exposure levels above 85 dBA. One mill worker who was not wearing hearing protectors had an exposure of 96 dBA. Everyone else was wearing protectors because someone had gone out and bought some since my first visit. With the supply of protectors finally replenished, the company made sure that the workers were wearing them on the day I returned to sample.

Interviews with supervisors and employees confirmed that workers had not been given training in noise hazards or in the use of the protectors. Only a small fraction of the work force had received a required baseline hearing test, and annual tests were overdue by several months. No one could explain this negligence.

Though it does not happen often, companies sometimes do not give hearing tests because they are afraid of discovering that workers have suffered hearing loss. Workers so harmed and informed of their rights will sometimes seek compensation, opening the company up to a possible avalanche of claims and resultant increases in its insurance premiums. The first wrong is in not controlling the excessive noise. The second is in preventing the just compensation of claims. A worker caught in this cycle can file a complaint with the local OSHA office and hope for rightful protection and compensation.

There was plenty of evidence that the company was aware of the high noise levels and knew about the applicable OSHA standards.

After all, it had conducted some hearing tests and made protectors available, albeit on an inconsistent and limited basis. Indeed, I discovered during the inspection that the company had received several reports about the noise problem more than a year and a half before from its workers' compensation insurance carrier. Furthermore, I learned that the insurance company had conducted several noise surveys and had identified areas where the OSHA hearing conservation standard applied. The insurance company had even outlined the requirements for hearing tests and training. Further, the previous OSHA inspector had determined that the punch press operators were exposed to noise levels above 85 dBA and had cited the company for not providing noise hazard training and had issued a written warning about the need to perform hearing tests.

I proposed to my office that Huntington Tables be issued a willful/repeat/general violation for failure to train and a willful/general violation for failure to provide baseline hearing tests. The general, or nonserious, classification was proposed based on the theory, and a history of appeal decisions, that failure to comply with these requirements will not result in "serious physical harm."

A serious violation could have been issued for failure to provide and require workers to wear protectors, in that the excessive noise could have caused direct harm. This was supported by the observation on the first day of the inspection that many workers overexposed to noise on a chronic basis, documented by representative sampling, were not using protectors, most likely because the company had run out of them weeks before. The serious violation would give the message that unprotected overexposure is serious and penalizable and that positive steps must be taken to protect workers' hearing and prevent additional fines. I was certain that without a penalty, the warning would be ignored.

Requiring engineering controls for the noise was considered, but only one piece of equipment, an air-operated boring machine, could be controlled with an enclosure. No enforceable means existed to quiet the saws and routers, at least none that I or several other inspectors I consulted were aware of. The company was thus informed of the feasibility of quieting only the one boring machine.

In contrast, engineering controls were feasible, and needed, to control the wood dust. Eleven mill workers were found to have exposure levels that exceeded the legal limits, and others might have been likewise overexposed. Values ranged from 6.2 to 42 mg/m^3.

Exposure to the 5 mg/m^3 limit over a work shift will leave an operator well dusted.

I proposed that the company be issued a serious violation for overexposing eleven workers to wood dust. Overexposure was occurring on a daily basis. The citation required that the dust levels be brought below the limit using engineering controls such as ventilation equipment. Until the controls were installed and working, the company was required to issue and fit all exposed employees with approved respirators.

I held the closing conference with Mr. Taylor, the owner who had become upset when the unguarded punch press was shut down. Robles was out of the country. A safety inspector, who had conducted a complete safety inspection based on my referral, was also present, as was one of the union stewards. The union steward sat straight across from me, his face somber.

Mr. Taylor initially challenged the presence of the steward when I called to set up the appointment for the conference. In a gruff tone, he complained that his employee had already spent company time on the walkaround, and now he would have to take time off from work again. I explained that under OSHA law the employee representative had a right to be present but that if Mr. Taylor wished, I could hold separate conferences with him and the union steward. The owner unhappily relented, and a joint conference was held.

As I read down my list of violations, I periodically looked up to see Mr. Taylor's expression. The allegations were serious, including the charges of willfully and repetitively ignoring the regulation requiring hearing protection. The owner maintained his unhappy expression as I explained all ten violations.

Before discussing the fines, I commented that if Mr. Taylor did half as well putting together a safety and health program as he did building the company, he would have no problems. Unfortunately, Mr. Taylor didn't realize that the company would be more successful if it had a hearing conservation program and an adequate ventilation system.

I then presented the penalty. "The total fine is $4,960," I said.

Mr. Taylor's expression grew increasingly serious. I looked over at the steward, who, looking down at his copy of the citation, attempted to restrain a tight grin.

The safety inspector followed with his list of citations, which included several serious violations and a fine of $2,445.

The fine for both inspections totaled $7,405. Mr. Taylor was visibly irritated, but, encouragingly and to his credit, he discussed how the company could comply.

After the safety inspector explained the rights of appeal, we excused ourselves without delay. Before leaving the room, I looked over at the union steward, who had remained silent throughout the meeting. He still looked somber. Undoubtedly he knew that it was a time to remain expressionless.

Inspections that uncover serious violations are not usually over with the closing conference, and this was no exception. Within the deadline of fifteen working days, the company appealed. The appeals board soon sent our office the notice of contest in which one of the owners challenged the existence of the violations and the amount of the fine. A hearing was scheduled for ten months after the closing date of the inspection. During this time the company was free to ignore the cited violations if it wished.

Almost ten months later, just five days before the day of the hearing, a deal was struck. Neither I nor the safety inspector was surprised.

In the meantime, the assigned OSHA attorney had done his homework, researching the cited hazards and reviewing the files. He had even received a "this is what we have done" tour, escorted by Mr. Taylor. According to the attorney, the company was now in compliance. I was uncertain how he could make this determination, however, since he had never conducted a safety or health inspection or been trained in hazard recognition and control.

During a prehearing meeting with the attorney, I tried to impress upon him that the company managers had willfully and negligently disregarded the safety and health of its employees.

"Yeah, they're all assholes, right?" he replied sarcastically.

"No, they just didn't care enough," I countered, disappointed by his implication that we were imagining that the company was negligent or were otherwise prejudiced.

In spite of all my documentation, the attorney told me that the evidence for a willful citation was weak. He lost the argument with the regional supervisor but prevailed in downgrading other violations and successfully played "let's make a deal" with the owner.

The citation for the overexposure to the wood dust was reduced from a serious to a general violation, which carried no first-instance fine. The attorney based his decision on library research on the cancer risk of wood dust, past appeal decisions, and the definition of a serious hazard in the OSH Act, which requires in part that there be "a substantial probability that death or serious physical harm could result." The attorney reasoned, and convinced OSHA management, that since the human carcinogenicity of hardwood dusts such as oak is inconclusive (that is, not enough deaths have conclusively been linked to oak dust, and OSHA has not seen fit to regulate it as a carcinogen), cancer risk could not be a factor in determining the gravity of the violation. Further, based on his reasoning, having prolonged and more frequent colds, more frequent ear infections, increased mucous production, "minor" irritation of the eyes and respiratory system, and discomfort from inhaling wood dust all day could not be considered serious physical harm.

Because a first-time general violation carries no fine, an uncaring company has little incentive to comply and reduce the risks until it receives an OSHA inspection. Even then, many companies wait for a follow-up inspection before complying. Unfortunately, not all businesses are inspected, and only a small percentage of those that are cited receive a follow-up.

The original $7,405 fine was reduced to $3,000. One willful and several repeat violations remained. Mr. Taylor accepted the settlement rather than face an administrative law judge. Based on the company's past experience but unknown to Mr. Taylor, the judge probably would have lowered the fine even more.

I assisted another inspector in the follow-up inspection a month and a half after the settlement and nearly a year after I had issued my original citations. Mr. Taylor greeted us, saying he had a busy work schedule and all his other management people were gone, making it an inappropriate day for an inspection. I was sympathetic but firm. Unannounced inspections are the only way to evaluate compliance.

We found that the workers had been given noise hazard training and hearing tests, that they had a selection of hearing protectors and were using them, and that approved respirators had been issued and were being worn. Little had been done to improve the dust-collection system. The collection hood on the particularly problematic router had not been modified, and the exhaust duct had a major rip in it, critically reducing the efficiency of the system. It was apparent that the company had not taken seriously the "general" violation requiring engineering controls for overexposure to wood dust.

Because of the possibility of noncompliance, we were again forced to monitor the workers and to establish the nearly forgone conclusion that there was overexposure to wood dust. If this was the case, the company could have been issued a "failure to abate" violation.

The other inspector conducted the monitoring. Before the monitoring was completed, however, the company had improved the router by increasing the fan capacity and enclosing the hood more efficiently. An edge sander had also been adapted with a ventilation system so that dust was effectively captured before it could fly out.

The company had finally come into compliance. It had taken more than a year since my first inspection and more than two years since the company had first been inspected.

Though the improvements cost the company several thousand dollars—money that should have been spent long before and that would have prevented the years of excessive exposure and risk—the cost to the government, even after deducting the fines, was probably more than that. OSHA's costs included the various inspectors' time to conduct three complete health inspections, not to mention the costs of the laboratory to analyze the samples and for the attorney to review the appeal. Over the years, the company would benefit from the reduction in claims for hearing loss and amputations and from the better employee morale and production that result when a safety program is started. More important, far fewer workers would suffer hearing loss or wood-induced diseases and irritation.

5. LEAD

Lead has been a useful metal for thousands of years and still has many beneficial applications. The primary use for lead today is in the manufacture of car batteries. Lead is also used in producing solder, an essential component of the electronics industry, and in certain metal alloys, which in turn have abundant valuable applications.

In several instances, however, lead-containing products have presented an extreme risk to public health. An important example is lead-based household paint for walls, furniture, and toys. In 1973, the Consumer Products Safety Commission banned paints containing more than 0.50 percent lead from use for these purposes. The ban was ordered after many children were poisoned from ingesting flakes of the paint. The CPSC went further in 1978 and lowered the permissible lead content for household paints to 0.06 percent. Lead-based paint may still be used for other less risky applications.

The gasoline additive tetraethyl lead is another important lead-based product whose use has been restricted. The Environmental Protection Agency, which has regulatory purview over the general environment, in 1973 required that the level of lead in gasoline be reduced after it was determined that it was a significant contaminant of the ambient air and the probable primary source of the increasing body burden of lead in the public. A further reduction was ordered in 1985, and the lead in gasoline has now been replaced by additives that do not contain lead.

The potential of lead to cause disease was recognized thousands of years ago, although the full consequences of lead intoxication were not well characterized until the nineteenth and twentieth centuries. As adverse health effects were discovered, more protective regulations were passed, including the banning of some lead-based products. It was not until the 1970s, however, that exposure in the workplace was controlled in this country to the point where the gross symptoms of lead intoxication among workers became rare. The effects suffered in the past included loss of appetite, a metallic taste in the mouth, constipation, obstipation (extreme constipation due to an obstruction), anemia, malaise, weakness, insomnia, headaches, nervous irritability, muscle and joint pain, fine tremors, encephalopathy (brain degeneration and excess water on the brain), and colic. Even more serious overexposure caused death.

Recommended occupational exposure limits for airborne lead were first set in the United States between 1910 and 1930 in an effort to prevent the known, gross effects.[1] The first limits were recommendations only, and many companies did not heed the advice, partly because there was no agency like OSHA and some employers were not even aware of the recommendations. As efforts were made to recognize and control exposure by industry, in some cases with the help of government action, the gross symptoms became less prevalent.

OSHA began enforcing maximum air levels for lead in 1971, starting with an eight-hour time-weighted average of 200 micrograms of lead per cubic meter of air (200 μg/m^3). OSHA proposed and set today's level of 50 μg/m^3 in 1978. This limit is based on the notion that most workers can be exposed to the limit during an eight-hour day for a working lifetime "without undue risk" of ill health. As indicated by the phrase *without undue risk*, instead of *without risk*, some balance was struck. An even lower limit could have severely affected industry and resulted in the loss of jobs, which would have also produced ill health. OSHA acknowledged that the limit was not as protective as it could be.

The 1978 standard, which has multiple requirements, also established a maximum concentration of lead in the blood. The level since then has been 40 micrograms per 100 grams of blood (40 μg/100 g).

The lead standard has been argued vigorously in the courts over the years, in large part because some industrial and professional associations believe that airborne limits of 150 to 200 μg/m^3 and maximum blood concentrations of 80 μg/100 g are appropriate to prevent disease. Although OSHA has acknowledged that gross acute symptoms rarely occur at blood leads lower than 80 μg/100 g, the agency has found the lower limits to be necessary to prevent more subtle effects. In the final rulemaking, OSHA defended the lower limits by detailing the potential health effects at exposures lower than the previous limit of 200 $\mu g/m^3$.[2] For example, OSHA maintained that at lower levels enzyme activity is affected. One enzyme system helps construct hemoglobin, which transports oxygen throughout the body. Though frank anemia is not found at blood lead levels of less than 80 $\mu g/100$ g, enzyme functions are disturbed. One result is that at levels of about 50 $\mu g/100$ g, hemoglobin levels are measurably lowered, enough to be of concern to athletes and anemic individuals.

The nervous system is also affected at lower levels, so that an exposed person may feel tired, anxious, nervous, and lose sleep—symptoms one would not usually associate with the workplace. One research study OSHA cited in support of changing the standard found that about 50 percent of a group of workers who had an average blood level of 60 $\mu g/100$ g demonstrated these symptoms. Some reported that they had muscle soreness. Based on this and other studies, OSHA concluded that 40 $\mu g/100$ g was a threshold for behavioral effects in adults and 60 $\mu g/100$ g a threshold for long-term behavioral effects. Studies also indicate that at blood lead levels of 50 to 70 $\mu g/100$ g, the peripheral nervous system is affected, as demonstrated by slowness in the conduction of nerve impulses to the muscles. The studies did not state, however, whether those so exposed noticed any change in muscle function.

Kidney damage is also of concern. Another study cited by OSHA found a significant loss of kidney function, termed a loss of functional reserve without outward signs, in individuals with blood levels of less than 60 $\mu g/100$ g. The loss of a functional reserve would be detrimental to anyone who developed partial kidney dysfunction. It was thus stated that 40 $\mu g/100$ g in the blood was a maximum level to prevent a burden capable of causing kidney damage.

Finally, OSHA's documentation for lowering the limit cited studies of the effects of lead on the male and female reproductive systems. Males with mean blood lead levels of 53 $\mu g/100$ g, for example, have been found to have a higher than average number of malformed sperm, and those with mean levels of 41 $\mu g/100$ g to have fewer sperm than average and sperm with decreased motility. The exact significance of these effects is unknown, but some scientists believe they represent an increased risk of infertility and genetic damage. OSHA cited other effects, such as risk of miscarriage, stillbirth, decreased libido, impotence, decreased fertility, sterility in men, and abnormal menstrual cycles. It is not clear at what exposure levels these effects become a risk.

OSHA's emphasis on biochemical disturbances and preillness effects in the current lead standard may be difficult for some employers to understand. In defense of its actions, OSHA stated in the rule-making:

> The record in this rulemaking demonstrates conclusively that workers exposed to lead suffer material impairment of health at blood levels far below those previously considered hazardous. Inhibition of the heme biosynthesis pathway, early stages of peripheral and central nervous system disease, reduced renal function and adverse reproductive effects are all evidence of adverse health effects from exposure to lead in workers at blood levels of 40 μg/100 gm and above. Based on this record, OSHA has concluded that blood lead levels should be maintained at or below 40 μg/100 gm and even lower for workers who wish to plan pregnancies.[3]

The 1978 OSHA standard for lead is one of the most complex health standards that OSHA has passed. Some employers become dizzy just looking through it. What OSHA's regulatory staff essentially did was take a textbook prescription for the control of lead exposure and use it to create an enforceable standard. The complexity and detail are due in part to the mistrust that has built up between employer and employee and between companies and regulators.

Each requirement is detailed, specifying what is expected of the employer, including how and where to take air measurements and how to inform affected workers of the results. The standard requires employers to supply work clothes and to install showers and to "ensure" their use. It requires that ventilation or other physical controls be installed or adapted, whenever possible, to prevent the excessive release of lead. It details the use of respirators should engineering controls not be completely effective and explains how medical examinations and blood samples are to be taken. It directs the employer to provide employees with information on the hazards of lead, safe work practices, and the requirements of the standard. It also states that an opinion must be obtained from a second physician should an employee be suspicious of the company's own physician; when to remove employees from their jobs should the risk of disease become too great; and that employees so removed must be paid at least as much as they were receiving before their removal. There is more to the standard, but the good news for employers is that in those situations in which the exposure to airborne lead is lower than the action level of 30 $\mu g/m^3$ averaged over a workday, very little is required.

The prevention of newly recognized health effects does not necessarily always follow in a timely manner. The process of translating new knowledge into more healthful working conditions and reduced incidences of disease has historically been a difficult one. As science has improved the methods of detecting illness, groups and agencies concerned with public health have sought lower standards. There are numerous examples of this process, such as the legislation and concern that were generated after the connection between asbestos exposure and cancer was fully revealed. OSHA scientists and public health professionals who do not have a financial interest in industries that produce or use lead have become convinced of the need for a lower standard. Most people who are exposed to lead and at risk, similarly informed, would agree with the action taken.

The Price of Bronze Bushings

F inally I was getting a chance to inspect a company on OSHA's target list. Our office had been so busy with employee complaints and referrals from safety inspectors that the industrial hygienists were finding it difficult to inspect companies on OSHA's list of those in high-hazard industries. If our office had been much more short-staffed, or this company had not been randomly selected, this inspection probably would not have been assigned for many more years, if ever.

A check in the files revealed that the company had never had a health inspection. Nor was there a record of a safety inspection, at least not in the past three years. Safety inspections are conducted in response to immediate hazards. The records are thus purged three years after the closing date, unlike the records of health inspections, which are kept indefinitely because of the long latency period for many health hazards.

Arriving at the company's office, I presented my business card to the secretary and requested to see the owner or plant manager. The secretary took my card into a back room, where I overheard some discussion. An older man passed through a hallway into another room, and there was more discussion. The older man then came out and introduced himself as Owen Fisch, the head of sales and an owner of the company. In a pleasant manner, he said he had been given the duty of working with me. Mr. Fisch told me that the company sold bronze bushings and had been in business for more than ten years.

When I asked about the company's safety and health program, he had trouble answering my questions. After several attempts, Fisch called in his plant manager, John Howard. The young-looking man knew little more about the program than that his machinists were required to wear safety glasses. My conclusion was that the company did not have a safety and health program.

I next asked Howard for an overview of the manufacturing process in hopes of getting a feel for the hazards I might need to evaluate. He gave me a good but general overview of the operations of the foundry and machine shop and, at my request, told me the percentages of the metals they used to manufacture their bronze bushings. The bronze contained about 7 percent lead, he said, and the rest of the alloy was composed of a little tin and zinc, with the greater balance made up of copper. The lead, not normally in bronze, was added to give the alloy more "machinability."

Through Howard's description of the plant's operations, two health concerns became obvious—noise and lead. High noise levels were predictable; high lead levels were not. The amount of lead exposure would depend on the company's control efforts and could be significant if there was little control. Lead is relatively more volatile and has a much lower exposure limit than the other metals that made up the alloy, so I concluded that exposure to the other metal fumes would probably not be as significant.

Given the possibility of lead overexposure, I asked to review any relevant employee medical records the company had. The comprehensive OSHA standard for lead requires medical tests for workers exposed to airborne lead above the action level. Another OSHA standard gives an inspector, and employees, the right to request and review exposure records. Fisch got up and, after shuffling through a few files, handed me copies of the results of tests done on the company's foundry workers. Surprised, I immediately reviewed the records. The date on the reports indicated that the tests had been done three years earlier. The results showed that the foundry workers clearly had excessive levels of lead in their blood. Most were at about the 50 to 60 μg/100 g level, but one was 90 μg/100 g. All of the values were above the action level of 40 μg/100 g. I was told that many of the affected employees had worked in the foundry for as long as ten years. The individual with the 90 μg/100 g value was no longer working there, Fisch explained. Some time ago he had left for Mexico, and the story was that he had been shot in the head. Half joking, I suggested that he might have been shot because the lead exposure at work had made him a little crazy. Fisch and Howard laughed stiffly.

I asked if they knew about the OSHA regulations for lead.

"No," Fisch replied.

"Why did you have the medical monitoring done?" I asked.

"Oh, to check on things," he said.

I noted that the words "outside normal reference range" were printed on the blood lead reports of the workers with high levels.

After completing the opening conference and learning that nothing further had been done to comply with OSHA's lead regulations other than "to check on things," I conducted a walkaround of the plant. Fisch did the honors, beginning with the foundry.

On entering the foundry, where the metal ingots were melted and the red-yellow molten bronze metal was poured into a mold, I instantly heard a loud noise coming from two blowers that forced combustion air into each of two melting pots. The noise was so loud that workers had to shout at one another to be heard. Rising from each pot were clouds of fumes. Most of the fumes bypassed the small ineffective hoods hanging overhead, which presumably were installed to capture the fumes and send them to an air cleaner located outside the building. Instead, the uncaptured fumes rose to the ceiling, where they were diffused throughout the foundry.

The plant and the equipment were covered with the fallout from the fumes and were old and needed repair. The place had a look typical of dirty heavy industry. Many people unaccustomed to such places are genuinely surprised when they learn that people work under such conditions.

As I walked around, I noted that in spite of the fumes none of the foundry workers wore respirators, and although the noise was tremendous, none wore hearing protectors. At least they were wearing hardhats and face shields. The latter would save the casters' faces from scarring and ruin should they be in the wrong place when the melting pots spit out molten metal.

Fisch introduced me to the foreman of the foundry, "Red," a mild-mannered, gray-haired man. His genuine mild manner would have made any inspector feel at ease. At my request, he detailed the manufacturing process, showing me where the ingots were stacked near the melting pots to make sure they were free of water. Pointing to the pots, Red explained how they were heated with the tremendously noisy blowers. Next, he guided me around to the other side of the pots to show me how molten bronze was poured into the top of a mold and how a crude bronze bushing, like a pipe, grew by inches from underneath a water-cooled jacket.

Because the bronze pipe grew downward, the process required a lower basement with a pit that extended ten feet into the ground. We went down to the basement and observed how the bronze pipe steamed and cooled as it slid into the pit. Also in the basement was a cut-off saw that enabled the casters to cut the pipe to a specified length. A chain hung down into the pit, which the caster used to draw the pipe out with a powered winch fastened to a boom up above.

The pit was about three feet wide, and, as I stood near its edge, it seemed bottomless. I was quick to note that there was no guard rail around it. One false step on one of numerous trips to the basement could send a caster on a ten-foot fall, resulting in severe or fatal injuries.

Finished with the foundry, we next toured the machine shop area, which contained a row of lathes and other machining equipment. The lathes cut the pipe into bushings of the precise outer and inner dimensions demanded by buyers—other manufacturers that needed the bronze cylinders for their own products and businesses that needed hard-to-find replacement bushings for their worn-out equipment. The noise levels in the machine shop were too low to be of concern, and although it was doubtful that the machinists were receiving significant exposure to lead, I planned to monitor to be sure.

During the exit conference, I reviewed with Fisch and Howard the potential hazards I had observed and told them that I would request a safety inspection. I finished by saying I'd be back to monitor the levels of noise and fumes.

I returned several days later to conduct the all-day tests necessary to measure levels of fumes and noise. Levels of exposure have to be carefully documented to enforce any needed corrective action, for the burden of proof for a violation is on OSHA. Requiring that OSHA document and "prove" a violation aids in the enforcement of regulations and corrective actions that are needed and protects the employer from having to make needless changes.

On my second visit, the foundry workers were wearing brand-new repirators issued just days after my initial inspection. I was encouraged to see that management was taking action, but it had obviously been prompted solely by my visit. As I learned later, respirators had never been required before. Given the company's past record, I suspected that the attempt to comply would be short-lived.

I interviewed several workers, some of whom spoke no English. I had help with the Spanish-to-English translations from one of the safety inspectors from my office, who stopped by to conduct the safety inspection I had requested. Interviews are an important aid in determining whether there are violations and whether people have been informed of hazards or instructed in how to use safety equipment. They also help uncover when management is not being forthright, which probably occurs in at least half my inspections. In this case, I learned that, as Fisch had admitted, not much had been done over the years to control the exposure to the lead or the noise. I could sense from the workers that most appreciated my presence and their government's concern. There was one notable exception, however: an employee who was wearing an air pump for the purpose of determining exposure to lead fumes. On one occasion when I returned to his work area to take a rest, I found a stick lying on the seat, a nail pointing straight up.

Based on the interviews, I decided that the workers did not have any health problems they knew about. They came to work, made bushings, took breaks, made bushings, had lunch, made more bushings, and, at the end of the day, took their work clothes home with them. They were unaware of the health risks of having lead fumes and dust deposited in their lungs and on their clothes and hands throughout the day. Nor were most of them aware that their hearing was decreasing incrementally, leading, over the years, to deafness. Their greatest concern was maintaining their jobs to support their families. It struck me that our office receives few employee complaints from such small nonunion companies whose operations pose significant health risks to their employees.

I approached an employee on break who spoke English and asked him if he knew how to use the newly issued disposable respirator. He said he did. I then asked him to put it on. I was curious if he could get a good fit. If a respirator does not fit snugly to the face, it leaks and doesn't perform the intended filtering action. Suppressing a smile, I watched as the worker put on the respirator. It was upside down, rendering it useless. Management, in its haste to have the workers "protected" on the day of the monitoring, had apparently neglected to provide instructions on proper use.

That same day I asked Red if there were any showers available. He said there weren't, whereupon I mentioned that they were required if there was overexposure to lead. He jokingly said that his workers did not even take showers at home, adding, "What are they going to do with a shower here?" Red then complained about the hassles of putting a shower drain and extra plumbing in the bathroom.

Once my sampling was completed, I packed up the lead cassettes and sent them off to the laboratory. It took the routine three weeks to get the analysis back, and I was not surprised at the results: all the foundry employees I sampled were overexposed to airborne lead. The values for the machinists were also recordable, but they were safely under the action level. The air levels for the foundry workers ranged from 61 to 860 $\mu g/m^3$; the latter was from a man who operated a cut-off saw all day.

Upon receiving the monitoring data, I held a closing conference at the site, about two and a half months after the initial inspection. Fisch and Howard attended. Curiously, the principal owner did not.

The safety inspector had already issued violations for not having a guard rail around the open pits and for some other infractions. I issued nine general violations and nine serious violations. Most dealt with the unprotected overexposure to noise and lead. The citation required the company to ensure the proper use of respirators and hearing protectors; to inform employees of the hazards of noise and lead and means of protection against overexposure, including fit tests and the proper use of respirators; to install and require the use of showers; to provide a change of coveralls; to monitor the air quality quarterly; to prohibit cooking and eating in the foundry; to provide medical examinations; and to conduct blood tests for lead to determine the effectiveness of the control methods. The total fine was $2,930.

One of the best ways to control the lead fumes would have been to install more effective capture hoods over the melting pots in the foundry. This would have also relieved the employees of the burden of wearing tight-fitting respirators all day. It was obvious that the hoods over the pots were capturing only part of the fumes, allowing much to billow up and then back down into the plant. The hoods were undersized and probably needed larger fans to draw more air. Unfortunately, the sampling produced conflicting data, which did not enable me to require this improvement. To enforce engineering controls, the lead standard in California requires OSHA to demonstrate employee exposure above 150 $\mu g/m^3$, averaged over an eight-hour work shift, for more than thirty days per year. Monitoring data for the man using the cut-off saw, plus statements from Red and the operator that the job was the same every workday, provided the necessary documentation, and engineering control was ordered. My data for the workers inside the foundry were less conclusive on two separate days, however, and did not demonstrate that the workers were exposed to levels higher than 150 $\mu g/m^3$ for more than thirty days a year, although I was certain they were.

I warned the company during the closing conference that engineering improvements, such as a better fume-capture system, would undoubtedly be shown to be required and that these changes should be made as soon as possible. The initial cost might be high, I said, but it would pay for itself in the long run. I emphasized that if the improved ventilation and fume-capture system were effective, as was likely, the company could forego building the shower and change room. And, if the exposures were controlled, many of the requirements for respirators, coveralls, showers, and medical tests would be dropped. I noted that when people do not have to wear respirators and breathe hot gases all day, they feel that the company cares about them and, as a result, their productivity increases and the quality of their work improves.

The company was given thirty days to comply with the citations and report the results to my office. Additional time could be granted with good reason.

After forty days, I had still not received the required follow-up report, so I called Red to see what the problem was. He said he had forgotten about it and would send it in right away. I received it a week later. The report indicated that not much had been done but that the company had hired a consultant to help with its lead problem. I confirmed that the consultant had been called and then notified Red that he would have to submit a formal request for more time. Shortly thereafter, our office received a request for the appeal forms, which were soon filed. Follow-up by the OSHA office was thus prevented.

The company appealed *all* violations and penalties. In the meantime, we had no assurances that the employees were being protected. Could I have made so many gross mistakes, or was the appeal simply a tactic to delay action?

We attempted to arrange a conference with the owners, with the goal of getting a control program implemented immediately. My efforts at contacting the president over the phone to set up a meeting were stalled by several "He's not here, I'll have him call you back" replies. He never did call back. I suspected that the consultant had advised the company to appeal, thus allowing abatement at its leisure. I had observed abuses of the appeals process numerous times.

I sent in the request for OSHA legal representation for the appeal and, because of the ongoing overexposure, asked our legal department to arrange an early appeal date. The appeals board was otherwise booking hearing dates nine to twelve months after filing—an unreasonable amount of time when there were serious hazards.

Several more weeks passed without any reply from our legal department, so I finally called to inquire about the status of my request. The request had not yet been made. By the time the hearing date was finally set, seven months had passed since the inspection had been closed—not what I had in mind when I requested an early appeal date.

About a month before the appeal date, our attorney still hoped a settlement could be reached. Recalling my failed efforts to set up a meeting with the president, I suggested that the attorney call him. The attorney prevailed and got the president to meet with us. By this time, the notice for the early appeal date had been sent to all parties, and the new-found motivation for attending the conference was probably due to the cost and possible outcome of the impending appeal.

I, the president, and Red attended the conference, along with representatives of our medical and legal units, my supervisor, and the regional supervisor. We reviewed each violation and learned what the company had done to comply. A consultant had been at the site, and the president provided us with his report. The president also produced the results of recent blood sampling for lead, which had been required by one of the citations. Ten out of eleven foundry employees were significantly above the blood lead limit of 40 μg/100 g. Several employees had been so exposed for ten years. Many had also suffered reduced levels of hearing, as shown on the submitted audiograms, indicative of years of unprotected exposure.

I was surprised when many of the OSHA officials at the meeting offered compliments on the company's efforts. I was encouraged that the company was making an effort to protect its employees but dismayed by the persistence necessary to induce the company to comply. I was compelled to tell the president that the problems had existed for years and that other companies had protected their workers from such hazards. This was a fair representation of the facts but undoubtedly was an untactful and unwise remark. The president and foreman still appeared confused about the hundreds of dollars they were spending, so I asked them again to read some of the appendixes to the standard, which put in lay terms the hazards of lead and the purposes of the requirements. They complained about all of the requirements but left the meeting promising to do better.

After the conference, I and the other OSHA officials discussed whether to reduce the penalty. Our attorney was ready to make major cuts. I was not surprised. The "new nice guy on the scene" who has not studied the case well and is not aware of the history of the inspection will tend to be sympathetic when first meeting with "hurt" and complaining management representatives. The attorney had only my written report and comments to counter the company. Having never visited the plant himself, he was missing aspects of the inspection that could not be described, such as the faces of workers needlessly at risk.

"These people say they've complied with everything. What's the problem?" he said.

I had witnessed this attitude all too often in and out of OSHA: why issue a penalty if the company is starting to comply? I knew that taking such an attitude would certainly provide me with job security, but it does little to induce future compliance, particularly from companies with poor histories. Nor does such an attitude motivate the thousands of other noncomplying companies that are not inspected and may never be. All too often companies that have had serious hazards for years are given a break when caught and then are found to have the same hazards on subsequent follow-up. Even after three, four, or more inspections and minimal sanction, some companies still fail to address their workplace hazards responsibly. Imposing stiff penalties, especially for serious hazards, seems to catch the attention of the company and its neighbors. Further, when stiff penalties are imposed, we end up doing fewer inspections of the same companies and more of companies that have never been inspected.

Motivated by my strong feelings on when to reduce fines, I argued with our attorney. The result was a compromise. Two penalties, which were shown to deserve to be reduced, were lowered by a total of about $200.

Our attorney called the president of the company later in the week to present the proposed settlement. I listened and, sensing some hesitancy on the president's part, I quickly wrote down on a piece of paper "will not go willful." Our attorney stated that, in addition to the $200 reduction, we would not seek a willful citation. The characterization had some basis, in that the company had conducted blood lead monitoring three years before my inspection and had ignored the high results, demonstrating some willfulness to disregard the health risk. One reason I had not proposed earlier that we issue a willful citation was because Fisch had voluntarily provided the incriminating evidence, without attempting to hide or deny its existence. If the company had hidden the data and I had learned about the tests from the employees or an examining doctor, I surely would have issued the citation. In addition, we were missing other evidence needed to sustain such a citation.

The deal was struck and the appeal withdrawn. A follow-up could now begin.

The follow-up was initiated ten months after the initial inspection. I was accompanied by a physician from OSHA's medical unit, so that the medical surveillance program could be reviewed. On our way to the company's office, we peeked through the foundry doors and noted that employees were not wearing respirators. In the office, we met Red and went over the medical records. Six of the eleven foundry employees still had high enough blood lead levels to remove them from their work areas.

We then proceeded to the foundry, where we were amused to find that the workers were now wearing respirators. The disposable paper respirators they had been wearing on our last visit had been replaced by reusable rubber respirators, which many industrial hygienists believe provide a better fit. And the cut-off saw had been replaced by a wet-process saw, which was not producing a dust cloud. Interviews confirmed that the workers had received hazard training, protective equipment, coveralls, and medical examinations. A shower had been installed, but it looked unused. No improvements had been made to the fume-capture system, forcing me to return for monitoring.

I returned the following week to remonitor the airborne lead levels. I was certain that overexposure was occurring, but I could not require any changes in the hood system until I could prove that the exposure levels were above 150 $\mu g/m^3$ more than thirty days each year.

Monitoring during the follow-up inspection revealed, not surprisingly, the presence of high levels of lead fumes. My data, together with previous data and those of the consultant, now clearly demonstrated that engineering controls were required according to the standard.

Since the opening of the follow-up, the company had taken another set of blood samples. The samples again indicated that six employees should have been removed from the exposure area, as required by the standard, so that the excessive amounts of lead in their bodies could finally be excreted. Though the company had received the results weeks before, they had not done anything in response to them.

We suspected that the reasons for the high lead levels were that the workers were not wearing their respirators all the time or using good hygiene. Our suspicions were well founded, based on our peek through the foundry doors on the first day of the follow-up. Respirators are uncomfortable. Workers dislike having to strap a piece of rubber around their faces, as anyone would. Several times during the follow-up inspection I had to remove my respirator to empty out the sweat in the bottom of the face piece. There were also problems with the respirators. During the follow-up I examined one that was missing some parts, and when I asked another employee to perform a positive-pressure test by covering the exhalation valve and lightly blowing out, air leaked out his nose. With each breath, he was inhaling unfiltered lead-contaminated air through the leak. Either the respirator was the wrong size or it was not properly adjusted to his face.

Respirators are an unreliable way to control exposure and a poor alternative to engineering controls, as evidenced at the bronze foundry and at numerous other places I have inspected. The effective use of respirators depends on good training that is difficult to attain, especially in small companies. There is much wisdom in the occupational health regulations that require that controls other than respirators be used whenever possible.

The follow-up report was closed a little more than two months after it was opened. Various violations were again issued, including one for not having an adequate fume-capture system over the melting and pouring operations. Though the company had some designs in mind by this time, it was legally necessary to set a schedule for the installation of a better system. At this point, talk and promises had little meaning.

The company was also ordered to remove the employees with excessive lead levels. Removal was to occur within thirty days, allowing time to train replacements. The alternative was for the company to shut down the plant and lay off the workers.

The total penalty after the follow-up inspection was $1,590. I was beginning to think I would be making follow-up visits for a long time.

Several days after receiving the penalty notice, the company appealed again, contesting all the violations. I again requested an early appeal date, and our attorney again arranged a conference. The same group met as for the earlier conference, except that a company-appointed safety and health consultant also attended.

The consultant first reviewed the progress the company had made. Encouragingly, progress included transferring to other jobs those employees who had excessive lead in their bodies and installing a hood and ventilation system that lowered the fume levels to below the standard for airborne lead. The consultant and president were upset, however, because the company had been issued a violation for not having an adequate fume-capture system. They saw the violation as unwarranted since a new hood had been installed on the day the citation was issued.

I explained again why I had issued the citation for the hood, pointing out that the standard had become effective five years before and that it had taken five years for the company finally to comply. I also mentioned that the company had ignored the results of its first blood-sampling test for lead, conducted three years earlier, and had not responded to my repeated warnings about the need for the hoods. I had a legal responsibility to require the improvements, I said, and I could not rely on their continued promises. "What should I say to the families of the workers—that the company deserves a break, to let them install the legally required improvements when they find the time? Never mind that they were required five years ago?" I asked.

I had been pumped up by our attorney earlier when he had insulted me by asking whether I was out to get these guys. I doubted that he had reviewed the file and documentation, and he was again saying in effect, "These are nice guys, what's the problem?"

The consultant made a few valid points regarding the severity of some of the violations and, after that, the meeting was ended. In light of the company's progress, I reluctantly went along with my supervisor and the attorney, and we decided to lower the penalties to about half the proposed amounts. All violations were otherwise affirmed, including the requirement for engineering controls.

Coincidentally, while this inspection was progressing, a co-worker was conducting an inspection of another foundry that made products of brass that contained 6 percent lead. I was very disturbed to learn that tests were conducted about two months after he made first contact and explained the hazards he would be monitoring. I asked him why he had waited so long, to which he responded that he had pointed out various problems on the first walkaround and told the owner that if these problems were taken care of before he came back, "it would all be water under the bridge." I asked about the previous years of noncompliance and the possible excessive exposure the workers had suffered and what could be expected in the future. He weakly replied that there were many more places to inspect.

Monitoring revealed higher lead levels in the air than I had found at the bronze foundry, as well as high noise levels. The employees had been provided respirators but of the type one buys at a hardware store to wear while mowing the lawn. They are not approved or designed to provide protection from toxic metal fumes. Small-particle fumes pass right through the cheap contraption. In fact, the box the respirator comes in is usually labeled "for nontoxic dusts." Not surprisingly, achieving a proper fit is impossible because of the cheap design.

Despite the warning by my fellow inspector, the company issued unapproved respirators, failed to improve its ventilation system, and did not bother to comply with the noise standards. Citations for hazards were issued five and a half months after the initial inspection. There was no apparent reason for this delay, particularly given that the employees remained exposed and unprotected. There was an administrative reason to issue the citations before six months elapsed, however, since that is the OSHA statute of limitations once violations are identified.

Eight general violations and one serious violation carrying a total "stupendous" fine of $135 were issued. I had difficulty comprehending why the fine was so small, especially since several of the general violations deserved characterization as serious. How could a company take compliance with regulations seriously when it was fined such small penalties? The company had allowed its employees to be exposed unprotected to high levels of lead and noise year after year. Could it be expected to protect its employees after OSHA concluded such an inadequate inspection? Wouldn't other companies with similar problems put off making improvements knowing that, if they were caught, the penalties would be harmless?

The penalties seemed so out of line that I brought the matter to the attention of my supervisor. A discussion was held, with the result that all lead-related violations are now reviewed first by the medical unit. The penalties were not changed in this case since it was too late, but the inspector did make a follow-up a few months later with OSHA upper management looking over his shoulder. The blood sampling for lead required by the standard found most of the workers over the 40 μg/100 g level, and one worker's level was 80 μg/100 g. Several employees were later put on medical removal because of the accumulation of lead in their bodies. I shuddered to think that an inspector with such an important responsibility would make such a slipshod inspection and wondered whether the inspector would have returned on his own to enforce the removal provision had I not complained.

The foundry I inspected was not reinspected for about another year and a half after my last follow-up. During the interim it was learned that the company was having problems getting the blood levels of some of its more experienced workers to levels that would permit them to return to the foundry. As required by the OSHA standard, these workers had months before been transferred to "lead-free" areas to allow their bodies to excrete the lead. Also as required by OSHA, the company had had to maintain the workers' pay at their previous levels.

Follow-up revealed that the company had shut down the foundry six months earlier. The machine shop was still operating, using unfinished bronze castings purchased from another foundry. The inspector's report stated that the company had been "unable to lower airborne lead through engineering controls." Earlier reports had indicated that the levels had been controlled. The company had not requested an extension of its abatement dates or contacted the OSHA office to discuss any problems. The report did not indicate whether the overexposed workers who had been transferred out of the foundry were working in the machine shop or whether they had simply been laid off.

A Fairer Price for Batteries

S ome of the worst incidents of lead intoxication have occurred in the lead-battery industry, where overexposure is easy because of the nature of the manufacturing processes and the large quantity of lead used. In this case, the company manufactured car batteries.

Lead makes up the heart of a car battery, forming the charge plates hidden by the more familiar plastic case. The plates are manufactured by pouring molten lead into a mold that forms a grid pattern. Once they are solidified, the plates go through a process in which they are coated with a paste composed of an unlikely mixture of lead oxide dust and sulfuric acid. The coated plates when dry easily release lead-containing dust during their subsequent handling and assembly into completed batteries. High exposure can occur during most of the manufacturing steps through inhalation and ingestion if control procedures are not properly followed.

Because of the potential hazards, a complete wall-to-wall inspection of the plant was scheduled. I was accompanied by a Hispanic safety inspector who proved invaluable when we found that virtually all the production workers spoke Spanish and very little English.

On our first visit to the plant we were welcomed by the owner, a gentle, fatherly figure who seemed calm and pleasant. We took this to be a signal that the inspection would proceed smoothly and that we would not need a warrant. The owner explained that he had six battery-manufacturing plants and had just recently bought a seventh. A retired executive from another industry, he had gotten into the battery-manufacturing business as a pasttime, as a way to give young, inexperienced businesspeople a chance to learn a production process and prove themselves.

The owner introduced us to his plant manager, David Chapen, who was well mannered and clean-cut. The owner seemed proud of his manager, as if he had found a capable son and student. Forced to answer a call from his broker, the owner left his manager to assist in the inspection.

Chapen had all the records I had requested. I was quite surprised to see that blood sampling for lead had been conducted regularly for more than three years. Most of the levels were lower than the 40 μg/ 100 g action value, and those that had exceeded 40 had reached only the 50s and had gone back down within two months.

Chapen discussed the success of the firm's lead-control program with much pride. A ventilation system had been installed ten years before, he said, to control the lead dust generated during manufacturing. The company had assumed that this had solved its problems. The effectiveness of the system had not been monitored. OSHA had inspected shortly thereafter, however, and had found high overexposure to lead, largely because the new ventilation system was not working effectively. Exposure levels were as high as 1,640 μg/m^3, and many people tested at higher than 500. The limit at the time was 200 μg/m^3 as an eight-hour time-weighted average.

Because no comprehensive standard for lead existed at the time (the full standard became effective four years later), the inspector had issued a "special order" detailing corrective measures. Special orders are unique to California OSHA and not available to federal OSHA. The provision gives the agency the power to write a specific regulation when there is none, tailored to an individual company and hazard. The order results in no fines at the time of issuance and is appealable. The battery plant's special order had required that employees be given periodic blood lead tests and medical examinations. In addition, a citation had been issued requiring improvements in the ventilation system. The company had been unsure how to control the lead dust, in that the required tests had revealed that some workers indeed had blood levels as high as 130 μg/100 g with what was assumed to be a good ventilation system.

In its efforts to deal with the problem, Chapen explained, the company had hired a consultant and had participated in a feasibility study with the National Institute of Occupational Safety and Health, which at the time was developing methods to control lead exposure. With the help of the consultant and the judicious use of respirators, employee training, better hygiene, and improved ventilation, the company had been quite successful: records showed that the employees' body burden of lead had declined steadily over the years. Much of the success was due to the efforts and commitment of management (if only other companies could make half the effort).

During my walkaround of the plant, ten years after the first inspection, I found the housekeeping to be excellent, ventilation controls in place, and protection supplemented by the use of respirators.

Workers were given a change of clothes daily and were required to shower at the plant, in compliance with the comprehensive lead standard. A consultant's report showed that respirators were still necessary since airborne exposure exceeded the current limit of 50 $\mu g/m^3$ in many parts of the plant. Effective respirators were being used, and employees had received training in their use and fit tests to ensure that there was no leakage.

After finishing the tour of the plate-manufacturing area and battery-assembly line, we visited what Chapen called the "acid room." On entering, I immediately felt a moderate upper-respiratory irritation. The irritation was from the mist of sulfuric acid that pervaded the room, generated from the mixing, filling, and charging operations. The acid room was where the electrolyte was mixed and added to the batteries. First, superconcentrated sulfuric acid was diluted with water to the proper strength for battery acid, which was still corrosive. Next, a worker wearing a rubber apron, gloves, and what I noted was an acid-stained face shield filled the batteries with the acidic solution at the rate of more than six hundred each day. The employees had no complaints about the acid mist; they had adapted.

Nonetheless, I still conducted air quality tests on the mist several days after the walkaround. The results documented that the levels were one-quarter of the limit. The limit had been set to prevent not only upper-respiratory irritation, but also corrosion of the teeth.

The most important danger in the room, however, was not the possibility of tooth corrosion, but loss of eyesight or disfigurement of the face. Concentrated sulfuric acid is capable of charring wood black in seconds and can ignite combustible materials. Consider then what it can do to one's delicate eye tissue or face. The use of eye and face protection was thus imperative. I issued an order to repair an inoperative emergency eyewash.

The safety inspector found a few areas of concern but no serious violations. He discussed his concerns with Chapen before we left that day.

I returned later to conduct monitoring for exposure to lead dust and fumes and to the acid mist. I found that some air levels exceeded the 100 $\mu g/m^3$ limit for which engineering controls were required. (Engineering controls for battery manufacturers must now be controlled to 50 $\mu g/m^3$ as a workday average.)

On closing the inspection, I issued several general violations, in accordance with OSHA policy and procedure, one for failure to inform the workers fully of the health risks of lead exposure. Hazard communication for people at risk is a basic right; it also motivates people to follow proper work practices. The company also received a violation requiring it to improve the ventilation system. Control of airborne lead by engineering methods had been improved over the years, but the company had not kept up. A better system was necessary. No penalties were issued, and the inspection ended on a friendly note with Chapen thanking me for my help.

I returned for a follow-up two months after the closing conference. Chapen had sent in the notice of compliance on time but had been vague about whether he had completed the ventilation improvements. On inspection, I found that the system had just recently been completed, past the due date. The consultant's air monitoring revealed that the improved system was controlling the levels comfortably to below the 100 $\mu g/m^3$ standard then in effect. In some instances, exposure was now controlled to below the exposure limit of 50 $\mu g/m^3$, so that respirators were no longer necessary.

I learned from Chapen that the improvement had cost the company $20,000. Even if I had rated all the violations serious, the fine would have been less than this. The plant manager noted that the new arrangement actually increased production and that the company would save money by not having to conduct air monitoring or medical examinations or provide respirators as frequently as before. I found no violations during the follow-up.

I was satisfied that there was little health risk at this site, at least as the OSHA standard defined it. I hoped that the company would use engineering controls to reduce all the levels to below the limit. Then no one would have to wear a respirator.

The company impressed me. Perhaps I shouldn't have been so impressed. After all, management was doing the minimum that OSHA required.

6. CARBON MONOXIDE

Carbon monoxide is a simple molecule made up of one carbon atom and one oxygen atom. It has no odor, no taste, and no color. Undetectable by the senses, it exists as a gas that mixes easily with otherwise clean, fresh air.

It is an unpleasant fact of life that the carbon monoxide molecule binds to hemoglobin 240 times better than oxygen does. Hemoglobin is the protein in human blood responsible for transporting oxygen from the lungs to tissues throughout the body. Thus, when enough carbon monoxide is inhaled, the body's oxygen transport system is impaired, producing symptoms of oxygen deficiency. The brain and heart, which require more oxygen for proper functioning than other organs, are the first organs to be affected. In carbon monoxide poisonings, the brain is usually affected most, and destruction of brain cells can result.

Relatively low concentrations of carbon monoxide in the air can cause serious damage. One percent (10,000 ppm) to 4 percent (40,000 ppm) can cause death in minutes. Higher concentrations cause lethal effects in seconds. The results are the same at slightly lower concentrations but take longer to occur. And even at concentrations as low as 0.1 percent (1,000 ppm) to 1 percent (10,000 ppm) headaches or vomiting can occur in a matter of minutes. Early rescue of a seriously poisoned individual can prevent death but does not always prevent irreversible brain damage. Many who survive the coma and assault on the nervous system end up with personality changes and memory impairment.

Depending on the concentration and length of exposure, symptoms of poisoning can include headache, inattentiveness, nausea, vomiting, dizziness, weakness, collapse, coma, and death, though not all poisoned individuals experience each of these symptoms. Death can also occur from careless operation of dangerous machines or vehicles caused by mental impairment from mild carbon monoxide poisoning.

In addition to being a potent poison, carbon monoxide is highly flammable at a wide range of concentrations. Many people exposed to or working with carbon monoxide overlook this fact, with potentially serious consequences.

Exposure to subacute levels of carbon monoxide, that is, concentrations just below those that can produce mild poisoning, are thought to cause more subtle effects. Because there is reduced oxygen available, the heart has to work harder, which may exacerbate previously existing heart problems. The carbon monoxide inhaled with cigarette smoke is thought to have this effect. Some individuals exposed to subacute levels of carbon monoxide have also been reported to experience behavioral effects, including increased response time.

The occupational exposure limits for carbon monoxide were developed with great respect for its poisonous and lethal potential.[1] Federal OSHA currently enforces an eight-hour exposure limit of 35 ppm (0.0035 percent), which is supposed to be low enough to help protect workers with cardiovascular disease. The federal agency also has a ceiling limit of 200 ppm to help prevent the early symptoms of acute poisoning. From 1971 until September 1989, when the current limits were adopted, the day-long exposure limit was 50 ppm, and there was no ceiling limit. For quick-acting poisons such as carbon monoxide, ceiling limits are an absolute necessity and should be well respected.

The serious consequences of overexposure to carbon monoxide provide ample reason for industry to control tightly its production and use. The gas has the distinction of causing more industrial deaths each year than any other chemical. And these statistics do not include the great number of people who survive but have serious brain damage.

Most industrial poisonings occur as a result of carbon monoxide being produced as a by-product of the combustion of organic matter. The combustion of fuel for energy, for example, occurs in practically every industry. Incomplete combustion, which can generate high levels of carbon monoxide in the exhaust of furnaces, heaters, and internal combustion engines, can be caused by a lack of sufficient oxygen for burning or an improper fuel-to-air ratio.

Some businesses such as refineries use carbon monoxide in the production of other chemicals and handle and store large amounts. It is therefore essential that all containers and pipes containing carbon monoxide be well maintained and strict safety practices followed to prevent equipment failure or other accidental release of the gas.

Carbon monoxide is not just an industrial hazard. The gas is the number-one cause of chemical poisoning in the home. Improperly adjusted or vented fuel-burning heaters have killed many unsuspecting people in their sleep. Other needless deaths have occurred because people used hibachis as car heaters. Still others have been killed while barbecuing with charcoal in poorly ventilated areas. And leaks from mufflers and exhaust pipes into the passenger compartments of cars and trucks have caused some to pay dearly for failing to make timely repairs. Many of these people would be alive if they had known about the danger of carbon monoxide poisoning or had at least been aware of the symptoms so that they could have prevented further exposure and obtained immediate medical help.

The best way to prevent carbon monoxide poisoning at work or at home is to have well-trained people install and maintain fuel-burning equipment. Additionally, anyone who could be exposed should be informed about preventive measures, how exposure can occur, the symptoms of overexposure, what to do in the event of an accident, and what the outcome of overexposure can be.

1.6 Million Man-Hours without Lost Time

I didn't have much experience with refineries when I was given the accident report stating that thirteen employees of a local refinery had been sent to a hospital as a result of gas inhalation. What gas? I thought.

I knew that refineries were complex places that presented many opportunities for toxic exposure and fiery deaths. Gasoline is highly flammable and is produced in enormous quantities, greatly magnifying the hazard. Hydrogen sulfide, a deadly gas usefully recovered for production into sulfuric acid, accompanies the refinement of crude oil into gasoline. Another deadly gas, carbon monoxide, is used in large quantities to manufacture the hydrogen used to refine certain distillates of oil into high-quality fuel. With all the processes involved, there are many ways for a tragic accident to occur. That they do not occur regularly is a tribute to a plant's engineering staff or safety personnel.

It is not unusual for an inspector to spend time reviewing the manufacturing process of a company and the pertinent hazards and standards associated with the industry before beginning an inspection. I thus decided that, although I needed to get to the accident site as soon as possible, I would first read up on refineries.

I spent three hours reviewing the health hazards and chemical processes of refineries before leaving for the plant. When I arrived, fifteen hours after the accident, I found a large billboard at the guarded gate proclaiming "Safety Is Everyone's Job." I hoped top management came in through this entrance.

The sign also claimed that the refinery had not had a "lost-time" accident in 1.6 million man-hours. It meant that in 1.6 million man-hours no one had lost a day's work because of an accident. The claim was impressive, but not as impressive as it may have sounded. A million man-hours without lost time is quite different from a million man-hours without an accident. Management often ensures achievement of the former by assigning injured workers light duty the day after an accident—a good idea if medically permitted. Nonetheless, if the refinery's claim was true, it was one the employees and management could be proud of. As I drove through the gate, I wondered whether the results of my inspection would force the company to change its sign.

I drove over to the safety office, where I was met by the safety manager, Betty Leval, and her assistant, Wally Mason. After announcing my purpose, I requested a briefing on the accident. They were quick to point out that no refinery personnel had been involved, only employees of a construction firm at the site. As far as they knew, everyone sent to the hospital had been released without serious injuries. They were not sure what had caused the accident, perhaps exposure to hydrogen sulfide, they suggested.

I asked some basic questions about the part of the operation involved in the accident, but they acted annoyed by my ignorance and offered little more than an overview. I did learn that the construction firm had a contract to repair portions of the B-5 complex, which included hydrogen gas–generating units and a unit that produced naphtha, a fuel distillate of oil.

"Is it safe to tour the accident site?" I asked.

I was surprised by their less-than-confident "I think so." I hoped it was.

Before beginning the tour, I called over the construction company's safety engineer, Tom Lynch, and the site superintendent, Dick Rubio, after informing them that I wished to talk with them.

Lynch arrived first. Greeting me with bloodshot eyes, a friendly Texas drawl, and a warm handshake, he said he would much rather have gone home and gotten some sleep than participate in an OSHA inspection. He explained that he had been up all night dealing with the accident and its aftermath. I apologized for my intrusion but explained that I had to open the inspection. First, I wanted to know whether the leak had been stopped.

"Yes," he replied, adding that all the equipment that may have leaked was now installed and bolted tight. I was happy to hear that.

He also confirmed that the thirteen men who had been sent to the hospital had been released. He confided that he was not certain what gas had leaked. At this point, I wasn't sure whether the refinery and construction company personnel really didn't know what had happened or whether they just weren't motivated to tell me. An inspector soon learns to keep an open mind and not make snappy judgments and to never make judgments based on whether a person "looks" honest. From my experience, some of the nicest people have spun the greatest lies and some rather hot-tempered and ill-mannered folks have told the purest truth.

At the opening conference, I promised Lynch that I would not keep him long and explained that I was inspecting only the work of the construction company and not the refinery since none of the refinery's employees appeared to have been involved in the accident. Lynch was already depressed about the accident, and my presence didn't cheer him up any.

I learned that the construction company had a surprisingly decent safety program, which I took to mean that the refinery was selective in obtaining contractors. Careless and irresponsible contractors can present a great risk for a place that manufactures flammable gases and liquids. I was also impressed by Tom Lynch, who not only gracefully put up with my questions but seemed to take the accident personally, even though it was unclear whether he was at all responsible. I would later learn during interviews that Lynch was active in training employees and frequently shouted at workers to correct unsafe conditions he found on his many walkthroughs.

After spending about a half-hour with him, I asked to speak to his superintendent, adding that maybe he should go home and get some sleep. He left for what would now be a good day's rest.

The construction superintendent, Rubio, soon appeared and, after introductions, sat down with relief. He had also been up all night, after being released from the emergency room.

I asked him to relate the previous night's events. He recalled that at about 10:00 or 11:00 he had heard shouting coming from the area of the heat exchangers in the B-5 complex, where two crews of three men each were installing two exchangers. He ran over and found one man collapsed in the corner of a sixteen-foot-high scaffold. Two other workers on the scaffold appeared sick and were having trouble responding to the apparent emergency. All three had been working on the south exchanger. He instinctively thought a leak had developed, possibly from the exchanger. After first giving orders to a couple of workers to obtain nearby compressed air hoses, he ran over to the emergency respirator station and grabbed two self-contained breathing apparatuses, or SCBAs. (Similar to SCUBA gear, SCBAs have their own supply of air in a pressurized tank.) Donning one of the SCBAs, he climbed up on the scaffold and asked someone to hand the other SCBA up to him. Meanwhile, the air hoses had begun spraying fresh air around the unbolted flange on the south heat exchanger.

I interrupted Rubio's story at this point to ask who the other men involved were and whether they were wearing respirators. He replied that he could not remember whether they were wearing respirators or who was helping him. He quickly went on, saying that once he was on the scaffold, he placed a SCBA on the man who had collapsed. At about the same time, he recalled, a large front-end loader was preparing to remove the collapsed worker from the scaffold. He next attended to the other two workers, with whom he shared the respirator's facepiece and bottled air. With the aid of workers on the ground, he then helped the two semi-conscious workers down a ladder. In the meantime, the unconscious worker was lifted off with the front-end loader. Everyone evacuated the area, he said, then reported to the hospital for treatment or evaluation. I later learned that several other workers near the area complained of dizziness and had also been taken to the emergency room. In total, five workers had passed out. Thirteen workers, including the superintendent, had been checked by a doctor and released. To my surprise, even the three workers who had been on the scaffold had not been held overnight.

Concerned about the manner of the rescue, I asked Rubio why he had taken off his respirator when he suspected there was a gas leak, particularly of toxic gas. He did not think it was a problem, he replied, since compressed breathable air was being blown into the area.

Based on the facts I had so far, I could not decide whether the superintendent had been a hero or a fool for risking his life and that of others. But removing his respirator, having other people respond without adequate protection, and using a vehicle that could have ignited flammable gases or vapors were the wrong responses in the face of a potentially toxic and flammable gas leak. If the leak had been more serious, he would have been a dead fool rather than a hero. After ruling out an imminent explosion, which would have necessitated evacuation, all the rescuers should have worn maximum respiratory protection, such as SCBAs. It would now be difficult to convince those who felt like heroes that their actions had been foolish. The company's emergency response program clearly needed improvement.

I next asked Rubio what had caused the accident. He replied that perhaps nitrogen or hydrogen sulfide had leaked, but he didn't know exactly where it could have come from. He had since learned that on the night of the accident one of his crews had been replacing tubing on a high-pressure separator and that gas may have been released. He was quick to add that the refinery had given the go-ahead for the job. I paused for a moment. He did not know the details of the accident—what had leaked or where—but if the tube replacement had anything to do with it, the accident was the refinery's fault.

"One final question," I said, "did you at any time smell or see any gas or feel any respiratory irritation?"

"No."

That ruled out hydrogen sulfide, the sulfur oxides, and petroleum distillate vapors. I was growing increasingly suspicious of an odorless and colorless deadly gas.

Rubio was eager to get back to work. The accident had caused production setbacks, and every day lost meant thousands of dollars of gasoline that the refinery could not produce and sell, which contractually could mean thousands of dollars of penalty to the construction firm. Refineries sometimes offer bonuses to contractors who finish ahead of time. Such strategies carry a risk, however, since the chance of accidents increases when a job is pushed too fast by contractors with hot palms.

It was time to visit the accident site. Mason from the refinery, Rubio, and I drove out to the unit under construction, and, at my request, we got out and walked around.

The technology was astounding. I was struck by the capacity and dinosaurlike size of the pipes and towers where the crude oil was transformed into sophisticated fuels. The massive configurations of pipes and tanks of the B-5 unit extended over tens of thousands of square feet and constituted only a small part of the refinery. Standing among the towers and superstructures, I had an insight into why some construction people worship such massive structures to the point that they can see a human life lost here or there as insignificant. Unfortunately, companies don't achieve such monumental feats vis-à-vis the safety of their employees.

After walking around the site, we stopped in front of the rows of heat exchangers where the accident had occurred. Like most refining equipment, the exchangers were in the open air. I sketched out the exchanger system and its connections to the structures that Rubio designated as the reactors and the high-pressure separator, and I took several photographs. After each, Mason, the safety engineer, stood where I had, taking an identical shot.

The installation of the south heat exchanger had been completed that morning, although the scaffolding on which the workers had been overcome remained. Work proceeded on the north exchanger.

I asked to interview the workers who had been overcome. Only one was back at work, and he was sent over to me. I introduced myself and, after explaining to Rubio that interviews are confidential, the worker and I walked out of listening distance.

I learned that he was a nonunion, temporary worker who had been on the job for only a couple of months. He had a job for as long as the construction lasted, and, from what I gathered, it was a job he needed.

In response to my questions about the previous night, he related that he and two other workers had been assigned to insert and bolt in the repaired south heat exchanger. They had been working for most of the shift, he said, when suddenly one of the men sitting on top of a pipe began to slide off. He and another worker grabbed their co-worker, who was only semi-conscious, and helped him off the pipe. As soon as they got the worker down, he and the other worker began to feel dizzy and disoriented. He remembered that the worker they rescued lumbered toward the end of the scaffold and then collapsed. Rescuers arrived, and shortly afterward the workers were transported to the hospital. The doctor didn't find anything wrong, the worker said, and, feeling all right, he was released at about 2:00 A.M.

I asked him what he thought had happened.

"I think it was something we ate for dinner," he replied.

I considered his explanation for a moment. "Did you all eat at the same restaurant?" I asked.

"No." They had each brought their dinners from home, he said.

His theory was humorous and inconsistent with the facts I had gathered so far. I told him that I hoped he did not really believe it was something they had eaten.

At that moment, for some reason, I looked behind me to see if anyone was listening. Rubio was watching us from about twenty feet away, far enough not to hear the conversation but close enough for my interviewee to read his concerned face. I continued with my questioning.

I learned that the three men had been working for several hours on the south heat exchanger without any problems. They had been overcome just as they were about to bolt the last flange to a matching flange. He said he did not smell, see, or feel anything unusual. When I asked whether he heard anything, like a hissing sound, he replied that he hadn't. On further questioning, however, he acknowledged that the background noise at the site could easily have masked a sound.

I concluded the interview, and, as soon as the worker walked away, Rubio caught up and talked to him, out of earshot. Mason and I drove back to the training office.

I next interviewed Allan Purdy, the operations manager of the refinery, who was responsible for the B-5 unit and for overseeing the work of the contractor. He seemed to be an honest and sincere man, but it took great effort to get enough information to piece together even part of the story.

I learned that the B-5 unit, which was temporarily shut down for the repair work, normally produced refined naphtha, a relatively volatile mixture of hydrocarbons, which the refinery used chiefly as a blending agent for gasoline and other fuels. In the B-5 unit, crude naphtha was upgraded in a reaction in which it was mixed with hydrogen gas in several reactors that were over fifty feet tall. The reaction that took place added hydrogen atoms to the "unsaturated" hydrocarbons in the mixture. The more hydrogen atoms on the hydrocarbons, the better the fuel. The mixture was next cooled by passing it through a bank of heat exchangers. The now partially cooled hydrocarbon mixture was then routed to a cooling tower the size of a large apartment building for further temperature reduction and then into the high-pressure separator, a tall, narrow tower. There, the refined naphtha was separated out and the unreacted material returned to the reactors.

Once I understood what normally occurred and how the equipment was interrelated, I next asked about the repair job that was taking place on the day of the accident. Under shutdown conditions, I learned, no product is made, and the reactors are "blinded" from the heat exchangers. In other words, a metal plate or other block is placed at an appropriate valve or flange, physically preventing the flow of gas or liquid. Setting a blind is a common technique required by OSHA standards to help prevent a product from being released from an inadvertently opened valve and those on the end of the line being overcome by a flesh-eating chemical, a poisonous gas, or, worse, a ball of fire.

Before beginning the repair work, the heat exchangers were blinded from the rest of the refinery and set in shutdown condition. Two of the three heat exchangers were then removed for repair and replaced with a temporary connecting pipe.

For a week before the accident, pipe lines in the system had been dried out by recirculating warm nitrogen through the remaining exchanger, cooling towers, and separator. The morning before the accident, the drying was completed. The system was now ready for the insertion of the repaired heat exchangers. All that remained in the system lines, said the operations manager, was unpressurized, warm nitrogen gas and perhaps trace amounts of volatile product.

My questions and the operation manager's terse answers finally brought us to the moment of the accident. Purdy stated that the construction crews had worked without incident inserting the two heat exchangers until about 10:30, when their problems began.

"But what about the tube replacement?" I asked, referring to what Rubio had thought caused the accident. It seemed the most important part may have been left out of our game of three thousand questions.

Finally Purdy admitted that the construction company had received a work order from his department to replace a piece of bent copper tubing on top of the high-pressure separator—a minor job.

"Could it have caused the accident?" I asked.

He didn't know. Maybe.

"Was there any other operation going on that could have caused a gas leak?"

Purdy replied that a hydrogen-generating unit next to the naphtha production unit had started up the day before. Its product, "HC-fuel," was sent to a flare stack, a supertall structure used to burn waste gases.

"What is HC-fuel composed of?" I asked.

"Mostly hydrogen and carbon monoxide."

"What concentrations?"

"I don't know exactly. But the lab has done an analysis, and we can get those numbers."

"Who was overseeing the crew replacing the tubing?"

He named a maintenance foreman from the refinery.

"Were refinery people required to walk around the site inspecting the construction?"

"Yes," Purdy replied. "Several foremen inspected the contractor's work."

I had more than a vague feeling that I was getting somewhere. Carbon monoxide, the one deadly gas I suspected of having leaked, was now in the picture.

Weary, I broke off the inspection. It was getting late, and I had already kept Mason, the safety engineer, an hour past his leave time.

The next morning in the office, I reviewed the information I had collected. In doing so, I realized I still had some unanswered questions. My last interview with Purdy had worn me down and I had missed asking him for some critical information. How could the HC-fuel leak into the exchangers? Could the gas find its way through the maze of pipes? Or, for some reason, was the nitrogen remaining from the drying operation pouring out of the exchanger? I still was not sure what gas had leaked out or how removal of the copper tubing could have resulted in the accident.

I needed a reliable diagram of the naphtha production unit, showing all the tanks, towers, and connecting pipes. The cause of the accident had to be related to the way the pipes and tanks were connected at the time of the accident. More important, why hadn't the accident been prevented? If hydrogen, and particularly carbon monoxide, had leaked, the accident could have been a major disaster.

I called Leval, the safety manager, that morning after reviewing my notes. I told her who I wanted to interview and informed her that my inspection would also include the refinery, since foremen had been at the site at the time of the accident. I also requested to talk with some of the operations people and someone who could draw a flow diagram for me.

When I arrived at the training office that afternoon, I was met by Leval; Mason; the plant engineer, Mike Po, who was my first interviewee; and a surprise guest—the refinery's attorney. Since my investigation now included the refinery, I was told, the attorney would be present at all interviews.

"Fine," I said.

We gathered in the room we had been in the day before, but the mood was noticeably different. Instead of the informal arrangement of chairs we had the previous day, we all sat in the middle of a long table. Po sat directly across from me, with the attorney and safety manager on either side of him. With the capacity to hold a hundred people, the room, to my dissatisfaction, now had the air of a courtroom.

At my request, Po drew a diagram of the pipes and vessels, including the main components I had viewed the day before—the reactors, heat exchangers, cooler, and high-pressure separator. He also drew the pipes connecting the high-pressure separator, the flare stack system, and the hydrogen-generating unit.

I learned from Po that the HC-fuel from the hydrogen-generating unit was composed of about 45 percent hydrogen and 45 percent carbon monoxide. The concentrations were certainly high enough for someone to get burned or poisoned.

Po explained that a vent valve, suspected of being somehow involved in the accident, connected the high-pressure separator in the naphtha production unit to the flare stack system. Opening the valve on the separator could cause the HC-fuel to flow toward the naphtha production unit if part of the unit was open to the outside and thus there was no back pressure to stop the flow. As Purdy, the operations manager, had explained the day before, the HC-fuel was being routed to the flare stack.

"What did the copper tubing have to do with it?" I asked.

If the copper tubing on the vent valve of the high-pressure separator was removed, Po explained, the valve would open, allowing the HC-fuel to flow into the separator and the naphtha production unit. The copper tubing contained compressed air that exerted pressure on a depression valve. This pressure kept the valve closed so that no gas could come into the separator from the flare stack system and no gas could leave the B-5 unit through the valve. If pressure was released because of a signal from the control room to connect the separator to the flare system or because the copper tubing was disconnected, the valve would open. In Po's opinion, it was possible for the HC-fuel to leak through an opening in the heat exchanger system if there was an opening to the outside air and there were no blinds along the way. I noted that Purdy would have to review the diagram and identify where there were blinds at the time of the accident. Po added that, assuming the conditions existed for a HC-fuel leak, the nitrogen gas in the exchanger system would probably have been pushed out by the incoming HC-fuel gas. He was uncertain, however, whether the valve on the separator, assuming it had a part in the accident, had been open long enough to allow the HC-fuel to leak in full strength to the exchangers.

The half-hour spent with Po was invaluable. If I had interviewed him first, I would have been able to ask more intelligent questions of the other people I interviewed. But at least my questions were now answered. Po also pulled together some other loose ends. Had my reconstruction of the accident been inaccurate and a citation issued based on it, the attorney for the refinery would have been more than delighted to embarrass me at an appeal hearing, and rightfully so.

I next interviewed the construction foreman who was supervising the replacement of the copper tubing on the night of the accident. He was a young, tough-looking construction worker with a deep southern accent. He introduced himself as the second-shift maintenance foreman for the construction company. I introduced myself and began asking questions about the accident. His manner was subdued, in contrast to his appearance. I sensed he had already felt an accusing finger.

The foreman related that he had received a work list, called a "punch list," at the beginning of his shift on the day of the accident, as he did every day. He then started his crew on the night's assignment, which included replacing a damaged piece of copper tubing. He noted that there were no special instructions on the handwritten list.

He had discussed the job with the refinery foreman overseeing the work, he said. He recalled that he had asked his permission to go ahead with the job and had received a "go-ahead." By all appearances, it was a minor job, so he hadn't obtained a written permit certifying that the job was safe.

At about 9:00 on the night of the accident, he climbed up the fifty-foot-tall high-pressure separator to look over the piece of tubing that needed replacing. He then climbed back down and assigned one of his men to do the work. Some time after 10:00—he was not sure of the exact time—he heard shouting coming from the area of the heat exchanger. He ran over and found one guy stumbling away. He immediately suspected a gas leak.

"Did you receive any instructions or information from your supervisor or the refinery foreman about whether gases could be released when the tubing was removed?"

"No," he replied quietly.

"Are you going to be working the second shift the rest of the week, in case I have more questions?" I asked.

"No, I'm flying out of here tomorrow. I got assigned to another job in Texas."

I suspected that the foreman was being pinned with the blame, perhaps unfairly. I thanked him and asked him to send over the worker who had replaced the tubing.

I learned from the worker that he had disconnected the tubing on top of the separator at about 10:30. He had heard a hissing sound, he said, when he first unbolted the tubing from his manifold, as expected when tubing holding compressed air is removed. It took about twenty minutes to complete the job, he estimated. He was in no rush, he said. No one had told him that removing the tubing could release a toxic gas.

My interviews ran late again as I stayed to interview workers on the second shift. The tired faces of the refinery safety personnel and the attorney told me that I had better quit for the day.

Several days passed as I attended to other inspections and mulled over my notes. It was disappointing to spend so much time on an investigation, but no one else was going to hand me an objective evaluation or signed affidavits that I could rely on.

To the dismay of Leval, the safety manager who had been coordinating my visits, I still needed to do more interviews. I called and set up a final round with the foreman of the refinery, who had allegedly given the go-ahead to replace the tubing.

The foreman began by explaining that he monitored the contractor's work, which included coordinating unplanned assignments. The normal routine was to provide the construction company superintendent with the punch list of assignments to be completed over the next few days. The list was first reviewed and signed by the operations manager of the refinery.

"Can any work proceed with a verbal okay?" I asked.

"Yes, if it's minor," he replied.

"On the night of the accident, did you give the construction foreman a verbal go-ahead to do the tube replacement job on the high-pressure separator?"

The foreman paused for a moment and shifted in his chair. After a thoughtful delay, he replied, "No."

He seemed to be trying not to lie. It was as if he was saying "no" for the benefit of the refinery personnel and his job yet saying "yes" for the benefit of his conscience. I felt more sure of this after he answered my next question.

"Were you aware that a toxic gas could be released in the heat exchangers if the copper tubing on the separator was disconnected?"

Without pause, he replied, "No."

After several more questions, I thanked him and let him start his shift. I did not like to put people under such pressure, but knowing the truth about the accident would, I hoped, prevent another possibly worse accident from occurring. Some mistakes are forgiveable; mistakes repeated are not.

I next interviewed Allan Purdy, the operations manager, whom I had interviewed at length some days before. I pulled out the diagram Po had drawn for me. At my request, Purdy drew in the nitrogen recycle lines that had been in use just before the accident. More questions revealed that there were heaters, one-way-flow check valves, and quench lines I had not known about and that the plant engineer had not mentioned. Next, I asked where the blinds had been placed.

To avoid misunderstandings, Purdy and I together traced the multiple routes the HC-fuel gas could have followed on its way to the openings at the heat exchangers. It was like playing a game in which one is required to draw a line through a maze in an effort to reach the center. The operations manager marked where the blinds were placed and whether valves were opened or closed.

One short-cut route we traced indicated that large quantities of gas that could have been released at the north exchanger were blocked by a blind, at least according to Purdy and other foremen. The north exchanger was otherwise susceptible to a massive leak since it had not yet been connected at the time of the accident and a line was open to the outside, so that the gas could have drifted toward the south exchanger.

Another more tortuous path through the nitrogen recycle lines would have resulted in a leak at both open exchangers. This route was possible, however, only if a one-way-flow valve, set to prevent flow in the direction of the exchangers, had itself leaked, which, as Purdy said, could have happened if there was not a perfect seal.

The third route, which followed the reverse course of the production process, was surprisingly unhindered by blinds and would have resulted in a leak at the unbolted flange of the south exchanger. It appeared that a mistake could have been made in relying on the vent valve being closed and not putting in a blind. This explanation was a bit unsatisfying, however, since the laborer working on the south exchanger at the time of the accident said that the pipe and flanges in the exchanger were unbolted but nearly flush, which would have prevented the release of a large volume of gas. Nonetheless, it wouldn't take much of a highly toxic gas such as carbon monoxide to knock people down.

Purdy would not offer an explanation of how and where the HC-fuel leaked at the time of the accident. He left that to me. He did not disagree that the HC-fuel could have leaked, and he had no other explanations for the accident.

"You were aware that the hydrogen-generating units had been started up the day before the accident and were putting out hydrogen and carbon monoxide through the flare stack lines?" I asked.

"Yes," Purdy answered.

"Did you know that if the copper tubing operating the vent valve on the high-pressure separators were removed, HC-fuel could be released into the naphtha production unit, where construction crews were working?"

The attorney, who was sitting in on the interview, interrupted before Purdy could answer. He asked me to clarify my question, perhaps in an effort to give the manager more time to think about his answer.

After I rephrased the question, Purdy answered. "Yes," he said, "I knew of the potential for release of the gas." The man had the courage to be honest.

I next pulled out a copy of the punch list Leval had given me. One of the items on the list was the work order for the copper tube replacement. There were no warnings or special instructions. I asked Purdy if his signature was at the bottom.

"Yes," he replied.

The strain of the interview was now showing on his face. I ignored an impulse to state the obvious: a serious oversight had occurred, or at least faulty and dangerous communication. My conclusion would be presented later at the closing conference, after I had time to review the entire file and discuss the case with OSHA management. I did not wish to blame the manager unjustly, though I was confident that he was at least partly responsible. Purdy appeared to be an honest and sincere person who would presumably learn from this experience. I hated to think he might be replaced by someone less capable.

I thanked Purdy for his time. The attorney copied my flow diagram and my copy of the punch list. I left, saying I would soon be contacting Leval to set up a closing conference. She was less than thrilled.

Provided I was not being severely misled by my interviewees, I was now able to reconstruct the events leading up to the accident. On that day, the pumps used to dry the insides of the pipes and naphtha production unit had been shut off and the pressure on the system released. Once the construction crews finished reinserting the repaired heat exchangers, the naphtha unit would be ready to start up again.

At about the time that the day's punch list was being prepared, the construction workers were getting set to lift the heat exchangers into place. It took the rest of the afternoon to insert the south heat exchanger and make the preliminary connections. Drifts of nitrogen gas, left over from the drying process, leaked from the disconnected pipes into the open air, but the air provided plenty of dilution for the relatively nontoxic nitrogen. The second shift continued the first shift's work of installing the exchangers.

At about 10:00 P.M. another crew of workers was positioning the north heat exchanger onto its mount, using an oversized forklift truck. The pipe connecting the exchanger to the naphtha production unit was open, its flanges ready to be mated to the flanges of the heat exchanger. At about the same time, and about a hundred feet south, the south heat exchanger was about to be bolted into place.

Also at about 10:00, another construction worker was making the long climb to the top of the high-pressure separator to replace the piece of copper tubing. Before beginning his work, the worker looked over his assignment, making sure he had all the necessary tools. It was almost 10:30 when he began loosening the nut that joined the copper tubing to a manifold. As he loosened the nut, he noticed a hissing sound that lasted only a moment. At the same instant, the loss of pressure opened a valve a few feet away, where the other end of the copper tubing was still connected.

The valve that was inadvertently opened was the vent valve of the high-pressure separator, designed to open only under critical circumstances during production. When naphtha was being produced and the pressure in the separator increased to a near-dangerous level, a sensor would send a signal via copper tubing to open the valve. When the valve was opened, the pressure was reduced by safely routing extra gas and vapor to the flare stack system, where they were vented and burned. The release mechanism saved the high-pressure separator from otherwise certain damage or complete destruction.

Inadvertently opening the valve under the shutdown conditions present the night of the accident connected the entire naphtha production unit with the flare stack system, as it was designed to do, but this time there was no highly pressurized gas to be vented. Instead, the system, shut down for repair, was at atmospheric pressure. Once the naphtha unit was connected to the flare stack, some of the HC-fuel, under production since the day before when the hydrogen-generating unit had been coincidentally started, was routed toward the naphtha unit. Following a simple law of physics, the pressurized gas headed toward the area with the lower pressure, through a path unhindered by blinds or closed valves, and most likely ended up at the south heat exchanger, which was still open to the outside air.

Shortly after 10:30, the three men on the south heat exchanger were becoming dizzy and disoriented. Unknown to them, an invisible, odorless, disabling gas had replaced their life-sustaining air. The gas that rushed toward the heat exchanger packed a deadly two-way punch. First, at 45 percent, carbon monoxide is instantaneously lethal. Second, hydrogen and carbon monoxide both at 45 percent are extremely flammable. This as-yet-undiluted fire and poison cocktail poured into the high-pressure separator. Being a large-sized vessel, the separator diluted the HC-fuel, mixing the highly concentrated hydrogen and carbon monoxide with the 100 percent nitrogen in the naphtha production unit.

Because the HC-fuel was diluted in the early stages of the accident, we were unable to determine the exact concentrations of carbon monoxide or hydrogen that leaked. In any event, 100 percent nitrogen was immediately pushed out of the openings at one or both of the heat exchangers and mixed with the outside air. Nitrogen at atmospheric pressure is harmful only in concentrations high enough to dilute out breathable oxygen. (Air is composed of 78 percent nitrogen and 21 percent oxygen.) Carbon monoxide, the substance that probably leaked out in ever-increasing concentrations, is capable of robbing the body of oxygen even when there is an oversupply.

As the rescue was in progress, the worker on top of the separator bent the new piece of copper tubing into shape and bolted it into place, thereby restoring pressure to the vent valve actuator and stopping the HC-fuel from flowing through the naphtha production unit.

Until the third day of the inspection, when most of the facts were brought out, the construction crew and refinery personnel did not understand how close they had come to death from poisoning or explosion. The worker on the high-pressure separator had no idea that he could release a deadly gas cocktail by removing the copper tubing. He was also oblivious to the emergency occurring on the ground. If he had decided to rest for a while after removing the tubing or, worse yet, had seen the emergency and left without reconnecting the tubing, a greater volume and higher concentrations of hydrogen and carbon monoxide would have been released. If the tubing had been removed a few hours earlier, the connections to the south heat exchanger would have been wide open, allowing more gas to rush out. Under any of these conditions, many construction and refinery employees, including would-be rescuers, would most likely have been killed. Finally, had the flammable concentrations of hydrogen and carbon monoxide been somehow ignited, the result would have been a highly destructive explosion and fire.

The accident could easily have been prevented. At the time the operations manager reviewed the punch list for the day, he should have flagged the copper tubing assignment and warned the foreman and workers of the dangers. Also, the replacement could have been delayed a day until the exchangers were bolted and sealed. Regardless, a blind should have been installed on the vent valve.

The contractor's employees had obviously considered replacement of the copper tubing an inconsequential job that would take thirty minutes at most. No need for a written permit, they thought, since the naphtha production unit was down.

The operations manager was not completely to blame. The foremen of the refinery and of the construction company, as well as the construction superintendent, who also reviewed the punch list, should have recognized that the tubing probably operated a valve. Those working in such situations must take positive action to avert hazards. The recurrence of accidents because of such negligence has resulted in the adoption of a specific set of safety standards just for refineries.

I completed my investigation and closed the inspection three and a half weeks after the accident. The refinery and the construction company were issued serious citations for the same violation: failure to instruct employees about the contents of pipelines and the necessary safety precautions before opening valves. The construction company received a fine of $600, adjusted down from a maximum of $1,000 for serious violations. The refinery received a fine of $700 because of its poorer safety record in the previous three years.

Before leaving, I requested to review the refinery's OSHA 200 form for the year, which by law it was required to maintain. I had never reviewed the record before and was startled to see every injury described as "hurt arm," "hurt leg," or "hurt index finger." None of the descriptions began with an adjective other than "hurt," such as "broken," "lacerated," "bruised," or "amputated," which would have better described their severity. The refinery had certainly had accidents, but apparently the workers were not injured severely enough to prevent them from returning to work the following day. The company could thus maintain its record of a million-plus man-hours without a time loss. Contracting out the more dangerous work has made it easier for refineries to achieve such records. A refinery under construction can be very dangerous; pipes and equipment are open and, as evident in this case, mix-ups can result in the deadly release of gases or vapors. In years past, a refinery's own employees were assigned maintenance and construction duties. Now this work is almost always contracted out, with a concomitant shift in liability.

Both the refinery and the construction company appealed, and an appeal hearing was set for eight months after the issuance of the citations. The construction company later requested and received a continuance from the appeals board. The company must have "reasoned" that eight months was too short a time to prepare for the hearing or, rather, that it did not want to be subject to a follow-up inspection or repeat violation. A few weeks before their respective hearings, both companies withdrew their appeals.

About three months after the closing conference another carbon monoxide accident involving a contractor occurred in a different area of the plant. The problem was again failure to review the potential hazards, to formulate a safety plan, and to inform the workers of the plan and hazards. One of the contractor's employees was hospitalized for four days.

As a result of the second accident, the refinery was issued a general citation for failure to monitor carbon monoxide and hydrogen sulfide exposures properly and for failure to place a warning label on a storage tank containing hazardous gases. No fines were issued. Potential overexposure could not be documented, although the potential may have existed during past jobs involving the same storage tank. And because no applicable standard existed at the time, a citation could not be issued for failure to inform the contractor about the hazards. (The new hazard communication standard requires that contractors be informed of possible hazardous chemicals to which employees may be exposed.)

In the closing conference regarding this accident, the office manager for the contractor put full blame on the refinery. "They should have warned us and provided my employees with monitors, alarms, and respirators," he complained. I was sympathetic but not completely since no one from his company had asked any questions or conducted a proper safety review of the job. The refinery could maintain, with some validity, that it had selected the company for its experience in handling chemicals and that it expected the company to maintain its own safety program, as the law requires.

I gave the office manager a presentation similar to the one I had given the refinery personnel about the need for prejob safety reviews. The office manager quickly replied that his company could not possibly conduct safety reviews for every job it did at the refinery.

"Why not?" I asked. "How many types of jobs does the company do at the refinery, fifty?"

"Maybe that many," he replied.

I explained that his company did not do fifty different jobs in a day but rather that many in several months, if not years. It was not much to expect, I told him, to determine the safety precautions necessary for each job while working up a contract. Furthermore, OSHA places overall responsibility for the safety of workers on their immediate employers.

The contractor received a serious citation for failure to provide its employees with information on the hazards and precautions of the operation involved in the accident. The fine totaled $550. The citation was not appealed.

Surprisingly, the refinery did not appeal the citation. Instead, the plant manager sent a letter saying that, although he would not appeal, he felt the refinery had done nothing wrong and had been cited unjustly. I replied in a letter of my own that the company had to engage in more prejob safety planning with contractors. Otherwise, I warned, the company would miss the point of the citations and risk yet another accident, one that could be catastrophic. Luck would not serve them much longer.

No More Coffee and Croissants

Mr. and Mrs. Greenbriar's cafe was decorated in a European style consistent with the row of trendy shops nearby. The cafe's French pastries were made each night in an adjacent kitchen.

Carlos had worked before as a baker for Mr. and Mrs. Greenbriar. He had decided to come back in spite of a long commute from his home to the exclusive shopping center where the bakery was located.

The owner reintroduced Carlos to his job on his first night back. He toured Carlos through the kitchen, where he would spend most of his time. It was a functional kitchen with a large oven and plenty of table space to fold and spread dough. In the back were a few rooms where the workers could take short naps.

To help Carlos get back into the routine, the head chef, Marla Dubois, stopped by the kitchen early the first evening to review Carlos's baking assignment and to help him prepare part of the next day's sales. The next day was Saturday, a good business day for the shopping center and thus for the cafe.

Confident that Carlos was reacquainted enough to get by, Marla left. As she started out the door, she turned on the oven. With the chef gone, Carlos returned to preparing the goods at his own rate. He was not alone. The dishwasher, Raphael, was there with him.

A little later Raphael and Carlos began to feel sleepy. Since it was only about 9:00 and they were on their own for the night, they decided to take a nap. Surely he had time to finish preparing the croissants and other baked goods, Carlos reasoned. After all, the store didn't open until the next morning. Even the head chef had slept while the goods baked, and Carlos knew it wasn't against the rules to take a short nap. They had plenty of time, he thought.

The next morning at 7:30, shortly before the cafe would open, Marla arrived to find two employees waiting outside. Usually they entered on their own through the back door to the kitchen, which was often unlocked, or knocked to get the bakers' attention. For some reason the door was locked and no one was answering. And, surprisingly, the windows were also locked. The bakers routinely kept them open for ventilation.

Marla unlocked the door, and they all entered. Immediately, she saw that nothing had been baked; seven to eight trays of unbaked goods sat on a table. Her first thought was that Carlos had taken off, quitting after only one night.

Continuing through the kitchen, Marla noticed that the oven was still on, uselessly burning natural gas. As she passed by, she turned it off.

Next, Marla informed the counter employees that they would have to help prepare the goods for baking while she opened the store. One of the employees said he would call the owner to give him the bad news that none of the day's items had been baked. It was going to be tough opening the cafe without its renowned croissants.

After checking to make sure everything was in order in the cafe, Marla proceeded to inspect the equipment and stock in the storage rooms. As she was doing so, she found what she thought was an amusing discovery. "Here's Carlos, over here on the floor, sleeping!" she yelled.

The counter employees rushed in from the cafe to get in on the fun.

"Carlos, wake up!" Marla demanded, probably annoyed by now.

Carlos did not respond.

In an instant, the fun ended. Marla sensed that something might be wrong, and, just as quickly, she noticed that Carlos's head was in an awkward position, right under the noodle machine, an odd place to fall asleep. Suspicious, she leaned down for a closer look. "I THINK HE'S DEAD!"

Disbelieving his boss's sudden pronouncement, one of the counter employees leaned down and touched Carlos's body. It was hard—dead hard. He rushed to the phone to call the owners.

Marla continued to look around, not sure what she would find next. Had Raphael gone home, she wondered, or had he met a fate similar to Carlos's?

Marla found Raphael, the teenaged dishwasher, not far from Carlos's still body, on the floor in another room. The deep and labored rise and fall of Raphael's chest indicated he was still alive, but barely. Marla ran to the cafe to call paramedics.

Within a few minutes, the paramedics arrived and administered first aid to Raphael. They were quick to suspect gas poisoning based on his labored breathing and the cherry-red color of his skin. He was rushed to the hospital.

Raphael survived, but there was nothing the paramedics or hospital staff could do for Carlos. His body was left for the county coroner.

The message service for the OSHA office reached Dave, the district manager of the local office, at his home on that fateful Saturday morning and informed him of the accident at the bakery. Minutes before, the responding fire department had called in the accident to the OSHA office, as required by state law. Dave, in turn, immediately called Greg, one of his safety inspectors, who lived close to the site of the accident.

Greg had made inspections of fatal accidents before and knew the importance of beginning the investigation promptly. He arrived at the bakery at 10:45 in the morning, forty-five minutes after Dave first received the call.

There was a crowd of people outside the bakery when Greg arrived. A fatality usually elicits concern from several agencies, some with more curiosity than jurisdiction. The number represented here was unusually high, indicating that something very serious must have happened.

Greg met first with a detective from the Homicide Bureau, who told Greg that two victims had been found in the bakery at about 7:30 that morning. The older guy was dead, he said, and the younger one had been rushed to the hospital near death. The detective relayed the conclusion of the coroner, who was busy working over the body, that the probable cause of death was carbon monoxide poisoning.

Because the death was apparently the result of an industrial accident, OSHA had prime jurisdiction over the case. In an attempt to get control of the scene, Greg thus began introducing himself and finding out who was there and why. By the end of the day, Greg had met everyone in the crowd, including the captain of the fire department's hazardous materials response team, the county coroner, two inspectors from the county health department, three employees of the bakery, and seven concerned officials from the gas company. The owners of the cafe were not at the scene.

Greg next met with the county coroner, who showed him Carlos's body. From the position of the body, it appeared that Carlos had become at least semi-conscious in his final moments, perhaps because of a severe headache or stomach cramps, which are known to occur in carbon monoxide poisonings. He had apparently attempted to crawl away but had missed the door leading out of the storage room by a few feet and had ended up in a literal dead end, underneath a noodle machine parked against an unyielding wall. It would later be determined that there would have been less hope beyond the storage room since the kitchen area had even greater concentrations of the life-robbing gas.

Inspecting industrial tragedies was not new to Greg. He had seen victims of other industrial accidents and had conducted interviews with seriously hurt survivors on numerous occasions. But such cases are never routine. The loss of life or limb always weighs heavy.

Noting the visible effects of death by carbon monoxide poisoning, the coroner pointed out the bluish lips and extreme redness of Carlos's skin. He added that he had heard that the owner of the bakery had had trouble before with carbon monoxide leaking from the oven.

Finishing with the coroner, Greg met again with the detective, who had just finished talking with the hospital staff. Raphael was being transferred to another hospital where he would receive oxygen at elevated pressures, which would speed up removal of the poisonous gas from his body. The emergency room doctors had found more than ten times the normal level of carbon monoxide in Raphael's blood.

What Greg needed more than anything was to speak to Mr. or Mrs. Greenbriar. The investigation had even greater importance now after it was learned that the bakery may have had a history of problems. The accident was developing into more than just an act of God or a mechanical failure. The detective explained that Mrs. Greenbriar, who had been on the scene earlier, had told the sheriff that she and her husband could be contacted later that day at home. It was standard policy to meet first with the owner or someone in management to explain the reason for an investigation before actually inspecting the place of business, but under the circumstances Greg was forced to find an employee who could act as a temporary management representative. Greg approached the next person in charge, Marla Dubois, the head chef, and promptly began the opening conference.

After completing the conference, Greg conducted the necessary interviews. He took statements from Marla and from the two counter clerks who had arrived on the morning of the tragedy. He also interviewed some of the representatives of the gas company.

Greg also spoke with investigators from the county health department, who planned to measure the amount of carbon monoxide released from the oven. After reviewing this idea, Greg quickly put a halt to their plans. Even though the oven was most likely producing lethal quantities of carbon monoxide, the investigators had made no plans to use self-contained breathing apparatuses (SCBAs). Greg was certain that they could not "hold their breaths" long enough to conduct the test.

The health department employees put together a sounder testing plan, and later that day, wearing SCBAs, they ran the oven. Within fifteen minutes of turning it on, it was producing lethal concentrations of carbon monoxide gas. The needle on the meter steadily rose from its resting position of zero until it could go no higher. The concentration of carbon monoxide was significantly higher than the maximum lethal concentration of 600 ppm that the meter could register. Unable to get any more information, they ended the test. The oven was shut off, and the doors and windows were opened to ventilate the room.

Greg now had the necessary documentation to prove that Carlos and Raphael had been poisoned by carbon monoxide from the oven. With the doors and windows closed, the odorless and colorless gas would have insidiously spread throughout the bakery, increasing to deadlier and deadlier concentrations as time passed and the oven ran.

Later that day, the owners were contacted at home and asked to come to the bakery. When they arrived, Greg held a formal opening conference, making sure every item required by law was discussed. Greg had many years of experience and knew this case was too important to be lost on a technicality. Shortly into the interview, however, Mr. and Mrs. Greenbriar became too distraught to continue. Greg arranged for an interview at a later time and issued the necessary paperwork preventing use of the oven. He also issued an accompanying citation for failure to train the employees on the hazards of carbon monoxide. Before leaving the site, Greg fastened a bright orange tag to the front of the oven which read:

USE FORBIDDEN!
USO PROHIBIDO
THIS OVEN IS DANGEROUS
and all work at this machine, equipment, location,

or under this condition is a violation of the
law, punishable by fine or imprisonment or both.
This notice must not be removed except by
an authorized representative of the Division of
Industrial Safety. Violation of this requirement
constitutes a misdemeanor, punishable by
fine or imprisonment or both.
WORK PROHIBITED TAG
SENAL DE TRABAJO PROHIBIDO

The oven had baked its last croissant for a while.

Greg reinterviewed the owners three days later at the bakery. He began by repeating the mandatory explanations regarding an OSHA inspection and, just in case, reminded them that it is unlawful according to OSHA procedures to discriminate against employees who are interviewed by OSHA inspectors. One of the first questions Greg posed had been on his mind since the day of the accident, and he was quick to ask it: "Did you have any problems with the oven in the past?"

Mr. Greenbriar recalled that there had been one problem about four years before. The bakery had been open for only three to four weeks, he said, when three of his employees had to be carried out by the fire department because of an oven leak. He added defensively that he had told his employees to keep the back door to the kitchen open whenever the oven was in use.

"Did you do anything to correct the leak?" Greg asked.

Mr. Greenbriar explained that the county health department, the building and safety department, and the gas company had done an investigation after the incident and had closed him down for four days. They did some leak tests, he said, gave him some recommendations about fixing the oven, and then let him reopen.

"What were the recommendations?" Greg asked.

Mr. Greenbriar replied that it had happened so long ago, he couldn't remember. Mrs. Greenbriar recalled that she had been told that there was a problem with the burners, but she could not remember who had told her that. Her husband interrupted before Greg could ask his next question. "Do you think I should have an attorney?" he asked.

Greg wanted to get his information that night and did not want an attorney chopping Greenbriar's answers into meaningless statements. The owner had the right to an attorney, but it was not Greg's duty to inform him about this right or to encourage him to retain one. Nevertheless, Greg replied that he did not object to the presence of an attorney. In an attempt to calm the owner, he again explained about the purpose and manner of an OSHA inspection. Mr. Greenbriar agreed to continue with the interview.

Greg next asked whether the owners ever provided their employees with specific information about the dangers of exposure to carbon monoxide or its symptoms. The owners replied that they only told the employees to keep the back door open.

"Have you ever had any routine work done on the oven?" Greg asked.

Servicemen from a contractor had come out on two occasions, Mr. Greenbriar answered.

"Did you ever receive any complaints from your employees about the oven making them sick?"

No, Mr. Greenbriar replied, adding that he hadn't had any accidents except for the one just after the bakery opened.

Greg concluded the interview convinced that Mr. and Mrs. Greenbriar were being less than candid. Interviews with county officials and with current and former employees of the bakery were telling a different story.

On a December morning, at about 6:30, four years earlier, the county fire department and sheriff's office had responded to an emergency call from a bakery that had just recently opened. A patrolling sheriff took the call in his car and, being close to the bakery, arrived first. All the doors were closed. Forcing an entry, he found two employees passed out in the adjoining cafe and one unconscious in front of the oven. After trying to revive them, the sheriff soon started feeling dizzy. Recognizing the possibility of a gas leak, he grabbed one of the employees and dragged him outside. The sheriff was then met by paramedics, who rushed back in and retrieved the other two workers. The paramedics noted that the employees' lips were purple and their skin reddish-purple. From the odor and mess on the victims' faces, the paramedics concluded that they had vomited on themselves. The problem was diagnosed as probable carbon monoxide poisoning, and the victims were given oxygen and hooked up to an intravenous solution. After several minutes of emergency first aid, all three workers were revived and saved from their near-fatal sleep. They were soon transported to the hospital for further treatment and evaluation.

Mr. Greenbriar was called and informed of the accident but did not come down to the bakery. The responding sheriff, who first informed the owner, recalled four years later that Mr. Greenbriar had acted quite cavalier. He had warned his employees to keep the back door open, he said.

The sheriff did not stop here. He called the county building and safety department and spoke with inspectors who told him that the oven was probably not vented properly and that the bakery could be shut down until it passed inspection.

Shortly afterward, inspectors from the county building and safety department visited the bakery and ordered that the oven not be used. They also made some recommendations about how the ventilation could be improved. When interviewed four years later, the inspectors recalled that the oven had been shut down for about four days. They could find no records of a follow-up inspection, however.

The gas company had also learned of the accident and had conducted some leak and pressure tests and inspected the duct work. Finding no leaks or obstructions, the representatives had concluded that the burner on the oven was not getting enough air for combustion. They had met with the owners and recommended that they install a fan to provide outside air to the oven and an interlock system to shut off the oven should the fan lose power.

Neither the affected employees nor any of the county agencies informed OSHA of the accident. The county building and safety department and the gas company must have assumed that any reasonable person would take action. They were wrong.

Throughout the year following the accident, employees complained to the owner, but nothing changed. After receiving reports of recurring illness at the bakery, a county inspector visited the site and issued the owner written recommendations regarding ventilation for the oven. In an interview, a former employee recalled watching the owner tear up the notice as soon as the county inspector left.

Another incident occurred about three years later. Two bakers, whom Greg interviewed, were working as usual when they started feeling dizzy and sick to their stomach. One of the bakers, who had worked there longer, suggested they go outside for some fresh air. They soon felt better. Several such incidents had occurred, the bakers said. They soon came to realize that their symptoms were related to the oven. Both reported that they complained to the owner but that he repeated his tried-and-true remedy: keep the back door open, adding that he did not want to spend a lot of money to get the oven fixed.

Greg also learned that the gas company had received a tip about this incident and once again had inspected. The gas company representative later recalled that he spent two hours with the owner explaining the need for a fan and an interlock system to shut down the oven if the fan failed. The representative closed his service call by urging the owner to consult a ventilation engineer.

Another baker recalled an incident that had occurred one time when he returned to the bakery at about 4:00 A.M. to pick up something he had forgotten. He found a co-worker passed out in front of the oven. He immediately dragged him outside, and, after a few moments of breathing the cold morning air, the worker woke up. The baker said he called the owner later that day and pleaded with him to get the oven fixed, saying that someone was going to be killed. If he didn't do something, the baker warned, he would call the health department. The following day the owner told him not to panic; all they had to do was leave the back door open.

OSHA was never notified of the first accident nearly four years before or of the subsequent incidents. For some reason, the county building and safety department and the gas company felt their authority and recommendations were sufficient.

As Greg's inspection progressed and evidence grew for establishing willful violations, Dave, the district manager for my OSHA office, and Greg decided that they had better cover all bases in documenting the case. This was particularly important if the case was to be forwarded to the district attorney's office for criminal prosecution, which requires unequivocal evidence.

There was added pressure, too. The DA had been throwing barbs at the OSHA office recently for the way it was collecting evidence of wrongful actions in work-related fatalities. One case in particular had been severely criticized because the safety inspector had taken pictures of the victim, a fatality as a result of a head injury, in which only the torso was shown and not the head or the agent of injury.

Part of Dave's and Greg's strategy was to issue a legal order prohibiting Mr. Greenbriar from dismantling or removing the tagged-out oven. This was done in quick response to the owner's telling Greg that he was about to remove it, at the request of the gas company.

The oven needed to be intact for additional evidence gathering. Dave and his boss decided to hire a consulting engineer to inspect it. The expert was an independent consultant, paid for by OSHA, and not associated with the gas company.

During the time the oven was tested and evaluated and the consultant wrote up his report, Greg completed the rest of his investigation. He talked with everyone who could provide information on the history of the carbon monoxide poisonings at the bakery. He found, not surprisingly, that former employees were very upset about the latest accident. One told Greg that he had repeatedly pleaded with the owner to correct the problem, and his worst fears had come true. He told Greg that he would gladly testify against his former employer.

Based on the numerous interviews and inspections of the site and with the help of an OSHA industrial hygienist and the consultant's report, Greg finally put together a summary of the mechanical problems with the oven and the accompanying human failures that had caused the accident. It turned out that there had been a question about where to put the vent when the oven was installed. The first plan was to run the vent straight up through the ceiling and onto the roof. But the landlord for the bakery had protested that he would lose a parking spot on the roof and that the shopkeepers on the block would complain that the vent was unsightly rising up from the parking lot. Mr. Greenbriar had decided to run the vent across the ceiling of the kitchen toward the back wall. It then turned 90 degrees where it punched through the ceiling, another 90 degrees for a straight run farther back under the parking lot, and finally yet another 90 degrees before emerging on the roof in a parking spot already taken up by other equipment.

Setting up a vent in this manner was contrary to the oven manufacturer's instructions and building codes. The long and tortuous ducting used to vent the oven's burners created resistance for the released combustion gases. Also contrary to building codes, the room with the oven did not have a fail-safe source of air to ensure that the oven could burn the gas cleanly and with minimal production of carbon monoxide, providing the burners were operating properly. The kitchen had fans, several in fact. But consistent with the chain of errors and negligence, they had all been installed to blow air out of the kitchen, rather than to provide combustion air inside.

In addition to the venting system, there were other critical problems. Tests conducted by the consultant engineer revealed that the oven leaked large amounts of carbon monoxide even when the back door was open. By measuring the flow of gas to the burners, he determined that the burner was being supplied with enough gas to operate at 500,000 BTUs per hour, although the manufacturer had recommended that it operate at only 365,000. Conclusion: too much fuel was being supplied to the combustion chamber. The consultant also found that the air-intake valve for the burners opened only one-fourth of the way, causing inefficient combustion and contributing to the production of the carbon monoxide. Tests also verified that the oven leaked in several places, sending combustion products into the kitchen instead of up the chimney and outdoors.

Keeping the back door to the kitchen open provided fresh air that diluted the carbon monoxide being produced by the oven. Hence the owners instructed their employees to keep the door open, or, more plainly, to keep the door open or die.

Both the venting system and the burners should have been operating properly, of course, but even if only one system had been up to code, the tragedy could have been prevented. A properly operating vent would have sent the poisonous gas to the roof, where it would have been safely diluted. A properly operating burner would have produced sublethal concentrations of carbon monoxide, at least for the conditions in the bakery. Ultimately, human failure caused the accident. The owners were negligent for failing to follow proper installation procedures, for failing to ensure that the malfunctioning burner was properly adjusted or repaired, and, most important, for failing to respond responsibly to the first warning of danger or the many warnings that followed.

The building and safety department and the gas company did not respond well either, for they both let the mechanical problems remain uncorrected. If they did not have the authority to force the life-saving changes to be made, then they had a duty to inform government agencies that did.

Toward the end of the inspection, I was asked to check out an oven that had been brought in as a replacement and a new ventilation system, which OSHA and the building and safety department had required that the owners install. We arrived at the bakery at about 6:00 P.M. with our carbon monoxide meter and were met by Mrs. Greenbriar. Greg and the other industrial hygienist who accompanied me exchanged friendly greetings with her and joked for a few minutes. Over the past few weeks they had developed quite a friendship with the owners, which that night struck me as strange and undesirable.

After a cup of the cafe's gourmet coffee, we warmed up our meter and turned on the oven. As Mrs. Greenbriar left, she offered us several meat and cheese croissants. They had been baked in an oven at another bakery, she said.

Greg and the other industrial hygienist quickly accepted her offer. I declined. "Aren't you guys being too friendly with the owners?" I asked. "You acted like she was a relative. In a few days you're going to be fining them tens of thousands of dollars, calling their actions willful, and possibly sending their case to the DA's office for criminal prosecution. How can you act so nice?"

They both laughed at the thought that there would be no coffee and croissants at the closing conference.

"Hey, don't worry about it," Greg replied. "So we issue them a serious/willful next week. There's no reason to be mean. Might as well be friendly. It makes it easier. Go ahead, eat your croissant."

After eating my croissant, I set about with the other industrial hygienist measuring the emissions from the oven. Within less than a minute, the meter indicated that the concentration of gas inside the exhaust duct was at least 600 ppm carbon monoxide, the maximum our meter would register. The levels in front of the oven were the same as outdoors, less than 10 ppm. We let the oven go for an hour to see if the poisonous gas would leak into the kitchen. Our plan was to shut off the oven and leave immediately if the meter indicated that the leak was becoming toxic. The levels in the kitchen and around the oven stayed at a comfortably safe concentration of less than 10 ppm.

The improvements to the vent system prevented the release of toxic concentrations of carbon monoxide into the kitchen. Nonetheless, the high levels in the exhaust duct still bothered us. Should a leak in the system or a complication in the vent stack occur, there could be trouble again. On closer inspection, we found that the concentration in the flue of the oven was always above 600 ppm when one row of burners was operating.

The next day, the industrial hygienist called Mr. and Mrs. Greenbriar and told them that they could not use the replacement oven until the defective burners were replaced. The oven was later tested again after repair and found to be releasing less than 100 ppm carbon monoxide into the vent system. Shortly thereafter, the store was baking croissants again.

The owners received four serious/willful citations related to the fatality and the near-fatality for failure to provide engineering controls, such as a proper vent system, which would have helped prevent the release of excessive levels of carbon monoxide into the bakery; failure to have a properly designed ventilation system; failure to train and warn employees about the hazards of carbon monoxide; and, finally, failure to schedule periodic inspections to identify and correct unsafe conditions. The inspectors hoped to inflict much more than the slap on the wrist usually required by the OSHA penalty schedule.

The penalty sheet was mailed via certified letter within a few days after Greg held the closing conference and issued the citations. Inside the envelope was a fine for $30,000.

The owner retained an attorney and appealed.

Our legal unit referred the case to the local district attorney, who initially prepared criminal charges related to the death. The criminal charges were dropped, however, long before OSHA had settled the case after it was learned that Mr. Greenbriar had recently been diagnosed as having terminal cancer.

The hearing date for the serious/willful violations was put off for so long that a deal was eventually struck. Just short of three years after the accident, the case was settled with Mrs. Greenbriar. By this time, her husband had died. The settlement was a major disappointment to OSHA personnel familiar with the case. All characterizations of willful were dropped, and the original $30,000 penalty was reduced to a total of $3,025. Mrs. Greenbriar agreed to pay the fine and withdrew the appeal.

7. FORMALDEHYDE

Many former anatomy and biology students never forget how formaldehyde gas caused their eyes to tear. The dull, haylike odor can often be detected even before one enters the laboratory.

Formaldehyde can be detected at very low levels, less than 0.1 ppm. At higher levels, the eyes become irritated and, beginning at about 0.5 ppm, the throat feels sore. Some individuals, however, have been known to suffer irritation and asthmatic attacks at levels far below 0.5 ppm.

As in the case of other potentially hazardous substances, the regulatory history of formaldehyde has been marked by controversy. Until 1988, formaldehyde gas in the workplace was regulated by state and federal health standards, with the aim of preventing acute eye and respiratory irritation. The first limit set by federal OSHA was 3.0 ppm as an eight-hour time-weighted average, with peak exposures allowed up to 10.0 ppm. The limits set by some states were more restrictive but were still intended to prevent irritation. California, for example, had a ceiling limit of 2.0 ppm, which was thought to be "adequate to prevent serious or persistent effects."[1] This standard was established based on observations that most people adapt to the symptoms experienced at exposures below 2.0 ppm but not necessarily to the potentially more severe effects experienced at higher levels.

When federal OSHA set the first limit on formaldehyde, at 3.0 ppm, in 1971, most health officials thought it was not low enough to prevent eye and respiratory irritation. In response, in 1976, the National Institute for Occupational Safety and Health (NIOSH), the government agency created in part to propose new standards for OSHA, recommended that the limit be lowered to 1.0 ppm, as measured over any thirty-minute period. OSHA did not lower the limit, however.

Then, in 1979, preliminary data were presented that made NIOSH recommend lowering the limit further. A report released by the Chemical Industry Institute of Toxicology revealed that formaldehyde caused cancer in animals. The final report documented that a significant number of rats exposed to 5.9 to 14.3 ppm and mice exposed to 14.3 ppm formaldehyde in the air six hours a day, five days a week, over a twenty-four-month period (nearly a rodent's lifetime) developed nasal cancer. These findings induced NIOSH to publish an information bulletin entitled "Formaldehyde—Evidence of Carcinogenicity," which recommended that formaldehyde be considered a potential occupational carcinogen.[2] Both the report and NIOSH's bulletin alarmed other interested groups, including those representing exposed workers.

The same year of the report, the Automobile, Aerospace, and Agricultural Implement Workers of America and thirteen other unions petitioned federal OSHA to issue an emergency standard lowering the exposure limit. Federal OSHA, under the Reagan administration, was not impressed, however, and turned down the petition. The unions went to court in an effort to force OSHA to act, and, after several court proceedings, fact-finding commissions, and calls by OSHA for information, the agency announced in April 1985, three and a half years after the original petition, that it was initiating the process of lowering the limit. Admitting that the 3.0 ppm and 10.0 ppm levels were too high to prevent even the acute effects of formaldehyde, let alone the carcinogenic effects, OSHA stated, "The ability of formaldehyde to cause a reversible sensory irritation of the eyes, nose, and throat at levels permitted by the present standard has been well documented."[3]

Another organization influential among safety and health professionals, the American Conference of Governmental Industrial Hygienists (ACGIH), responded to the 1981 report before OSHA, and in 1983, calling formaldehyde a suspect carcinogen for humans, lowered its recommended exposure limit from 2.0 to 1.0 ppm.

Likewise, in 1982, the Consumer Products Safety Commission (CPSC) banned the use of urea-formaldehyde foam insulation under some conditions, particularly in mobile homes. The foam was a relatively inexpensive and useful product that was easily applied between walls. The problem was that some people could not live in the home after it was applied. Newly installed, the insulation could release unreacted formaldehyde and cause acute symptoms. The ban on urea-formaldehyde foam was overturned by the courts seven months after it was passed by the CPSC, but the commission plodded on, issuing consumer alerts on other formaldehyde-containing products. The alerts were directed primarily to individuals sensitive to formaldehyde and pertained to a number of products made from textiles, paper, and pressed woods. Some of the affected manufacturers fought the CPSC, while others made great strides in reducing the amount of formaldehyde that could be released from their products.

Federal OSHA finally adopted a new standard in December 1987, six years after the original petition by the unions and not without much bureaucratic gut-wrenching.[4] The record for the rulemaking was composed of 1,400 exhibits and 30,000 pages of testimony. In the end, federal OSHA set forth comprehensive requirements for the control of both airborne and liquid formulations of formaldehyde. The current limit, which became effective on February 2, 1988, is 1.0 ppm as an eight-hour time-weighted average and 2.0 ppm as a ceiling level, averaged over any fifteen-minute period. The standard also includes mandatory requirements for monitoring, posting of warning signs, recordkeeping, employee training, and medical surveillance of employees. It requires that safety procedures be followed in "regulated areas" of overexposure and outlines methods of compliance; use of respirators, protective equipment, and clothing; and responsibility for emergency preparedness and housekeeping.

Generally, products made from formaldehyde now pose little health hazard to consumers, although formaldehyde can and in many instances does pose a significant threat in places that make or use it commercially. OSHA has stated that compliance with the new standard can prevent about six thousand cases of respiratory irritation and nearly eleven thousand cases of dermatitis and reduce the risk of cancer among those exposed. Estimates are that for identified industries with prestandard exposure levels above 1.0 ppm formaldehyde, 6.5 to 47.5 cases of respiratory cancer will be prevented over a period of forty-five years, out of 13,180 exposed, as a result of compliance with the standard.[5]

Hundreds of millions of pounds of formaldehyde are produced each year, most of which is used in the manufacture of resins and plastics. The chemical, which can react so well with human protein, can also react with itself and other chemicals used to make hundreds of plastic products. The chemical is also used in the production of cosmetics, fertilizers, textiles, leather, and photographic chemicals and as an antiseptic, a fungicide and germicide, and a preservative.

The use of formaldehyde as a preservative in embalming solutions poses a risk to a large number of workers in the funeral service business. Though the annual tonnage used ranks well below the amounts used in other industries, the number of workers exposed is sizable, estimated to be about 30,000.[6] Most embalmers are probably exposed to less than the earlier limit of 3.0 ppm averaged over eight hours, but a significant number are exposed to levels exceeding the 2.0 ppm ceiling limit now enforced by federal and state OSHA programs.

No one should have to suffer the acute effects of formaldehyde. With proper training, protective equipment, and, above all, ventilation, everyone should be free from the acute effects, and, most important, everyone will have significantly reduced their risk of contracting cancer from formaldehyde exposure.

A Preservative Only for the Dead

I knew that none of the inspectors in my office wanted this assignment. It was thus with some apprehension that I read the complaint form alleging that two funeral homes had excessive exposure to formaldehyde. I was not surprised that no one wanted to view dead bodies, let alone go inside a mortuary, but I reminded myself, before volunteering, that, like other workers, embalmers are covered by the labor code and have a right to a safe and healthful workplace.

As I read the complaint, I was amused that the name of one of the mortuaries, Roberts, Howell, and Peal, sounded like that of a law firm. The other, Roswell and Sons, could well have been owned by a long-standing member of the community.

The Roberts, Howell, and Peal building could best be described as a large, cheap reproduction of a European cottage. But getting out of the car and following the walkway, I didn't know what to expect, and I entered the building with some anxiety. The small lobby looked like a dentist's or doctor's waiting room. A receptionist sat behind a sliding glass window, and there were several seats for clients. The receptionist promptly greeted me. I asked to see the owner but was introduced to the manager. Presenting my identification card, I introduced myself as an inspector from OSHA.

We sat down in his office and had the opening conference. I explained the OSHA program, pointing out that under the labor law, the employer is responsible for providing workers with a safe and healthful workplace. I went down the items we were required to discuss about rights of appeal, the walkaround, unlawful discrimination against employees who raise safety and health issues, and the issuance of citations. I added that the aim was to have voluntary compliance with the safety and health laws but that OSHA was available to enforce the laws as needed. As happens occasionally, the manager responded by launching into a critique of OSHA.

After further discussion, I was surprised to learn that there was no Mr. Roberts, Howell, or Peal and that the home was owned by a large corporation that owned mortuaries across the nation. The manager also mentioned that the corporation owned nearby Roswell and Sons, which I planned to inspect later that day.

Most of the homes had been locally owned, the manager explained, but the corporation had bought them out and in many cases kept the original names. I guessed it would be poor marketing to publicize that a neighborhood mortuary was actually owned by a national corporation, not unlike the fast-food restaurant on the corner.

After the opening conference, I was led back to the embalming room. As we walked back, I peered down the dark hallways, not sure what to expect. I was more accustomed to plating shops and foundries. The embalming room was near the end of one of the hallways and next to a garage that contained a hearse and stacks of new caskets.

The manager called to the two embalmers on duty, introduced me, and then excused himself. Referring to themselves as counselors, the embalmers explained in a friendly manner that they spent most of their time conducting and arranging funeral services, not embalming. On questioning, one admitted that they sometimes experienced strong eye and throat irritation from the gas during embalmings. "The autopsied cases are the worst ones," one embalmer explained, adding, "There isn't much fresh air in the room, as the fan doesn't do much and the doors have to be kept closed."

The two men gave me a tour of the embalming room, which didn't take long. Filled with gurneys and other equipment, it seemed to be about twelve feet wide by twenty feet long. The first thing I noticed was the empty embalming table. It had a porcelainlike finish, cold and white, and measured about three feet by seven feet. The table had a gutter along the outer edge, presumably to collect runoff. A large block of rubber rested on one end of the table. I was told that it was put under the neck of the deceased to prop the head up. On the other side of the room was a draped client, silently resting on a gurney, his stockinged feet sticking out.

Lining the embalming room were cabinets filled with bottles of all types. Many of the smaller bottles were clearly women's cosmetics. I was told that they were used to make the body look more natural, less dead-looking. I asked about a bottle of phenol, a toxic chemical, and was told that it was applied to the skin of the deceased to bleach out bruises or dark spots.

One cabinet contained many larger bottles of bright orange and red embalming solutions. They were labeled in an oddly mystical style, more appropriate for a box of magic tricks or an 1890s hair tonic. The colorful labels indicated that the bottles contained different strengths of formaldehyde, from 18 to 36 percent. The balance of the solutions was made up of water and methanol to help trap the gaseous formaldehyde and slow its vaporization. The methanol also prevented the dissolved formaldehyde from polymerizing into a crude plastic.

I next turned my attention to the ventilation in the room. Formaldehyde is a volatile chemical. Depending on the method of embalming and the amount of solution exposed to the air, the amount of ventilation could determine whether the embalmers were overexposed or not. Based on what the embalmer had said earlier, I was already suspicious.

The room had two doors. If they were left open during embalmment, there would be a good cross-draft, which could dilute the formaldehyde. But, as the embalmers informed me, this source of ventilation was unavailable because a state law required that the doors be kept closed during an embalmment to prevent the public from viewing the procedure.

The only powered ventilation available was a small fan in the ceiling. The fan was positioned right over the embalming table, where it most likely exacerbated exposure by drawing the formaldehyde right past the embalmers, rather than away from their breathing area. On closer inspection, I also found that the fan did not have any duct system to carry the gas-laden air outside but instead exhausted into a crawl space above the ceiling. I asked the embalmers what was above the room, and they told me that the ceiling of the crawl space was the floor of an apartment. I had to wonder whether the upstairs residents ever had tearing eyes and irritated throats.

I was doubtful about the effectiveness of this whole arrangement. To help determine the severity of exposure, I asked the embalmers how many cases the mortuary handled each year. One said about two hundred, but added that not all of the clients were embalmed. Embalming was not required by law, he explained; it was merely an option available to a client's family. The process prevents the body from decomposing, and thus makes viewing an open casket more pleasant. Refrigeration and a funeral service within a day or two of death can substitute for embalmment, he said. If refrigeration is not available, he concluded, mortuary employees certainly prefer to have clients embalmed as a way to prevent odors.

Finishing with my tour and interviews, I caught up with the manager and had him place me on call for both a regular (nonposted) and an autopsied (posted) embalmment. "This depends on God's will," the manager stated. He tacked my business card outside the embalming room, next to the list of upcoming burials, and said he'd be in touch.

It began to rain as I drove over to Roswell and Sons later that day. The Roswell building looked as much like a house as one can make a mortuary look like a home. The lobby, which was much larger than the one at Roberts, Howell, and Peal, had satin-draped doorways and framed prints of flowers on the walls. But although attempts had been made to make the lobby look like a living room, I didn't feel comfortable. The somber organ music coming from a back room and the dim lighting didn't help any.

I looked through several doorways into adjoining rooms, but no one was around. I pressed a call button. Minutes passed, and still no one came. Growing impatient, I slowly entered a dark hallway leading away from the lobby. Halfway into the hallway, I sensed something moving toward me. I stopped, considered my escape route, and strained my eyes until I recognized the face of an old woman, her body slowly emerging from the darkness. I backed into the better lit lobby and introduced myself and asked to see the manager.

The woman disappeared back into the darkness and soon the manager came into the lobby to greet me. As we walked into his office, I explained the reason for my visit. Speaking in pleasant, soothing tones, as if I were a grieving customer, he politely asked about the inspection. I was still feeling on edge, in spite of his congenial manner, when suddenly the wall panel on my right began to rumble from the floor to the ceiling. I turned quickly, not knowing what might jump out. The wall continued to rumble for a moment while I sat motionless. The manager understood my reaction and calmly assured me that it was only the wind. I finished my opening conference without delay, and we went back to the embalming room.

The embalming room at Roswell was larger than the one at Roberts, Howell, and Peal, and I was encouraged to see that it had a much better ventilation system. Two fans were located in the wall opposite each end of the two embalming tables, arranged to exhaust to the outside parking lot. The embalmer commented that the ventilation here was much better than at most mortuaries. Completing my tour I asked to be placed on call for either a posted or a nonposted embalmment.

Two days later, I was called and told that a nonposted case was ready at Roberts, Howell, and Peal. The deceased was an elderly woman who had died at a nursing home. The embalmer was already dressed in gown and gloves and was washing the deceased's body and hair when I arrived. Rubbing soap over her body with his latex-protected hands, the embalmer commented that the woman was in pretty good shape for someone who had come from a nursing home, adding that some cases showed real evidence of inattention and poor hygiene. "We report those nursing homes to the state," he said.

I hooked the embalmer up with the sampling equipment for formaldehyde, which consisted of a pump connected with plastic tubing to a special glass jar called an impinger. The impinger, which contained a trapping solution for formaldehyde, fit into a leather holster that I pinned to the outside of the embalmer's gown, on his shoulder. The pump, which bubbled the air he was breathing through the trapping solution in the impinger, was hooked on his belt under the gown. The trapping solution would later by analyzed for formaldehyde and reported as parts formaldehyde per million parts of air. At the time the ceiling limit for formaldehyde was 2.0 ppm in California.[7]

The embalmer was ready to perform. Dressed in gown and gloves and hooked up with my equipment, he talked about his family. It seemed odd for him to be talking so casually while performing an embalmment, but the job was routine for him, and his banter made me feel more comfortable.

He selected an embalming solution with a high concentration of formaldehyde, which he explained was needed since the woman had been dead longer than the optimal time for embalming. This solution would preserve her better, and the dye in the solution would help take away the gray hue in her skin.

He poured several bottles of the "industrial-strength" solution into a tall, clear-plastic cylinder with a mixing blade and motor connected at the bottom and topped the cylinder off with water. Covering the top with a lid from a kitchen pot, he set the machine on mix. The device also acted as a pump for the dilute embalming solution.

Picking up a scalpel, the embalmer cut a small incision in the woman's neck, opened the carotid artery, and inserted a metal tube, which he secured to the artery with thread. The metal tube was then connected using a rubber hose to the plastic cylinder. He next opened a vein in the woman's leg and inserted a second tube, which would function as a drain. With the tube secured, the embalmer had completed tapping into the body's circulatory system. The two openings would allow him to replace lifeless fluid with preservative.

Next, the embalmer turned on the pump, and the diluted 4 percent formaldehyde solution flowed through the circulatory system and into the brain, the still heart, and through the rest of the circulatory system and organs, permeating the tissues. A deep burgundy-colored liquid flowed out of the vein in the woman's leg, into the gutter around the table, and finally into a nearby sink. Additional preservative was injected directly into the chest cavity with a long spike.

I asked the embalmer if he liked his job.

"Yes," he replied. Then, after a pause, he said that embalming really didn't bother him, that it was only a small part of his job. What he enjoyed most, he said, was counseling and providing services to grieving families. Yep, sounded like fun, I thought.

During the twenty minutes it took to pump the several quarts of embalming solution through the body and clear out the hemolyzed blood, my eyes felt a slight burning sensation. I attributed the discomfort to the formaldehyde gas in the air. I wore a respirator but pulled it away from my face several times to check on the level of respiratory irritation. The odor of formaldehyde was detectable and mildly unpleasant.

The embalmer had no symptoms and said he didn't usually have any trouble with nonposted cases, that is, those that had not been autopsied. He either had a higher tolerance than I or had become desensitized from chronic exposure, a known physiological response and one sometimes considered in setting regulatory standards.

The embalmer finished the procedure by removing the tubes and sewing up the incisions. The circulatory system was now closed and the formaldehyde sealed in. The gas would slowly continue to permeate the body. Eventually, the preservative would evaporate and break down and the decay process begin again.

I didn't sleep well that night. I had been forcefully reminded of my own mortality.

I turned my sample into the state laboratory for analysis the next day. The results ranged from 0.3 to 0.6 ppm for the twenty-to-thirty-minute samples. The embalmer was significantly under the 2.0 ppm celing exposure limit, but it was not clear whether a room with such a small exhaust fan and little fresh air would be adequate for an autopsied case, when much greater amounts of formaldehyde would probably be released. Lab results in hand, I held a conference with the manager of Roberts, Howell, and Peal and explained that I still needed to sample a client who had been "posted" (autopsied). The manager acted quite concerned, in contrast to the mild disapproval he first expressed, and belligerently stated that it was impossible for mortuaries to comply with OSHA. By his challenge, he was admitting that he knew the formaldehyde levels could get high during an embalmment of an autopsied case. I explained that, if necessary, the existing ventilation system could be greatly improved by increasing the amount of exhaust, providing a system for fresh-air replacement, and positioning the ventilation inlets and outlets more strategically. I added that controlling exposure to chemicals was done all the time. He wasn't convinced, having been blinded by his contempt of OSHA and his ignorance of proper ventilation design. He also expressed concern about the prospect of being fined.

Within a week after completing my sampling at Roberts, I got a call from the OSHA answering service one weekend telling me that Roswell had a nonposted case. I went to my office, packed my equipment, and headed over to the home.

The embalmer was experienced and, other than using slightly less formaldehyde, he followed the procedures I had observed at Roberts. The embalming went quickly and smoothly. There was little detectable odor, and the two fans across from the embalming tables appeared to work well.

The lab later reported readings of 0.4, 0.5, and surprisingly, 2.1 ppm. The last value was slightly higher than the exposure limit of 2.0 ppm, but allowing for a statistical error, as required by our legal department, it was not high enough to enforce any changes.

Two more weeks passed without a phone call from either mortuary about a posted case. I called both homes and was assured by the managers that no posted cases had come in yet.

After four weeks, I received a phone call from a complainant alleging that another mortuary in the chain, Franklin Family, had poor ventilation for embalming. The complainant also said that a company conspiracy had developed to stall my inspections at Roberts and at Roswell. Their managers had met with the regional manager at Franklin, he said, and had been given instructions to ignore me and stall further sampling. I imagined that the managers had pegged me as a stereotypical government worker who would fumble the inspection in one of three ways: by growing weary of the delays and giving up; by forgetting about the need to complete the inspection; or by misplacing the file. Unfortunately, the perception of government workers as ineffectual is occasionally validated.

What also worried me was how many more complaints we would receive. The corporation had about ten more funeral homes in our district and many more statewide. The number of complaints could mushroom as more and more embalmers became concerned. It was conceivable that the entire industry needed a "sweep." Though the corporation that owned Franklin Family and the two others may have needed targeting, OSHA could not just focus on the one corporation. A task force for the industry could be considered, but it was hard to imagine conducting the necessary number of inspections given the limited number of inspectors in OSHA, other targeting schemes under way, and the number of employee complaints streaming into each OSHA office. I had to hope that the threat of inspections and fines and the few more inspections that would probably be done statewide over the year would motivate the rest of the funeral homes to review their safety and health status. So far, that appeared doubtful.

The most recent complaint against the corporation could not be ignored, and the case was accepted by my supervisor, who in turn assigned it to me. By now the other inspectors in the office were calling me "the cutting room specialist."

Within a few days of being assigned the case, I met with the regional manager at Franklin Family. He seemed cooperative and acknowledged that he knew about the inspections at Roberts and at Roswell.

After the opening conference, I was introduced to the supervising embalmer, who ushered us into the embalming room. The room was larger and better kept than the rooms at the other two mortuaries. As at Roswell, it had two embalming tables, but I noted that none of the windows or doors opened to the outside.

When I asked about the ventilation system, the manager admitted that the air-conditioning unit, which provided some fresh air, had not been working properly for several months. With his help, I found the inlets for the air conditioning and, on the opposite wall, two exhaust outlets with a common duct to the roof.

To estimate the room's ability to dilute the formaldehyde released from an embalmment, I climbed up to the roof and measured the air output from the exhaust duct. Using this estimate and the dimensions of the room, I was able to approximate the number of air changes per hour. Comparing this number to values described in the literature as being adequate, I found that the embalming room had about half the minimum recommended ventilation.

I also learned that clients were sometimes embalmed one right after another, allowing formaldehyde to build up, and occasionally two clients were embalmed at once. The supervising embalmer explained that Franklin had more than five hundred cases a year, of which forty to fifty were autopsied, making it one of the busiest mortuaries in the corporation.

I concluded my initial inspection of Franklin by telling the manager that I was obliged to sample during an autopsied case, adding that I was still waiting to sample such a case at the other two homes. With assurances that I would be called, the manager tacked my card on the burial board outside the embalming room.

As another four weeks passed without a call from any of the three homes, I began to believe that the management of the corporation was making a deliberate effort to avoid having the homes fully inspected. Such ploys, while not common, are used. Some inspectors end up returning several times unannounced in hopes of being able to complete an inspection. Others give up.

I called our legal department and explained my problem. I was told to go back to the homes and inspect their embalming records. If I found evidence that they had embalmed posted cases and made no attempt to call me, we could then consider their actions evidence of a refusal of inspection and obtain an inspection warrant from the Superior Court. Further refusals on the mortuaries' part would prove costly and embarrassing. Either they would have to take us to court to quash the warrant, an unlikely possibility since probable cause was established, or face arrest by state police.

Armed with the advice of our legal department, I prepared to go back to the mortuaries. The visit would be stressful since the suspicion of deceit and conspiracy would be obvious. I was angered by their possible attempts to avoid a legal inspection and sweep hazards under the rug. Perhaps more so, I was angered at the thought that they probably considered me an ineffectual government worker who could easily be pushed around.

I planned to inspect all three homes in one day, unannounced, starting with Roberts, Howell, and Peal. I was met there by the manager and, checking some embarrassment, I explained that I suspected the mortuary of purposefully refusing to allow sampling of a posted case. I then asked him for the embalming records for the past three months. Feeling like a district attorney, I followed him over to a file cabinet and looked over his shoulder as he pulled three files. Taking a seat, I thumbed through about fifty death certificates and embalming records. None had been posted.

After politely returning the files, I asked to speak with the embalmers, in private. The two embalmers on duty confirmed the record—there had been no posted cases. I caught up with the manager and thanked him for his time, reminding him that I was still on call should a posted case come in.

My next stop was Roswell. The manager there was surprised by my request to make the embalmment records available, but, without hesitation, he opened the file cabinet and pointed at the pertinent files so I could help myself. A review revealed that there had been two posted cases in the past three months but that only one had been embalmed. I asked the manager why I hadn't been called. He thought for a moment and recalled that the case had come in over the recent holiday and that OSHA's answering service was unable to reach me. I checked the date and confirmed that he was right. I was almost humbled.

That afternoon I met with the regional manager at Franklin. He became stiff and shifted in his chair as I explained the purpose of my visit. He did not know why I had not been called, he said. He had given instructions otherwise. "Maybe they didn't receive any posted cases yet," he said, adding that he would straighten out any problems for me.

During our exchanges, I read a plaque on the wall, right over my shoulder. It promoted the value of honesty and truth.

We went down to the embalming room together and reviewed a ledger of all the cases that had been received and shipped. Four posted cases had been received within the past three weeks and were clearly marked "embalmed." The manager called in the supervising embalmer and asked why I had not been called. The embalmer, who

I had interviewed several weeks before, replied that he didn't know. I noted that my business card was still on the board right above where the ledger was kept. Written on the card were instructions to call me when a posted case for embalmment came in.

I curtly explained to the manager that I had consulted with our legal department and that I would have to obtain a court order or inspection warrant if I did not receive cooperation. "It could be embarrassing," I said. He promised that I would be called in for the very next posted case for embalmment and that an inspection warrant would not be needed. I added that I was also waiting to sample posted cases at Roberts and at Roswell. So far I had spent thirteen weeks trying to arrange my sampling.

Just then, the supervising embalmer suggested that since Franklin received so many posted cases, maybe the embalmers there could ship a few to the other mortuaries. I watched the manager's face to see if the embalmer had broken some policy. The manager agreed without expression. I was still suspicious, however. If it was that easy for Franklin to ship cases to other mortuaries, the other mortuaries could have shipped cases to Franklin before the inspection there was even opened. This shell game would explain why there were no records of an embalming of an autopsied case at the other mortuaries.

Over the next two weeks I was finally able to sample a posted case at each of the three mortuaries. Sometimes cooperation needs to be motivated.

Sampling at Roberts, Howell, and Peal was arranged first. Embalming was scheduled for 9:00 P.M. Although I was not thrilled with the prospect of visiting a mortuary at night, I was eager to finish the inspections. I arrived early and found out from the night attendant that the body was en route from Franklin.

The embalmment was to be performed by the Franklin Family embalmers, including the supervising embalmer. Roberts had its first-string team on this assignment.

The body was pulled out of the hearse and wheeled on a gurney into the small embalming room, where the two embalmers pushed the draped body onto the table. They then began preparing the equipment and themselves for their work.

The supervising embalmer was the one who would be doing all of the mixing and injecting, so I placed the sampling equipment on him. I then put on my respirator and stood back to watch. The embalmer began the procedure by cutting the pathologist's sutures, put in during the autopsy, from just below the neck to just below the stomach. He next opened up the chest, pulled back the already-divided rib cage, and, to my surprise, removed a plastic trash bag. I was told that the bag contained most of the body's organs. The pathologist had removed them for examination, and, without a reason to return them to their former anatomical position, he had dumped them in the bag, tied it, and placed it back in the chest cavity. The embalmer then simply added a sawdustlike para-formaldehyde formulation, mixed in some embalming solution, and tied the bag. With the "shake and bake" mix complete, the supervisor placed the bagged organs, now embalmed, on the floor for later.

The embalmer then prepared the embalming solution for injection by mixing the concentrated formulation with water. During the autopsy the pathologist had obviously severed the circulatory system in numerous places while removing the organs, so that it no longer had a closed loop. Rather, it functioned more like a sieve.

As the embalmer proceeded to inject the embalming solution, a mixture of the solution and hemolyzed blood leaked from numerous vessels into the hollow chest cavity, releasing formaldehyde into the room. I noted that, although one of the embalmers periodically suctioned the chest cavity, the formaldehyde was being released nonetheless.

In spite of the formaldehyde in the air, I didn't feel any irritation in my nose or throat. The half-mask respirator that covered my chin, mouth, and nose filtered out the gas with each breath. The chemicals in the embalming solution caused my eyes to tear slightly, however, since they were not protected.

I asked the embalmers if they had any symptoms. They were not wearing respirators and had reported earlier that they never did.

"No," they replied, "no trouble at all."

Regardless of their responses, I was certain that more formaldehyde was released in a posted case than in a nonposted one. Nonposted cases require only one drain tube that runs straight out from a vein in the leg. The single drainage point and otherwise intact body mean that there is no pooling of blood and less liquid-to-air contact than during posted cases. Furthermore, because the body has been autopsied, posted cases are more complex to embalm and therefore take longer.

As my eyes continued to feel a prickly sensation, I was prompted to survey the ventilation system in the room as I had on the first day of the inspection. To my surprise, someone had made improvements. The room now had a new, more powerful exhaust fan overhead, and the exhaust was ducted to the outside parking lot rather than to the upstairs apartment. Part of a brick wall had been knocked out in order to duct the exhaust outside, and a new air conditioner had been installed on the wall. I noted that the air conditioner allowed for the introduction of much-needed fresh outside air. As a result, the exhaust fan could work efficiently. As I adjusted the air conditioner to allow for the maximum introduction of fresh air, I explained to the embalmers the importance of having good make-up air.

Someone at Roberts had indeed been busy since my last sampling. The improvement in the ventilation system, though not the best designed, was clearly aimed at better controlling the exposure to formaldehyde. I suspected that it was a strategy on management's part to avoid the possibility of a fine rather than an altruistic attempt to protect the employees. I was sure that had I not insisted on sampling a posted case, the ventilation system would have been left as it was.

About halfway through the procedure, the supervising embalmer, still dressed in gown and gloves, lit a cigarette. He offered me one, but I replied that I didn't smoke. He took a few drags, put the cigarette down, and resumed his work. After suctioning out the chest cavity of the deceased, changing his injection sites, and sewing the artery to the injection pipe, he took a few more drags. I felt obliged to tell him that he shouldn't smoke during an embalming since he could contaminate his cigarette with his gloved hand and transfer infectious contaminants into his mouth. He wasn't concerned and continued to smoke.

The embalming was concluded as smoothly as it had begun. The inspection had been interesting, so much so that I had another sleepless night pondering my own mortality.

The laboratory reported the exposures to be 0.35, 2.0, and 0.25 ppm. Two of the values were comfortably below the standard, and one was right at the exposure limit but still legal. From my observations and sampling, it was clear that had the new ventilation system not been added, overexposure certainly would have been recorded and Roberts given a serious violation with a penalty. My evaluation was corroborated by what I had learned during my initial interviews: the embalmers at Roberts, as desensitized as they were, had been experiencing severe irritation when they embalmed posted cases.

Some companies that have no intention of complying voluntarily with health regulations choose to comply when they are discovered and either through trickery or weak enforcement avoid penalty. I was not certain in this case whether such an approach had been adopted, but, based on the employees' complaints and the well-known chemical properties of formaldehyde, I was certain management knew that excessive exposure was possible if not likely. Many companies recognize that this approach is shortsighted and unethical. Unethical companies exist, however, and many never receive the OSHA inspections they need to motivate them to comply.

Roswell's posted case came in a few days after the inspection at Roberts. It had also been sent from Franklin.

The manager introduced me to the two embalmers as they were washing down their client, a very large, overweight woman. The two embalmers looked as if they had just finished embalming school, which I soon learned was the case. Roswell had lined up its third-string team for this one, and I sensed trouble.

I asked the embalmers whether they ever had any symptoms from the formaldehyde. One mentioned that he occasionally had sinus problems and eye irritation. He showed me a respirator he had purchased himself. There were embalming rooms where he had to use it, he said. The other embalmer said he had only minor irritation.

I set up the embalmers with the sampling equipment and watched them as they began the procedure. Neither wore respirators. The embalming of the bagged organs was simple enough and went smoothly, but the procedure went from the comical to the grotesque. The injection hoses popped out several times, squirting embalming solution into the air and onto the floor. At one point, the puddle on the floor grew so large that I had to request that they throw down towels to prevent someone from slipping. Then, while they were attempting to embalm the head, a vessel in the left side of the cranium developed a leak and, as a result, the left side of the face remained unembalmed and ashen. In their effort to embalm the right half, a blockage developed, and the side of the face became puffed up. Being responsible embalmers, they became frantic over the situation.

Having one side of the face underembalmed and the other overembalmed was not going to make it at a service with an open casket.

Meanwhile, the chest cavity developed a large pool of a grisly solution as the embalmers tried to deal with the yards and yards of intestines that the pathologist had not bothered to bag. Attempting to embalm the intestines with a spike injector, they broke the organ in several places, spilling its foul contents into the chest cavity. The odor and progressively disgusting mess finally drove me from the room.

It took two hours for the men to complete the job, twice the time it normally takes one embalmer. They were both worn out, and when I asked them if they had any trouble with the formaldehyde in the air, they replied that they had some throat irritation but were bothered mostly by the odor. Their embalmment procedure was a stringent test of the ventilation system.

The exposure levels to formaldehyde turned out to be 0.9, 0.3, 0.6, 1.3, and a high of 4.4 ppm. Because only one out of the five values exceeded the 2.0-ppm standard, I didn't issue a citation. Better work practices would have prevented the one high value and reduced the exposure overall. As I told the manager, the embalmers needed better supervision and easier cases to learn on. The ventilation system was adequately designed, though not optimal. If it were up to the embalmers, more ventilation would have been added regardless of the legal limits.

Only Franklin Family remained to be sampled. I got a call from the manager one morning, and he informed me that he had a posted case for that afternoon. When I arrived, I found two men in their sixties or seventies about to be embalmed. I was assured that the clients had been sent from a hospital after being autopsied by a pathologist.

As soon as the embalmers got gowned and gloved, I hooked them up with the sampling equipment. The supervising embalmer for Franklin, who had performed the job at Roberts, was to be assisted by a junior embalmer. I put on a respirator, although the embalmers did not.

They embalmed the bagged organs quickly and injected the bodies at several sites. As their work progressed, my eyes became increasingly irritated to the point where I had to leave the room. The supervising embalmer said he detected an odor and felt a slight irritation. The other embalmer said he was also suffering. I noted that his eyes were red and he was blinking repeatedly. My suspicions that the formaldehyde levels were high were confirmed a couple of weeks later when the laboratory reported that the concentrations in the air were 3.9 to 4.4 ppm, or about two times the allowable level.

After receiving the laboratory reports, I closed the Franklin inspection by issuing a serious violation for overexposure to formaldehyde. The citation required that the mortuary immediately obtain respirators with formaldehyde-purifying cartridges and that the embalmers use them during posted cases. The citation also required that Franklin upgrade its ventilation system within thirty days so that the respirators would not be necessary. Additional time could be granted for good reason, I explained.

During the closing conference, the regional manager expressed concern that Franklin would receive a fine. From the way he fretted, it was evident that the corporation was on his back for every dime spent. He was relieved to learn that the fine was only $185, a ridiculously insignificant amount for a national corporation and a fraction of the cost a private consultant would charge to conduct similar monitoring. The manager thanked me for keeping the fine low, though the penalty was "unmercifully" derived straight by the book. He didn't thank me for helping him protect the health of his employees.

I also closed the inspections at Roberts, Howell, and Peal and at Roswell. Their ventilation systems were found to be adequate.

All three mortuaries received general violations without fines for failure to have an adequate emergency eyewash. A splash of concentrated embalming solution into the eyes could have caused temporary or permanent blindness if adequate first aid was not provided promptly. All three mortuaries had pint-sized bottles hanging on the wall for emergency use, but unfortunately they did not provide enough solution for the recommended fifteen-minute water flush for eye contact with damaging chemicals. Furthermore, if the accident victim was alone, he or she first had to find the bottle, break the seal, and then squeeze the solution into the eyes. In contrast, the eyewash required by the citation has a large handle that stays in the "on" position when it is hit once, thus freeing the person's hands. The required eyewash also comes with dual nozzles so that both eyes can be flushed simultaneously. The unit connects to the plumbing system, allowing the water to flow for fifteen minutes or longer. Though chemical eye burns are not a common injury among embalmers, the $100 cost of the better eyewash is sensible insurance against eye damage, particularly when the use of eye protection is lax or unsupervised.

The three mortuaries also received general violations for failure to provide training in chemical hazards or, as it is currently called, hazard communication or material safety data sheet (MSDS) training. To comply with this "burdensome" regulation one must order MSDSs over the phone or through the mail and spend about an hour with one's employees reviewing the information on the sheet and the company's chemical safety rules.

I shouldn't have had to order the mortuaries to protect their employees. The corporation certainly had no excuses now for noncompliance at the mortuaries I had inspected or at any of its others. At the very least, the corporation had a responsibility to send a memo or a representative to its other mortuaries and have their safety programs reviewed.

Seven months passed before I could conduct the follow-up at Franklin Family, as required when serious violations are issued. The manager had long before signed and returned the OSHA compliance report form, stating that the ventilation had been improved and all the violations corrected. Neither Franklin nor the other two mortuaries appealed. Follow-up inspections at the other two mortuaries were not mandatory since no serious violations had been issued, and they were not done because of the OSHA office's workload.

I opened the follow-up at Franklin with the regional manager, who explained that a new air conditioner had been installed that introduced fresh air and that the former exhaust fan had been replaced with a more powerful model. The improvements were not optimally designed, but they would probably prove adequate, I thought. I requested and received a copy of the bill, stamped "paid," for the improvements as partial documentation of compliance. Franklin had spent several thousand dollars, most of it for the new air-conditioning system, which was required regardless of the citation if clients were to be stored in the embalming room. The citation may have given the regional manager some leverage to get corporate funds to replace the air-conditioning system, which he said he had wanted to do before the inspection in order to keep his clients properly cool.

I explained to the regional manager that I had to sample one more posted case in order to document that the overexposure to formaldehyde had been controlled. The manager placed me on call.

Within a week, the assistant manager called to say a posted case was in. Another inspector who was curious about the embalming procedure accompanied me.

The embalming procedure went routinely. Although the odor of formaldehyde was fairly detectable, the embalmer said he could not even detect an odor, and our sampling found that the ventilation system had been upgraded to the point where the exposure was only about 0.3 ppm.

Success at last—at least for the three mortuaries I inspected. I could only hope that the corporation would evaluate its other mortuaries and install better ventilation systems where necessary. Based on the management's attitudes and the threat of a $185 fine, I was at best doubtful.

8. FROM THE FIELD

A ssessing the benefits of the 1970 OSH Act and the state acts that followed is a controversial and difficult undertaking. One method researchers use to estimate the impact of OSHA is to examine statistical parameters of occupationally related injuries, illnesses, and deaths that have occurred since the creation of OSHA and determine if there have been any reductions over the years. Overall, the results of these analyses have proven ambiguous to slightly favorable to OSHA. Assessing OSHA's impact by such methods is complicated, however, by the limited availability and inconsistent quality of the data.

As reviewed in a 1985 report by the U.S. Office of Technology Assessment, the results of studies of safety-related injury and death rates (e.g., deaths and injuries due to explosions, falls, moving machinery, motor vehicle accidents, or electrocutions) show that OSHA's effect has been minimal at best.[1] Nonetheless, even small decreases in injury rates and safety-related deaths can add up to thousands of injuries prevented and hundreds of lives saved.

OSHA's overall effectiveness in preventing health-related illnesses and deaths (e.g., due to chronic exposure to chemicals and hearing loss due to noise) is equally unclear. One of the problems is that no reliable reporting system exists on which to base assessments. As the report by the U.S. Office of Technology concludes, "[OSHA] has had some effect on several clearly defined health hazards, but its effect on the many hazards it has not addressed is still in doubt."[2] Summarizing, the report states:

> Measuring OSHA's impact is difficult. To detect the impact of a small
> Federal program on something as large as the Nation's entire work force

might be asking too much. Regarding workplace-related illnesses, even if data were reliable, it is too early to expect that OSHA regulations would have much impact on occupational disease. On the positive side, however, OSHA standards for vinyl chloride, cotton dust, and lead have clearly reduced workplace exposures. Furthermore, increased productivity accompanied compliance with both the vinyl chloride and cotton dust regulations.[3]

Another less scientific but useful way to assess the benefits of the OSH Act is to review a series of inspections, as was done in this book, with the goal of determining whether hazards were abated and injuries and illnesses prevented. In each inspection discussed, people were found to be at risk while performing their jobs and, as a result of the inspection, were somehow protected.

Chapter 2 described a case in which, because of an inspection, workers on a demolition job received information on asbestos and training in its handling. The demolition site was protected from massive asbestos contamination and consequently from becoming a major health hazard for new occupants as well as the workers.

Chapter 3 concerned an airplane manufacturer in which a few management personnel allowed production to rule over basic safety procedures. Well-devised OSHA procedures were ignored, which nearly caused the death of a tank mechanic.

The two narratives in chapter 4 dealt with the decades-old problem of hearing loss from excessive noise. As a result of inspections, enforcement of OSHA's hearing conservation standard provided several hundred employees with training and protection and a better chance at maintaining their hearing.

Chapter 5 discussed a case involving foundry workers at risk of lead intoxication because they were not given respirators or provided with adequate ventilation. OSHA ordered the company to make corrections, and, assuming the company continued to comply over time, workers were protected from chronic overexposure.

The dangers of disregarding basic OSHA safety procedures for hazardous gases were hightlighted in chapter 6, which described a near catastrophe at a refinery and a death from carbon monoxide poisoning at a bakery and cafe.

Finally, chapter 7 described a case in which OSHA enforcement resulted in needed changes in ventilation and reduced unhealthful exposure to formaldehyde for workers in several funeral homes. Safety and health inspectors in federal and state OSHA programs across the nation have conducted many inspections similar to those recounted in this book in which employees were found to be at risk and corrections were made as a result of an inspection.

Besides the tens of thousands of inspections OSHA conducts each year, the mere presence of OSHA as an institution puts pressure on companies to maintain safety and health programs. Many of these companies established programs as a result of the passage of the act, taking the cue from Congress and the public that such programs were necessary. Many take advantage of the resources provided through the act, including the consultation services and NIOSH. Some complying employers appreciate the pressure OSHA can exert on their noncomplying competitors to make investments in safety and health, thus creating a fairer marketplace. The presence of OSHA also helps safety and health professionals in the private sector motivate their managers to correct problems rather than risk the embarrassment if not the threat of an OSHA citation. Finally, when OSHA uses its authority to set new limits or standards, the result can be protection where none existed before for tens of thousands of workers. In short, the act has generated a level of safety and health consciousness that never before existed.

Increasingly, however, the OSH Act and state and federal OSHA programs have been criticized by legislators, workers, and the business community for not meeting their goals. This chapter addresses some of the criticisms and problems with OSHA and discusses how the goals of the OSH Act might better be achieved.

A Response to Criticisms of OSHA Law and Policy

Need for Unannounced Inspections   Many never-before-inspected employers challenge the requirement that OSHA inspections must be conducted without advance notice. "Why don't you come back next week when I'm not busy?" or "You'll have to make an appointment" are among the more polite responses inspectors hear on introducing themselves to a business owner or plant manager for the first time.

It is imperative that an inspector observe as well as possible a company's everyday safety profile and attitude. Providing notice of an inspection might be more convenient for employers, but it would also provide an opportunity to cover up hazards. Equipment can be turned off or employees removed from hazardous operations. Even without advance notice, machines get shut down and employees removed between the time an inspector introduces himself or herself and the walkaround begins. In a limited number of cases, maintenance personnel run ahead of inspectors, installing guards. Without "surprise" inspections that enable inspectors to evaluate a company's injury and illness prevention program as it actually functions, inspectors have little chance of finding problems and reducing risks.

OSHA law grants inspectors the right to enter and inspect a workplace "without delay and at reasonable times." The courts have qualified this authority and have granted the employer the right to refuse an inspection if the inspector does not have a warrant. From an employer's perspective, this is an important right since it makes the inspector responsible for proving probable cause before he or she can obtain a warrant and enter a place of business. But as some OSHA supporters have suggested, with this right a company can routinely refuse to be inspected and cover up problems while the inspector is getting a warrant.

OSHA generally has little trouble obtaining warrants if the inspection is conducted in response to a signed employee complaint, the company has been randomly selected from a list of businesses in high-hazard industries, or an inspector or other public official has observed a possible hazard. If necessary, a warrant can be obtained on the day or the day after one is requested and before inspecting those companies known to demand them. Establishing probable cause is usually not an issue since OSHA has established procedures for sending its limited number of inspectors to businesses in industries in which they are most likely needed. In practice, warrants are rarely demanded; most employers permit inspections without challenge, some because they fear that refusing an inspection will prejudice the inspector against them.

Written Citations Another requirement of the OSH Act that employers often criticize is that citations for safety and health violations must be in writing. A copy of the citation recording the wrongdoing and the date by which the hazard must be abated must be placed in a file at the OSHA office and another copy affixed on the company's bulletin board for employees to see; management keeps the original. Many employers understandably hate this "ticket" system. But as inspectors know all too well, many employers are unlikely to even look up a standard pertaining to a hazard an inspector merely discussed, and without a fixed date for abatement recorded on a citation, they are unlikely to give priority to abatement. Written records have a much better chance of receiving an employer's attention. They also establish the legal documentation necessary at appeals hearings and during follow-up or repeat inspections.

Employees' Right to File a Confidential Complaint Many employers loath the idea that employees have the right to file a confidential complaint with OSHA and request an inspection. This right is often mistakenly thought to promote government intervention in their business. Such employers overlook the fact that *voluntary* compliance with OSHA recommendations or standards minimizes the need to file complaints. The hope is that companies will have effective safety programs and their employees will feel free to bring their concerns to management. This is an immeasurably more effective way to address problems than having an inspector issue citations.

Another objection employers often express is that they do not have the right to confront their "accusers," a right granted by the sixth amendment to the Constitution and applicable in criminal law. Safety and health in the workplace are generally regulated through administrative, not criminal, law. The right of a complainant to remain anonymous is necessary to counter the inherent power difference between employer and employee. If workers knew that their identities would be revealed, few would complain for fear of discrimination by their employer. Without the right of confidentiality, employees could be forced to choose between working in unhealthful conditions and holding jobs that feed their families.

Hierarchy of Controls Over the years, the hierarchy of controls for correcting health hazards has also come under criticism from some employers and from the Office of Management and Budget. The basis for the criticism is that the costs (at least short term) of installing engineering controls, the method of control of first choice whenever possible, are much higher than the costs of having employees wear personal protective equipment.

The hierarchy establishes in the following order of preference generalized methods that may be used to control exposure to a range of harmful substances:

1. *engineering controls*—the containment or elimination of the hazard through physical means, such as a ventilation system to control exposure to a volatile toxic solvent;

2. *administrative controls*—the manipulation of work schedules to reduce exposure, such as limiting the time employees may spend in a noisy area (many OSHA programs have ranked administrative controls with engineering controls); or

3. *personal protective equipment*—the use of protective equipment such as earmuffs to attenuate noise or of respirators to filter out chemical vapors.

The use of *work practice controls*, the design and use of safe work procedures, often falls under class 1, but it can fit into class 2 or 3 depending on the circumstances of the risk.

OSHA will make limited exceptions to the hierarchy if implementation of engineering controls is infeasible for technical and/or economic reasons. The definition of feasibility has been determined through several court decisions. In some circumstances, personal protective equipment may be used instead of engineering controls or during emergencies (e.g., when responding to a fire or chemical leak).

The consequences of a change in OSHA policy and standards favoring the use of personal protective equipment are predictable. Inspectors often see the problems incurred when employers invert the hierarchy, usually in an effort to obtain control by the cheapest means possible. Industrial hygiene inspectors repeatedly observe companies in which respirators are used ineffectively as a cheaper alternative to installing a ventilation system and enclosures around machines emitting dangerously high levels of airborne contaminants. Ensuring consistent and effective use of each worker's protective equipment is a difficult undertaking for any but the most committed employers and employees.

One of the worst respirator-related violations, which occurs often and can be cited as serious, is that employees are found to be using air-purifying respirators that do not fit properly. As a result, there are leaks between the face and the outer edges of the respirator, as if a large hole had been drilled through the front of it. The poorly fitting respirators continue to leak, day after day. This and other problems occur because employers and employees fail to read the manufacturer's instructions and follow OSHA standards, which require that respirators be carefully selected and individually fitted. OSHA's standard specifies that anyone required to wear an air-purifying respirator be given a fit test to identify a size and model that provides at least minimal levels of protection.

Even if adequate respirators are selected and employees are properly fitted, efforts can easily fail soon after the respirators are introduced into the workplace. Only rarely are employees given adequate instructions on the limitations of their respirators and on their proper use and maintenance. As demonstrated by several of the narratives in this book, inspectors often find that respirators are missing vital parts or employees are wearing them improperly. And in many cases, employees do not wear respirators even though they have been issued.

One NIOSH survey of spray-painting operations, conducted in 1976, found that most of the respirators performed poorly, invariably as a result of the inattentiveness of the management and workers to their proper use.[4] The researchers reached this conclusion by sampling separately but at the same time the air outside the respirators, which workers would otherwise have been exposed to, and the air inside the respirators, which the workers were actually breathing. The conclusions of the report are still valid.

Hearing protectors also cause problems. Inspectors frequently find that employees are not using the hearing protectors issued to them, are wearing them in a manner so that there are noise leaks, or are using damaged protectors that provide only a fraction of the necessary reduction in noise. These problems occur because employers fail to require their workers to wear the protectors, fail to maintain a replacement supply, or fail to instruct employees on proper use and the risks of noise.

Although there are many circumstances when personal protective equipment is appropriate, the problems of ensuring that numerous individuals are using the equipment effectively makes preference for engineering controls a wise requirement.

Employees' Problems in Exercising OSHA Rights

Inspectors have many opportunities to learn employees' attitudes toward OSHA. OSHA procedures generally require that individual employees be interviewed during an inspection, usually privately, to determine if required training has been provided and safety procedures followed and to elicit any concerns the employees may have about the safety of their jobs. These interactions provide an opportunity for employees to express their feelings about OSHA and the problems they face in exercising the rights granted to them under the OSH Act.

Based on my own experiences, I would say that most employees support an inspector's presence in their plant and realize that benefits may result. Few employees will say outright that they think OSHA is helping them, but appreciative nods, questions about the risks they may face, and cooperation with the inspector indicate general approval. The depth of this support, however, varies considerably. Ignorance of workplace risks or a sense of powerlessness to control hazards can lead to an indifference regarding health and safety. A significant number of employees express such indifference to an inspection, perceiving more important priorities in their lives.

Union representatives often feel more free to express their opinions to OSHA inspectors than do rank-and-file members or nonunionized workers. Union representatives have acknowledged to me that many hazards in their plants have been corrected as a result of a complaint to OSHA. Other union representatives have learned not to expect OSHA to provide the degree of protection they desire. Still other union representatives place workplace safety and health as a low priority among their duties and consider OSHA regulations overprotective. And very infrequently, union representatives make minor or questionable complaints to place leverage on their employer regarding some matter such as wages that is being negotiated. This tactic is an abuse of the rights granted by the OSH Act and wastes an inspector's valuable time.

The OSH Act grants employees the important right to file a confidential complaint about workplace hazards with the local OSHA office.[5] It is a right some employers loath and many employees are afraid to exercise. Filing a complaint with OSHA or suffering with hazardous working conditions is a difficult choice for many employees. In some companies employees who file complaints sense that they face the risk of dismissal, demotion, a change of duties, or a hidden barrier to promotion, even though the complaint is confidential. In companies with a small number of employees, especially nonunion shops, or in large companies with small work groups, the risk of being suspected of filing a complaint can be great. Losing one's job and the means of support for one's family can be a high price to pay for exercising one's rights. Many of the complaints received by an OSHA office come from courageous people without union protection who put their jobs on the line for safety and health matters.

Discrimination by an employer against employees for exercising the rights granted to them under the OSH Act is against the law and is aggressively investigated by OSHA. Employees who have been discriminated against and who "win" their cases rarely come out unscathed, but at least they have the consolation that they and their coworkers have been protected. Unions can provide a shield for employees by presenting the health or safety concern to management and later if necessary to OSHA. The union representative thus takes any "heat."

A major share of OSHA's complaints come from generally dissatisfied employees, some of whom have been disciplined or terminated by their employers. Although some of these complainants may be motivated to file for other than legitimate reasons, most of their complaints turn out to be valid. (False allegations, motivated by revenge, have instigated a small minority of my inspections.) Inspectors may initially sympathize with the employer in such cases, but the sympathy quickly fades if there is demonstrable truth to the allegations. Not surprisingly, inspectors find it difficult to justify the need for an inspection to an employer who is the "victim" of an employee's "revenge."

Unfortunately, some companies with the most hazardous working conditions operate year after year, in many cases for their entire business lives, without ever having a complaint filed against them. Typically, such companies are small and nonunionized, have mostly women and minority employees, and the working conditions exemplify management's attitudes toward its workers. The employees in such companies are usually ignorant of their rights under OSHA, and those few who are aware of their rights are reluctant to file a complaint for fear of losing their much-needed jobs.

Some employees become frustrated with OSHA because their employers revert to noncompliance as soon as the inspector leaves (or as one construction safety inspector put it, "as soon as they see your tail lights"). Some become further upset when they learn that only employee witnesses can counter their employer's testimony at an appeal hearing unless an inspector observed the hazardous condition or documented it with physical evidence. "You expect me to put my job on the line?" the employee is likely to respond when asked if he or she is willing to testify. Some of these employees become even more disillusioned when they find out that their employer was fined only a few hundred dollars for a hazard for which they risked life or limb.

Employees express disappointment that certain standards are not as protective as they would like and that workers develop workplace-related cancers, lung sensitization, and other diseases or symptoms even though exposure limits were not exceeded. It amazes them to learn that although they were "underexposed" to chemicals such as formaldehyde, isocyanates, or xylene, they still suffered from the effects. Such was the reaction of a group of floor coaters when an inspector told them that they could work for four hours without being legally overexposed to the xylene in their work area. "You got to be kidding!" they replied. "If we stayed in there for one hour we would be feeling dizzy and sick. We know; it's happened enough times." Many such victims also know that their employer would purchase a ventilator or other protection only if OSHA ordered it.

Problems in Achieving Compliance

Before the legislative debates over the 1970 OSH Act, many businesses were against government control of safety and health in the workplace beyond the weak authority exercised by most states. So it was no surprise that business associations and lobbyists attacked the job safety and health bill (the forerunner of the 1970 OSH Act) when President Lyndon Johnson introduced it in Congress in January 1968. Fears were fueled by what may now be viewed as alarmist propaganda, such as a report in *Nation's Business* entitled "Life or Death for Your Business?"[6] The scenario described in the article is amusing now but was frightening for some employers in 1968: an inspector, whom the businessperson had once refused to hire, barges into his office, threatening to padlock the gate and fine the company $1,000 a day if it does not follow the inspector's instructions. The article also noted that if the bill was passed, the labor secretary would have wide-ranging powers over business, including possibly the power to "cancel any professional football game should he [the labor secretary] decide, say, that tag football would be safer and healthier than tackle." Though a significant amount of the rhetoric criticizing the proposed OSH Act was an attempt to achieve language favorable to business interests, the passage of the bill did not mean the end of tackle football. Nor were most of the fears of business people realized.

The early years of OSHA were undoubtedly frustrating for all affected, including labor, business, and OSHA staff. Some of the headaches were created because OSHA adopted consensus standards, many of which were ill designed for enforcement. Difficulties were also created by the numerous court challenges of OSHA's authority and as a result of the resistance generated by the hundreds of thousands of disapproving employers.

In a study comparing OSHA and the equivalent government agency in Britain (the Factory Inspectorate under the Health and Safety Executive), Graham K. Wilson found that British employers were much more accepting of their inspection agency than U.S. employers were of OSHA.[7] One reason may be that at the time of the study employers in Britain had been subject to safety inspections for 150 years. British employers came to accept the inspection system over time, the study concludes. Likewise, acceptance of OSHA among the business community in the United States has improved over time and in response to adjustments by both OSHA and business.

Nineteen years after the passage of the OSH Act, inspectors find that many business people no longer complain that OSHA regulations are too stringent, but rather that they are not protective enough. Many giant corporations, as well as medium- and small-sized companies, have more than complied with OSHA regulations. Some corporations have set and met much lower exposure limits for noise and chemicals, for instance, than OSHA is likely to propose in the next decade. Unfortunately, other companies have been slow to realize the benefits of even minimal compliance or to recognize OSHA's "threat."

Like any group, employers have diverse attitudes toward government regulation and differing perceptions of their responsibility to protect their employees' safety and health. Employers also differ in their levels of competence in managing a safety and health program. It appears from my vantage point that of the supercompliers, compliers, noncompliers, and those in between, the *noncompliers* constitute a significant percentage. Among this group are a surprising number of companies in hazardous industries that do not have even the rudiments of an injury and illness prevention program. The owners of many of these companies when inspected plead ignorance of OSHA laws and standards. And should an inspector issue a citation, often the inspector's greatest hope is that the employer will read it. Years of inspecting noncompliers (sometimes the same employer over and over again) can result in such desperate and meager expectations.

Ignorance of the responsibilities OSHA places on employers can no longer be accepted as an excuse. Business managers cannot claim ignorance of the Internal Revenue Service and the responsibility to pay taxes. Why shouldn't employers be expected to be equally responsible for their employees' safety and health?

There are diverse reasons employers do not comply, and inspectors are witness to most of them. Absolute greed is an underlying motivation for a relative few. Others claim, usually in a roundabout manner, that they do not have the time or money.

In many cases money management is the problem—the costs of not complying versus those of complying. One of the foremost considerations for a company inclined to comply is whether its competitors are likewise complying and thus including the costs of protecting their workers' safety and health in the price of their products. As one accident investigator noted around the turn of the century, employers, like everyone else, are "in the grips of economic motives."[8]

An oft-cited comment by employers is, "Why do I have to buy all of this safety stuff when my competitor down the street doesn't have to?" As this comment illustrates, because only a token number of companies in an industry are inspected and forced to comply, a competitive disadvantage can be created. Though the apparent solution is greater sanctions and more inspections, many companies that are inspected would not endorse this solution. They are not willing to name their noncomplying competitors and would rather OSHA just did not exist. And, as soon as possible, many undoubtedly return to their old noncompliant ways.

Some employers appear to lack the resources to comply. These employers have several options, including seeking help from their business associates, insurance carrier, or local OSHA office, which can refer them to OSHA's nonenforcement, no-cost consultation group.

Some employers report that they do not comply because of a sincere belief that there are no benefits in adhering to "regulation after regulation." They may also have philosophical or political objections to the idea of reducing risks under government pressure. My experience is that most of these companies have no alternatives to

OSHA's regulations. This is not surprising in that OSHA's basic standards for injury and illness prevention rely on fundamental methods for which there are few alternatives. Who can argue that a guard rail around a thirty-foot-high scaffold can prevent a fall and injury or that the proper use of an approved respirator can prevent a sandblaster from inhaling enough silica dust to cause lung disease?

Some employers still hold grudges against OSHA for intruding into the "sovereign domain" of their business, and most people are sympathetic to their cry for freedom to conduct their businesses in whatever lawful manner they choose. It is an important freedom for the country to maintain. But for one aspect of a business, the safety and health of employees, which historically has been unfavorably at the mercy of the employer, there is another freedom that must be considered: the right to work free from harm.[9] The United States has been blessed with a democratic form of government that grants all individuals the right to self-manage their business affairs. Poisoning or subjecting employees to undue risk of harm is not included in this right.

Some employers have a sincere belief that many OSHA requirements are unreasonable. They point out that the standards require an employer to spend money and perhaps change or slow production. In addition, they may complain that the standards cause their employees to become unduly concerned about risks of injury and illness that are "acceptably" low. Typically, such criticisms result from being forced to comply with well-devised and needed standards. During the legislative hearings before passage of the OSH Act, documentation was presented to prove that industrywide standards were needed and that preventable injuries and illnesses were inflicting a heavy toll on working people.[10] Since passage of the act, several influential court decisions have guided OSHA in determining acceptable and unacceptable risks for new standards (e.g., benzene), and the "cost versus benefits" controversy has entered into standards development, as imposed by the political process and partly by the courts.

One criticism that is sometimes valid is that some standards are applied to single work sites or entire industries although the risks are insignificant. The decision of whether to cite in such cases is determined in part by how burdensome compliance would be for the employer. OSHA administrators could do better at determining whether compliance with citations marked serious or costly to abate will result in significant risk reduction. Additional research on enforcement priorities could help improve this situation.

Some employers do not comply because they are unaware of all the benefits of compliance. Managers may be too busy, for example, to recognize that their workers' compensation insurance premium would be lower if they had an effective safety program. They may also fail to consider the costs associated with retraining replacements for injured workers, the loss to the company when experienced workers are injured, the production costs incurred when equipment is damaged, and the low morale associated with a disregard for employees' welfare. Many businesses have found that complying actually saves them money by cutting the losses resulting from injuries and increasing the morale and thus the production of their work force.

Another reason the benefits of compliance may not be clear, particularly for small businesses, is that many employers do not understand the concept of prevention—that preventing injury or illness benefits the company as well as potential victims and their families.[11] Many business owners, and many employees, find it hard to understand why a prevention program is needed, especially if their company has never had a fatality or serious accident. They fail to see that otherwise preventable events will happen in at least one out of every one hundred small shops. What they don't realize is that never having a serious injury or illness is often a matter of luck. The risks from chronic health hazards, which unlike safety-related accidents have no immediate and often no discernible consequences, are even less appreciated.

One of the problems is that preventing illnesses or deaths from chronic, long-term exposure can require a high initial investment. The "return" on the dollars is often long term, which goes against the goal of maximizing short-term profits, which many businesses hold as the golden rule. Furthermore, because it is difficult to document chronic workplace-related diseases and illnesses, many noncompliers escape the increases in their workers' compensation costs associated with more easily documented negligence. The method by which costs are diffused through the compensation insurance system also works against compliance if an employer's insurance premiums are low compared to the costs of adopting preventive measures, such as installing ventilation systems or other engineering controls. Companies have to have reasons to implement injury and illness prevention programs and attendant controls other than because it will save them money. When all the reasons and motives for not complying are considered—competitors are not making safety and health expenditures; the costs of compliance are high; the company lacks the resources; management has philosophical or political objections; management lacks an awareness of OSHA and of the benefits of compliance; the company has relatively low workers' compensation costs—the economic motive nearly always prevails.

The report *Preventing Illness and Injury in the Workplace* by the U.S. Office of Technology Assessment suggested seven incentives that may motivate employers to control hazards:

1. an enlightened self-interest and concern for others;

2. information on hazards and controls, which in turn stimulates voluntary compliance;

3. financial and tax incentives for compliance;

4. reductions in premiums for workers' compensation insurance on implementation of control or evidence of a decrease in injuries and illnesses;

5. tort liability—threat of third-party lawsuit;

6. employees who are exercising their rights granted by the OSH Act and unions that are bargaining for safety and health provisions; and

7. regulations.[12]

Too much reliance can be placed on number 2 above. Informing or educating employers about the hazards in their businesses and about the possible control options available does have a motivating effect, but information alone is often not enough. Many employers do not even request the material offered, let alone take action. Pages of guidelines are already available from OSHA and NIOSH, insurance companies, private consultants, universities, and other groups. This information is valuable to employers who recognize their responsibility to promote safety and health. But many employers disregard the information so that they can cite ignorance as a reason not to comply. Congress found it necessary to enforce regulation in large part because incentives 1 through 6 above were not enough.

How OSHA Works for Employers

There are several ways OSHA helps employers reduce their rate of workplace-related injuries and illnesses. Many of the standards, for example, take into consideration the technical and economic feasibility of compliance and thereby allow employers alternative control methods. Further, employers are not sanctioned by OSHA for acts resulting from misconduct by an employee, provided the employer has met certain conditions related to the implementation of an adequate safety and health program.[13] Penalties are imposed for most first-time violations only when they may result in "death or serious phyical harm" and the employer knew of the hazard or with "reasonable diligence" should have known, or for violations that were committed willfully.[14] Whenever a penalty is issued, employers are credited for their past history, their evidence of good faith toward compliance, the size of the company, the severity of the hazard, and the probability of harm. This sliding penalty schedule helps small employers, employers who made a mistake but are otherwise in compliance, and those who have a recalcitrant foreman. Furthermore, the appeal system provides a recourse if employers believe a mistake has been made or they are suffering from an abuse of authority by an inspector.

Need for Enforcement
through Deterrence

In establishing OSHA, the Occupational Safety and Health Act set forth a general method of enforcement for the agency to follow. It provided the right of entry into a business and the authority to conduct an inspection. The act gave the agency the responsibility to issue citations for violations of standards and the power to subpoena evidence and witnesses. It also prescribed a range of penalties for violations. But in writing the act, Congress could not possibly describe all the administrative procedures and policies necessary for the agency to perform its duties. The formulation and implementation of the multitude of procedures that enable any institution to run in an orderly, consistent, and flexible manner were left up to the agency itself. Interpretation of the act was left to the courts. Policy is administered within the bounds of the act, other laws, and appropriation riders by the legislature. (Changes in the act itself may be made only by the legislative branch.)

OSHA policy is directed internally by the top administrators of the agency.[15] Policy is influenced, however, by a number of overseers or pressure groups, including the executive branch of the ruling administration, the legislative branch, business and professional associations, labor unions, and agency staff. The most influential of these groups is the executive branch. Because the top administrators of most OSHA programs are politically appointed, the president, or governors for state programs, set the overall policy of the agency.

The effectiveness of federal and state OSHA programs in achieving compliance and thus in preventing injuries and illnesses depends on the enforcement policies implemented by each OSHA program. Major differences in policy, given sufficient time for the effects to be felt and recorded, have a significant impact on a program's effectiveness. Decisions about the following matters, for example, are subject to differences in enforcement policy:

- which companies get inspected;

- under what circumstances a company receives a partial or "wall-to-wall" inspection;

- whether penalties for first-instance serious violations are proposed;

- how actively serious, repeat, nonabate, and willful violations are pursued;

- whether penalties are imposed for each violation when there are multiple violations;

- penalties assessed;

- the degree of negotiation allowed over the amount of the penalty at the time it is calculated and before an appeal hearing;

- the number and type of cases sent for criminal prosecution;

- levels of staffing, which dictate whether there is time to document serious cases or time only for cursory inspections;

- whether the agency pursues appeal decisions unfavorable to OSHA; and

- the morale, competency, and thus effectiveness of the inspectors who implement the policies.

These policies and others have been tacitly changed over time, sometimes overtly, by political and pressure groups averse to enforcement.

The collective effect of these changes has been a weakening of enforcement policy and a shift toward the formation and adoption of a general policy of *forced consultation*.

Under a policy of forced consultation, OSHA's penalty schedule is used primarily as a threat and a bluff. Fines, if issued, are minimized by providing all possible credits and are further cut upon appeal. First-time and often repeat serious violators are given "fair" warnings rather than meaningful fines. Inspectors are encouraged to conduct "consultation visits" that a company cannot refuse. In short, most elements of enforcement are removed. Inspections become imposed information and safety audits without real sanction. In contrast, under a policy of *enforcement through deterrence*, penalties are imposed on serious noncompliers even after the first inspection.[16]

Some OSHA programs employ a policy of forced consultation, whereas others tend to use a policy of deterrence. Even within a program, some OSHA area offices implement one policy while others implement the other. The differences on a program level are most noticeable, however, under different presidential or gubernatorial administrations. Under Jimmy Carter, for example, deterrence was preferred, whereas forced consultation was preferred under Ronald Reagan. Similarly, deterrence was preferred under Jerry Brown in California and forced consultation under George Deukmejian. A policy of forced consultation currently exists in many OSHA programs.

Under a policy of forced consultation, the fines paid may be a fraction of what a company would have to invest to comply with a given standard or to hire a private consultant to make a similar health and safety audit. Initial small fines are reduced even further based on the employer's contriteness or willingness to comply as expressed throughout the inspection or appeal process. Under a policy of forced consultation, willful, repeat, and nonabate violations are not aggressively documented because such characterizations lead to high fines for which it is often difficult to rationalize sizable reductions. Also, high penalties run contrary to a consulting mode. A few OSHA supervisors actually encourage employers to appeal fines and ask their inspectors to encourage appeals if the fine is high.

The focus of forced consultation is on solving a company's safety and health problems, as observed during an inspection, using the threat of a penalty. The goal of the inspection is to achieve compliance with little or no sanction. The business community learns over time that the local OSHA enforcement office is willing to "work with them" and that an appeal will resolve any monetary discomfort.

The policy of forced consultation is an attractive one. Problems appear to be solved, OSHA inspectors do not have the stress-inducing conflicts that come with hard enforcement, and cited employers are relatively happy. But are problems really solved? Will a noncomplying company once cited become a complier after it is "visited"? Will noncomplying competitors and neighboring businesses that are not inspected be induced to comply?

Supporters of forced consultation point out that OSHA may penalize quite heavily if there is evidence during a follow-up that the employer has not abated the cited hazard. The theory is that the first inspection provides a warning and the second inspection the "shock" the company needs to force it to make corrections. Proponents of the theory also propose that the high penalties for nonabatement will motivate other employers to take first-time citations seriously. In practice, however, the theory fails.

A policy of forced consultation has a chance of succeeding only for a small fraction of the noncomplying companies that are inspected, even if they are inspected more than once. More important, the policy fails to achieve any significant compliance among the many noncomplying companies that are never inspected.

OSHA cannot inspect every place of business that may have serious hazards on a frequency that would enable forced consultation to be effective. There are just too many employers. For example, 1983 data indicate that federal and state OSHA programs inspect manufacturing plants, which receive "special emphasis," about once every six years.[17] The safety and health inspection rates for other fixed establishments are much lower. (Some nonfixed businesses, such as logging and certain types of construction, may receive safety inspections more often.) Health inspections, which are more time-consuming, are conducted the least frequently, and many employers never receive a health inspection. (Safety inspections are conducted more frequently than health inspections by a factor of ten.) The number of employers is far too great for even a greatly expanded OSHA inspection staff to hope to find the noncompliers, let alone give them a "fair" warning and then conduct timely follow-ups.

Relying solely on high penalties as threats for nonabatement may be appropriate if all businesses in critical industries receive an initial inspection and timely follow-ups. But even then, the policy is unlikely to achieve compliance over time. Businesses are dynamic operations in which management personnel come and go, equipment wears out, money becomes tight, and new processes are introduced. Some companies would need periodic inspections just to ensure that they were given "fair" warnings about new hazards.

To establish the threat of citing for nonabatement, a significant number of follow-up inspections have to be conducted. Because of understaffing, many OSHA offices have trouble conducting even the tiny fraction of one out of twenty. Consequently, few employers get caught for ignoring a "warning," and the threat of high penalties for nonabatement—the motivation many employers need to comply—vanishes. Finally, even when follow-ups are done, some OSHA offices knock down nonabatement penalties to insignificant sums at the appeal stage.

A common mistake among the public and even among some safety and health inspectors is failure to recognize that enforcement should deal not just with single problems in a business as they are found but should influence industry as a whole. Forced consultation, while having the benefits of frequently uncovering and solving problems at individual workplaces, fails to affect the much larger pool of noncomplying employers that are not inspected. These employers can simply wait without adverse consequences for the remote possibility of being inspected. In the meantime, employees are at risk and the number of injuries and illnesses mounts. Since the enactment of the OSH Act, employers have been required to comply *before* they are inspected. By reducing the first OSHA inspection to a warning, forced consultation softens the requirement in OSHA law for employers to be proactive in complying with OSHA regulations.

Another problem with forced consultation lies in the inherent limitations of an OSHA inspection. An inspection is conducted over a few hours to a few days and constitutes only a fraction of a business's life. Violations may be observed, but other violations are likely to be missed. An inspector may be able to ensure that observed violations are abated, but without the fear of another inspection and substantial sanction, many employers revert to noncompliance after the inspector leaves. A more successful enforcement policy is one that induces the noncomplier to maintain a functioning safety and health plan, to abate both cited and missed violations, and to abate hazards as they arise in the future. If employers are not made to feel responsible for health and safety *over time*, much of an inspector's efforts are wasted.

Further, because a policy of forced consultation forces compliance on only a few companies among many in a competitive industry, it induces inspected companies to accept a competitive disadvantage in the form of extra costs that are not shared by their uninspected competitors. Further pressure is thus exerted on the cited company to backslide.

The outcome of noncompliance is preventable injuries and illnesses. Proponents of forced consultation might well be shocked by how relatively little improvement has been made. Most inspectors who have conducted inspections in several hazardous industries will agree that nineteen years after enactment of OSHA, a significant number of employers still have serious safety and health problems. Of the inspections I have conducted, about 50 percent of the employers had major deficiencies in safety and health. It should come as no surprise that far too many workers, including those in companies that have been inspected, suffer preventable injuries or death or develop preventable hearing loss or fatal or debilitating diseases. Something broader and more effective than a policy of forced consultation must be pursued.

The more active use of *enforcement through deterrence*, as weakly or occasionally practiced by OSHA, may provide the more lasting and widespread compliance that is needed. Enforcement through deterrence includes the practice of firmly but fairly issuing *and collecting* penalties for valid citations in amounts that raise the concern of those noncomplying employers that have been inspected. Enough concern so generated will motivate many more noncompliers to comply.

A more extensive use of a deterrent policy by OSHA would mean that all inspectors would be supported by their supervisors and OSHA administrators to cite "serious" where it is due and to complete documentation and issue willful violations when they are discovered. Penalties would be calculated based on the objective criteria provided in OSHA policy and procedure manuals, as opposed to maximizing credits, as practiced by many inspectors and their supervisors. OSHA staffing levels would be increased to ensure that a significant number of businesses in target industries were inspected, complaints were addressed, appeals were resolved in a timely manner, and follow-ups occurred. Nonabatement would be properly assessed, based on a penalty schedule. Prosecution by local district attorneys for willful violations that resulted in the death of an employee would be vigorously supported, as already allowed by OSHA law. Appeals would not be encouraged, but cited employers would be expected to abate the hazard and pay the penalty. The appeal system would be respected more for what it should be: a process for resolving mistakes by inspectors and, more rarely, abuses of authority, rather than a means to delay compliance and to negotiate reductions in penalties.

The low penalty schedule used by OSHA programs is an important limitation to implementing a policy of enforcement through deterrence. To establish a true deterrent, the maximum penalty of $1,000 for serious violations would have to be increased. An increase in the penalty ceiling would require a change in the act, thus requiring legislative action. Several states have already taken this step. The maximum penalty for a serious violation in the state of Washington, for example, is $5,000. The maximum should be raised even higher. Currently, the maximum penalty is levied only when there is the greatest probability of death and is often not levied even when a fatality resulted from an infraction of a standard. Adjustments depending on the gravity of the hazard and the probability of death or serious physical harm can significantly decrease the penalty from the maximum, so that the average federal OSHA penalty for a serious violation was $239 in 1987, $216 in 1986, and $196 in 1985. The maximum penalty for willful and repeat violations combined was $5,441 in 1987, $1,558 in 1986, and $897 in 1985.[18] If the maximum figure for a first-instance serious violation is increased, the maximum figures for repeat, nonabate, and willful violations should be increased correspondingly.

John M. Gleason and Darold T. Barnum came to a similar conclusion regarding OSHA's procedures and policies for penalizing noncompliers:

> Expectancies of being cited for initial safety and health violations, and fine levels if cited, are so low under OSHA that they are of little value in preventing violations of the Act. Those employers who obey the law would do so regardless of the penalties. Employers at whom the sanctions are aimed—those who will correct violations only if it is economically profitable to do so—are not being affected. Thus the current sanctions antagonize employers who attempt to obey the law, while having little impact on those employers who will obey the law only if it is economically profitable.[19]

Gleason and Barnum's conclusion that sanctions antagonize employers who attempt to obey the law is not completely accurate. Those who comply voluntarily and abate their serious hazards without motivation from an inspector are free from sanction. Those who attempt to comply but still have a serious hazard receive an appropriately reduced penalty based on "good faith." Those who have attempted to comply but have failed miserably are fined depending on the good or bad faith found.

Critics of OSHA who support lowering fines often complain that high fines are imposed to "punish" employers for bad behavior. This is not the case. High fines are intended to motivate inspected companies and others to comply. Levels should be high enough to compete with economic motives for not complying.

Consideration should also be given to expanding federal OSHA's limited policy of penalizing for each instance of a serious or willful violation (e.g., the penalty for a single violation is multiplied based on the number of employees who are overexposed). Federal OSHA has limited use of this policy to a handful of employers characterized by the "egregious" nature of their violations.

In addition to major increases in the maximum and average penalty levels, consideration should be given to changing the penalty schedule to allow greater reductions based on evidence of good faith, past history with OSHA, and the quality of the company's accident and illness prevention program. Such allowances would permit greater distinction in levying fines between noncompliers with chronic or serious problems and compliers that have made a mistake. Additional credits should also be offered to small employers.

A shift toward enforcement through deterrence would have the greatest impact on small employers, for they represent a majority of the noncompliers. An increase in their demand for help should be anticipated. OSHA consultation services should be increased, for example, and NIOSH should resurrect and expand its program of publishing pamphlets detailing hazards and corrective methods. Other problems and needs of the small employer have been discussed elsewhere.[20]

The following examples demonstrate how a policy of enforcement through deterrence could be rationally applied.

Company 1 is inspected and found to be complying minimally or better with OSHA standards applicable to its business. There are a few nonserious violations, but they do not result in penalties, and the inspector is confident that the hazards will be abated. The inspector makes a few suggestions about better and perhaps easier methods of compliance. Otherwise, the inspection is pleasant and brief, and a follow-up inspection is not scheduled.

In contrast, a first-time inspection of company 2, which employs about one hundred workers, uncovers numerous serious hazards and no evidence of an injury and illness prevention program. Several suggestions are made of ways the company could be brought into compliance, and the inspector spends much more time evaluating and documenting the hazards than she did at company 1. On closing the inspection, six first-instance serious violations are cited, and more than $20,000 in penalties are imposed. The company proposes to appeal. An informal ccnference is held, and the OSHA office confirms that the inspector made no errors in documentation or judgment. No changes in the citation or penalty are proposed. The employer is encouraged to comply, and assistance and referral are again offered. The employer continues with the appeal, and OSHA continues to defend its position. OSHA prevails and a follow-up inspection is conducted during which instances of significant nonabatement are found and appropriately higher penalties are assessed. A second follow-up is scheduled.

The details for company 3 are more specific. The company is a demolition contractor, a business that by its nature is very hazardous. The company is found to have a good safety program; safety belts and other protective devices are used consistently; cranes are inspected and maintained regularly; and employees attend regularly held safety meetings. Further, the company is found to have complied with all the major elements of OSHA's complex asbestos regulations, except for one provision: asbestos demolition workers are using an air-supplied respirator at below the minimum required pressure. As a result, asbestos fibers are leaking in and exposing the employees—a potentially very serious violation. The inspector documents that a mix-up has occurred and the problem is corrected immediately. Based on the company's demonstrated commitment to its workers' safety, the behavior is deemed neither willful nor extremely negligent. The inspector cannot ignore the infraction, however, and a citation is issued. The violation is classed as serious, but the penalty is considerably lower than the average because of the employer's good faith and evidence of responsibility to its employees. In this instance the company needed no economic motive to comply since compliance entailed no cost. Noncompliers would hear about the action, however, and get the message that companies with a commitment to health and safety are treated reasonably and that companies without such demonstrated commitment may be penalized harshly.

One potential drawback of enforcement through deterrence is that by levying higher fines OSHA could increase employer resistance, which could initially result in more appeals and more companies refusing entry to inspectors. One could also expect serious resistance from those legislators who for political reasons want OSHA enforcement policy weakened.

Forced consultation may well be the policy of choice among the business community. Changing policy and law necessarily depends on the nation's voters. Unfortunately, many may have little understanding of OSHA's benefits or of how much protection they want in the workplace.

The Deal and Appeal System

All employers cited by OSHA have the right to appeal a citation, the amount of a fine, and the date by which a hazard must be corrected. The employer has fifteen working days after receipt of the citation in which to file the appeal. If the appeal is over the existence of a violation, elimination of the cited hazard is not required until a decision is rendered.[21] When a hearing is held, an administrative law judge assigned by the managing appeals board or review commission hears the case. (Appeals of federal OSHA citations are managed by the three-member Occupational Safety and Health Review Commission, appointed by the president; appeals of state OSHA citations are managed by an appeals board or its equivalent, appointed by the governor.) The burden of proof is fully on OSHA. Attorneys representing OSHA and the employer are often present at the hearing. Witnesses, including employees, management representatives, and experts, may be called and physical evidence introduced, under a semiformal system of evidence submission. Cross-examination is permitted.

After hearing the case, the administrative law judge will issue a written decision that affirms or throws out the violation and penalty or adjusts the amount. Should OSHA or the employer not be satisfied with the result, either party may appeal directly to the state appeals board or to the federal review commission, depending on whether the citation was issued by a state or federal OSHA program. The employer or OSHA may take the appeal all the way to the U.S. Supreme Court. Some appeal decisions have had major impact on the way OSHA conducts inspections and on the applicability of standards.

OSHA also has an established and well-used mechanism by which the enforcement agency or the employer may request a meeting, called an informal conference, before the formal appeal. At the informal conference, employer representatives and employee representatives, if requested by an employee group or union, meet with the management of the issuing OSHA office. The conference is intended to provide all involved parties with a chance to consider any new information regarding the alleged violation and to correct any mistakes in documentation and determination of the violation, penalty, or abatement date. Requests for extensions of the abatement date and for decreased penalties may also be considered.

The process for making appeals and holding informal conferences is important to OSHA and helps keep the OSHA program a fair one. Both stages of the process have been subject to abuse, however, by employers and OSHA administrators and staff.

In some OSHA offices, informal conferences routinely turn into deal-making sessions at which penalties are lowered in exchange for promises from the employer to abate cited hazards. Often the penalties are greatly reduced if the employer simply shows up. In such offices penalties are reduced even though the OSHA office already granted allowances for the severity of the hazard, the probability of harm, good faith, the company's history with OSHA, the size of the company, and the number of employees exposed. Employers frequently reject an offer made at an informal conference but receive an additional reduction during a conference before the hearing. In some parts of the country, a large number of companies appeal because they expect, correctly so, that the appeal process will result in their penalties being reduced automatically. Such deal-making is an integral part of a policy of forced consultation and counter to a policy of enforcement through deterrence.

OSHA management and attorneys can exercise great discretion in reducing penalties if OSHA administrators condone it. Under one Democratic administration in California, for example, deal-making was forbidden. Adjustments in penalties were allowed only if an inspector had made an error in judging, documenting, or assessing the fine. Under a later Republican administration, deal-making was encouraged in an effort to prevent further appeals and to achieve timely "compliance." Federal OSHA has gone through similar changes.

OSHA managers and attorneys face several pressures that make them prone to striking deals. One is that they are under pressure to do so from employers. Letters of appeal often put forth employers' allegations of overregulation and abuse by OSHA and carelessness by inspectors. The employers' concerns are also well represented during informal or pretrial settlement conferences, whereas employee representation is rare. Further, unlike inspectors, who continuously interact with employees at risk, OSHA managers rarely see employees in the workplace. This problem is shared by OSHA attorneys and administrative law judges. Also, because of understaffing, OSHA attorneys are sometimes forced into penalty-slashing settlements just to keep a burgeoning backlog of cases at bay. Perhaps more influential, OSHA managers and attorneys know that appeal judges often discount penalties regardless of the formal procedures OSHA used in calculating the fine. The net effect of these pressures is for managers and attorneys to cut deals that may look promising in the short term but ignore long-term implications. Once a cited employer and the rest of the noncomplying business community understand the deal-making system, the threat of a high penalty for noncompliance evaporates. Noncompliers feel free to continue in violation of standards, knowing that the probability of an inspection is remote and that even if it occurs, it will result, with little effort on the employer's part, in no significant fines.

Some OSHA personnel believe that deal-making saves the government money by discouraging employers to follow through with the more costly appeal process. Other OSHA personnel prefer deal-making for another reason: it lessens an employer's anger and makes inspectors' jobs easier and more pleasant. But what message do such deals convey to noncomplying employers, and how does deal-making affect the employees whom the inspection apparatus is supposed to protect?

The idea that deal-making saves the government money is questionable on two counts: it occurs at the workers' expense, and it may not be cost-effective over the long term. If deal-making diminishes OSHA's ability to obtain long-term compliance from cited and uncited noncompliers, then deal-making actually defeats the goals of the entire OSHA system. When noncompliance is significant, the costs to society of the resultant injuries and illnesses (e.g., workers' compensation and its administration) and to the injured and their families are also significant.

Another reason many OSHA supervisors and area directors practice deal-making is that it takes so long to hear an appeal. As many of the narratives in this book illustrate, appeals are often not heard for six to twelve months after a citation is issued. During the waiting period the employer is not legally required to abate the hazard and further sanctions may not be imposed. Not surprisingly, employers and inspectors often lose respect for a system that finds it important enough to issue a legally binding citation with a fixed abatement date but routinely puts off appeal hearings for six months or more past the date by which the inspector felt the hazard should have been eliminated. Likewise, having to wait so long to have an important case resolved puts tremendous pressure on OSHA to have an immediate promise of compliance from an employer and to cut a deal as quickly as possible.

The delays in hearing appeals provide opportunities for abuse. Though the OSH Act states that appeals by employers are to be done "in good faith and not solely for delay or avoidance of penalties," many companies appeal with the goal of putting off the date of abatement. Companies also make formal appeals to strengthen their hand in the deal-making game.

There are solutions to these problems. One is to increase the staff available for the hearing process so that appeals can be heard twenty-one to forty-five days after an employer appeals. Appeals concerning only the amount of a penalty or the validity of a nonserious violation or abatement dates should be heard in sixty to ninety days.

In some cases, simply having a union or an employee representative attend the informal conference greatly diminishes the temptation to make deals. An employee's presence reminds OSHA personnel of the workers back at the plant who may still be faced with the cited hazard and can check the bureaucratic tendency to "discount" facts so that the appeal process will go as "smoothly" as possible.

Restrictions must also be placed on the power of appeal judges and board or commission members to reduce penalties. The ability of each judge or board or commission member to impose his or her own policies for assessing penalties has often resulted in neutralizing their deterrent effect and demoralizing OSHA staff. Reductions in penalties could be limited to specialized circumstances. For example, reductions could be considered for employers who can demonstrate severe economic hardship and a willingness to stay in compliance. Reductions or increases could also be permitted for cases in which OSHA is found to be in error in its penalty calculations. Formalizing and restricting the procedure used to adjust penalties would help prevent abuses and provide the deterrence that is so needed.

Everyone involved in the appeal system must be committed to enforcement through deterrence. Without such a commitment, the policy has a short life. For example, increasing the understanding of appeal judges and board or commission members of accident and illness prevention would help them make fairer appeal decisions without diminishing the rights of employers to challenge honest mistakes and abuses of authority. Once the noncomplying business community learns that the appeal system is upholding penalties assessed in accordance with OSHA policy and that the system no longer promotes delay or dismissal based on a judge's ignorance of safety and health, the number of appeals will drop.

Currently, the appeal boards and review commissions are separate from OSHA. This arrangement may contribute to the problems. Organizational improvements that would keep policy within OSHA have been proposed elsewhere.[22]

Need for Competent Inspectors

OSHA's inspectors are its front-line "soldiers." It is essential that they have the social skills to interact with diverse employers and employees, expertise in industrial safety or health, and knowledge of the multitude of regulations they must enforce.

The job is demanding; an inspector is making judgments that affect workers' welfare and a company's budget. When an inspector confronts a potential hazard, he or she must be able to determine whether it is indeed a hazard and whether employees are exposed and at risk. Further, he or she must determine the degree and likelihood of harm and what control methods are available. Also, the inspector must document his or her decisions, often under less than cooperative circumstances. Finally, the inspector must be able to prove that a hazard is a problem and that the employer is in violation of a standard. Overlooking a violation can result in workers being hurt or becoming ill. And citing when there is no violation can result in an employer needlessly spending thousands of dollars.

Few overt rewards counter the pressure exerted on an inspector by his "client" companies. Rarely will the management of a noncomplying business thank an inspector for reducing the risks of harm to his or her employees, and few employees will thank an inspector for protecting them from harm, for fear of antagonizing their employer. Given these difficulties and responsibilities, OSHA administrators must make a continuing effort to ensure that inspectors are motivated and competent. New inspectors must be expertly trained in safety or health and in OSHA law and inspection techniques. When inspectors are deficient in some aspect of their jobs, they should be given appropriate remedial training.

Inspectors are required to inspect a broad range of industries and must be armed with as much information about the hazards and applicable standards for each industry as possible. Even experienced inspectors need periodic training to broaden and review their knowledge. Inspectors should have ready access to good reference materials and be required to attend periodic staff meetings for the purpose of exchanging information and experiences.

As important as having knowledge, resources, and experience, inspectors need to be reminded that their work is important. Safety inspectors see the results of noncompliance more often than industrial hygienists, who rarely see the death and disease that can result from harmful exposure. Consequently, industrial hygiene inspectors are sometimes lulled into minimizing workplace risks. Inspectors need support and motivation from their administrators, who sometimes appear to have been selected by presidential or gubernatorial administrations to provide just the opposite.

One aspect of an inspector's training that is significantly lacking is an appreciation of the need for comprehensive injury and illness prevention programs. Consequently, many inspectors concentrate solely on individual hazards and violations. Further, OSHA characterizes individual hazards as serious infractions but for the most part does not issue serious violations for failure to have and implement a prevention program. A complete prevention program would include, preferably in writing, identification of the hazards in the business and the organizational and physical control methods that are to be used. (OSHA and NIOSH and many private and public institutions and organizations have abundant literature to help any employer who wishes to devise an overall safety and health program.) Citing only for those hazards observed on a walkaround but not for failure to have a prevention program runs counter to OSHA's goal of achieving long-term compliance and of preventing accidents and illnesses.

Besides giving inspectors more training in setting up prevention programs and in evaluating those that are in place, OSHA programs, where needed, should probably amend the standards and laws so that inspectors can enforce, and where applicable penalize, for failure to have an overall safety and health program. Federal OSHA currently has no standards requiring employers to develop a comprehensive safety and health program, though the agency has requested comments on such a proposal.[23]

Better overall training would also enable inspectors to provide more useful guidance to companies they inspect. Inspectors need not and should not be expected to design engineering controls, but they should be able to offer suggestions on how to achieve compliance and be able to refer employers to appropriate sources of information. Citing and penalizing do not preclude cooperation toward abatement. In documenting a hazard, for example, inspectors sometimes find the perfect way to eliminate a hazard. And explaining why a control is needed may not convince every cited employer to comply, but it may produce more respect for OSHA from noncompliers who think OSHA has no reason to exist.

One way to help ensure that inspectors are competent is to hire the best people for the job. Recruiting such people, however, can be difficult. OSHA inspectors are paid less than inspectors in private industry, and many good professionals leave OSHA once they have field experience. The job is known to lack overt rewards and to have its political and on-site problems.

OSHA is currently having a difficult time hiring college-trained industrial hygienists. For the most part, this critical shortage is caused by a decrease in federal funding of NIOSH training grants to universities.

Under a policy of enforcement through deterrence, the need for well-trained and competent inspectors would be even greater. If more and higher penalties were issued, good judgment would be more important than ever, both to lessen criticism from the business community and to prevent needless heartache for undeserving businesses. But regardless of the enforcement policy, employers, employees, and OSHA benefit when inspectors are as competent as possible.

Conclusion

OSHA enforcement policies are directed toward those companies that challenge the goals of the act rather than those that choose to comply. Although the overall impact of enforcement may be less than what the framers of the act had hoped for, the risks of suffering occupationally related injuries and illnesses have been reduced as a result of the tens of thousands of inspections conducted each year. Further, thousands of workers in complying companies have been protected as a result of OSHA's standards. Unfortunately, many businesses still do not comply. This partly accounts for the commonly held view that the overall injury and illness rates have decreased only minimally since the inception of OSHA. Clearly, much can be done to improve the situation.

In *Crisis in the Workplace*, a comprehensive study of occupational health problems and OSHA published in 1976, Nicholas A. Ashford listed five requirements that OSHA must satisfy in order to achieve voluntary and involuntary compliance:

1. understandable and accessible standards and regulations;
2. a large enough inspection staff to present a significant threat to employers of random inspections;
3. significant penalties for violations;
4. well-qualified inspectors; and
5. employees who are well informed about workplace hazards and their rights of protection under the law.[24]

Ashford concluded that OSHA had failed to meet most of these requirements.[25] Some have still not been met. OSHA's staff is still not large enough to conduct random inspections of a significant percentage of the employers in hazardous industries (more critical for health inspections than safety). Significant penalties are not being levied. Inspectors are more qualified and dedicated than in 1976, but they are still not receiving adequate training. And most employees are still not well informed about workplace hazards and their OSHA rights.

After spending years enforcing OSHA standards, I conclude that they must be enforced in a manner so that they provide a strong deterrent for *serious noncompliers*. A policy of greater enforcement through deterrence would include higher first-instance penalties for serious violations in amounts that would compete with the economic motives not to comply. The policy would also include more active but objective pursuit of repeat, willful, and failure-to-abate violations and those more serious cases demanding criminal prosecution. Changes in the appeal system would prevent unjustified penalty reduction, which erodes an employer's accountability for safety and undermines enforcement. Additional changes would allow more timely hearings and increase understanding among appeal judges of injury and illness prevention. Furthermore, inspectors would be provided with the motivation, training, enforcement tools, and judgment needed to motivate noncompliers. Greater emphasis would be placed on developing priorities regarding which companies to inspect and which violations pose the greatest risk. Inspectors would also be better trained to evaluate comprehensive injury and illness prevention programs and be able to require changes when there were deficiencies. Because inspectors would be highly qualified and priorities clearly articulated, there would be less enforcement for insignificant risks and inspectors would make fewer mistakes. Cooperation with and assistance for compliers and those voluntarily attempting to comply would be equally pursued. Only by shifting toward a policy of enforcement through deterrence can we expect America's workers to receive the protection in the workplace to which they have a right and to which they are entitled under the OSH Act.

NOTES

I. Introduction

1. Occupational Safety and Health Act of 1970, Public Law No. 91–596.

2. For more information about OSHA, consult the following publications, which may be obtained from the OSHA Publications Office, U.S. Department of Labor, Room N–3101, Washington, D.C. 20210: *All about OSHA* (publication 2056); *Employer Rights and Responsibilities Following an OSHA Inspection* (publication 3000); *OSHA Inspections* (publication 2098); *Code of Federal Regulations, Title 29, Parts 1900–1910; The Occupational Safety and Health Act of 1970, PL–91–596* (publication 2001); *Chemical Hazard Communication* (publication 3084); *Consultation Services for the Employer* (publication 3047); *Emergency Response in the Workplace* (publication 3088); *OSHA Handbook for Small Business* (publication 2209); *Personal Protective Equipment* (publication 3077); *Safety and Health Is Our Middle Name* (publication 3076); *Safety and Health Guide for the Chemical Industry* (publication 3091). In states covered by a state OSHA plan, publications are also available from the state's OSHA office. Check the phonebook under your state's industrial safety and health program.

3. Not all OSHA or other recommended limits are based on the best and most current data, and limits are not always established with the aim of preventing all health effects. Concerns over the financial costs and ability of industry to achieve a lower exposure level, as well as disagreements over interpretation of toxicological data and what constitutes a "reasonable risk," can seriously affect the limit-setting process.

2. Asbestos

1. For additional information about products and uses of asbestos, contact the U.S. Consumer Products Safety Commission, Office of Information and Public Affairs, Washington, D.C. 20207, or phone 800–638-CPSC.

2. Paul Brodeur, *Outrageous Misconduct—The Asbestos Industry on Trial* (New York: Pantheon Books, 1985).

3. Respirable asbestos, generally invisible fibers in the air, is measured by passing the air to be sampled through a specially designed filter that traps the fibers. The filter is then treated and the fibers on the filter are counted with a microscope. The total number of fibers collected is then divided by the amount of air passed through the filter, giving a fiber concentration in the sampled air commonly expressed as fibers (f) per cubic centimeter of air (cc), abbreviated f/cc.

4. A limit of 0.5 f/cc over an eight-hour time-weighted average means that a worker who has breathed in about 350 cubic feet of air in a workday, or 10 million

cubic centimeters, will have breathed in, on average, 5 million fibers of asbestos by the end of the shift.

5. U.S. Department of Health, Education, and Welfare, National Institute of Health, *Asbestos: An Information Resource*, AHEW Publication No. (NIH) 79–1681, May 1978.

6. OSHA, "Occupational Exposure to Asbestos, Tremolite, Anthophyllite, and Actinolite: Final Rules," *Federal Register* 51:22643–46, June 20, 1986.

7. Ibid., p. 22648.

8. National Research Council, Committee on Nonoccupational Health Risks of Asbestiform Fibers, *Asbestiform Fibers: Nonoccupational Health Risks* (Washington, D.C.: National Academy Press, 1984).

9. U.S. Environmental Protection Agency, "Asbestos: Proposed Mining and Import Restrictions and Proposed Manufacturing Importation and Processing Prohibitions," *Federal Register* 51:3739, January 29, 1986.

10. The California act provides the state OSHA program with the administrative power to shut down equipment or operations that pose imminent risk of death or serious bodily harm to workers. Other state OSHA programs have similar laws. Federal OSHA inspectors do not have such quick-acting authority for high-hazard situations. Upon finding an imminent hazard, they cannot stop an operation or direct employees to leave. Rather, they must go through the more time-consuming process of contacting an OSHA attorney, who in turn assists the OSHA office in obtaining a temporary restraining order by presenting the case to a U.S. district court judge.

3. Solvents

1. National Institute of Occupational Safety and Health, *Organic Solvent Neurotoxicity*, Current Intelligence Bulletin 48, DHHS (NIOSH) Publication No. 87–104, March 31, 1987.

2. National Institute of Occupational Safety and Health, *Glycol Ethers*, Current Intelligence Bulletin 39, DHHS (NIOSH) Publication No. 83–112, May 2, 1983; National Institute of Occupational Safety and Health, *Methylene Chloride*, Current Intelligence Bulletin 46, DHHS (NIOSH) Publication No. 86–114, April 18, 1986.

4. Noise

1. OSHA, "Occupational Noise Exposure: Hearing Conservation Amendment," *Federal Register* 46:4078–179, June 16, 1981.

2. Ibid., p. 4107.

3. Ibid., p. 4084.

4. Ibid., pp. 4081–82.

5. Ibid., p. 4083.

6. National Institute of Occupational Safety and Health, *A Field Investigation of Noise Réduction Afforded by Insert-Type Hearing Protectors*, HEW (NIOSH) Publication No. 79–115, November 1978; Richard J. Goff and William J. Blank, "A Field Evaluation of Muff-Type Hearing Protection Devices," *Sound and Vibration* (October 1984).

7. Federal OSHA enforced a 15 mg/m³ limit for seventeen years until an appeal decision in early 1988 ruled that the limit for nuisance dusts did not apply to organic contaminants such as wood. A limit specifically for wood dust was promulgated on March 1, 1989. The workday limit was set at 5 mg/m³ for hard and softwood, except for western red cedar, which was set at 2.5 mg/m³. *Federal Register* 54:2528–33.

5. Lead

1. How much damage lead does depends on the amount a person breathes in or inadvertently eats. The former is generally dependent on the amount in the air and the length of time spent in the area of exposure. In cases of occupational exposure to

a chemical such as lead, which is excreted slowly and can accumulate in the body, chronic exposure, over months and years, can be serious. Damage is also dependent partly on individual susceptibility. Occupational exposure levels, however, are established with the aim of protecting most but not all of the working population. More sensitive workers, including pregnant women, are not usually considered when limits are developed. Other groups, such as children, the infirm, and the elderly, are not considered at all.

2. OSHA, "Occupational Exposure to Lead," *Federal Register* 43:52952–3014, November 14, 1978.

3. Ibid., p. 53006.

6. Carbon Monoxide

1. OSHA, "Airborne Contaminants: Final Rule," *Federal Register* 54:2651, January 19, 1989.

7. Formaldehyde

1. American Conference of Governmental Industrial Hygienists, *Documentation of the Threshold Limit Values*, 4th ed. (Cincinnati: American Conference of Governmental Hygienists, 1981), p. 198.

2. National Institute of Occupational Safety and Health, *Formaldehyde: Evidence of Carcinogenicity*, Current Intelligence Bulletin 34, DHHS (NIOSH) Publication No. 81–111, December 23, 1980.

3. OSHA, "Occupational Exposure to Formaldehyde," *Federal Register* 50:15180, April 17, 1985.

4. OSHA, "Occupational Exposure to Formaldehyde," *Federal Register* 52:46168–290, December 4, 1987.

5. Ibid., p. 46241.

6. Ibid., p. 46238.

7. The inspections were concluded before promulgation of federal OSHA's comprehensive carcinogen standard for formaldehyde.

8. From the Field

1. U.S. Congress, Office of Technology Assessment, *Preventing Illness and Injury in the Workplace* (Washington, D.C.: Office of Technology Assessment, OTA–H–256, April 1985), pp. 264–71.

2. Ibid., p. 269.

3. Ibid., p. 15.

4. National Institute of Occupational Safety and Health, *Performance Evaluation of Respiratory Protective Equipment Used in Paint Spray Operations*, HEW Publication (NIOSH) No. 76–177, June 1976.

5. Filing a confidential complaint with OSHA is a right provided by law. In some cases, inspectors suggest to potential complainants that they bring their safety or health concern to the attention of their employer before reporting to OSHA. This should be recommended *only* if the company is likely to respect the employee's concern and take needed action. Before filing a complaint with management rather than with OSHA, workers should first consider whether a safety committee exists, whether safety and health grievances are addressed in their labor contract, and whether their employer is indeed responsive to safety and health issues. If the employee has doubts about his or her employer's attitude, the worker may be better off calling in a confidential complaint to OSHA, thus preventing the possibility of discrimination. Exceptions may have to be made for instances of imminent danger in which the worker feels a duty to inform all concerned immediately.

6. "Life or Death for Your Business?" *Nation's Business*, April 1968, pp. 337–39.

7. Graham K. Wilson, *The Politics of Safety and Health—Occupational Safety and Health in the United States and Britain* (New York: Oxford University Press, 1985), p. 126.

8. Crystal Eastman, *Work Accidents and the Law* (1910; reprint, New York: Arno Press, 1969), p. 115.

9. David Bollier and Joan Claybrook, *Freedom from Harm—The Civilizing Influence of Health, Safety, and Environmental Regulation* (Washington, D.C.: Public Citizen and Democracy Project, 1986).

10. Bureau of National Affairs, *The Job Safety and Health Act of 1970* (Washington, D.C.: Bureau of National Affairs, 1971); Joseph A. Page and Mary-Win O'Brien, *Bitter Wages* (New York: Grossman Publishers, 1973).

11. Requiring employers and foremen to undergo first-aid training may help motivate them to comply with OSHA regulations and use preventive methods. Supervisors and foremen in the state of Washington, for example, must have training in both first aid and cardiopulmonary resuscitation, regardless of whether the work site is fixed, mobile, or remote. Learning how to bandage a bleeding limb or pack a severed limb for possible reattachment forcefully presents the benefits of accident prevention. The training probably has a "spinoff" effect in preventing occupational diseases in that the concept of prevention is favorably presented. All OSHA programs should consider having a first-aid training requirement for all industries. Washington Administrative Code, chap. 296–24, General Safety and Health Standards, sec. 060.

12. *Preventing Illness and Injury*, p. 11.

13. Gary Z. Nothstein, *The Law of Occupational Safety and Health* (New York: Free Press, 1981), pp. 420–26.

14. The act does not hold employers accountable for every possible hazard; allowances are made for hazards that are unpredictable or unforeseeable. The law requires that for a serious violation to be proposed and affirmed, the inspector must show that the employer knew of the hazard, or should have known, had he or she exercised "reasonable diligence." The 1970 OSH Act states that "a serious violation shall be deemed to exist in a place of employment if there is a substantial probability that death or serious physical harm could result from a condition which exists, or from one or more practices, means, methods, operations, or processes which have been adopted or are in use, in such place of employment unless the employer did not know, and could not with the exercise of reasonable diligence, know of the presence of the violation." Occupational Safety and Health Act of 1970, Public Law 91–596, sec. 17, paragraph k.

15. References to "OSHA" in this chapter include both federal and state OSHA programs.

16. As discussed in detail later, deterrence is limited because the penalty schedules are so low.

17. *Preventing Illness and Injury*, p. 236.

18. OSHA, *Report of the President to the Congress on Occupational Safety and Health for Calendar Year 1987*, 1988, p. 47.

19. John M. Gleason and Darold T. Barnum, "Effectiveness of OSHA Sanctions in Influencing Employer Behavior: Single and Multi-Period Decision Models," *Accident Analysis and Prevention* 10 (1978):44.

20. See, for example, Nicholas A. Ashford, *Crisis in the Workplace. Occupational Disease and Injury: A Report to the Ford Foundation* (Cambridge, Mass.: MIT Press, 1976), p. 366; *Preventing Illness and Injury*, p. 340.

21. There are limited remedies in situations of serious danger. If the hazard is imminent and there is a threat of serious injury or death, an OSHA program may

pursue a voluntary shutdown by the employer or, under some state programs, a legal shutdown via administrative order, or, as required of federal OSHA, a court-ordered temporary injunction.

22. Thomas O. McGarity and Sidney A. Shapiro, *Report to the Administrative Conference of the United States on OSHA Rulemaking: Regulatory Alternatives and Legislative Reform.* (Washington, D.C.: Administrative Conference of the United States, September 16, 1987), pp. 172–83.

23. OSHA, "General Safety and Health Programs: Request for Comments and Information," *Federal Register* 53:26790–96, July 15, 1988.

24. Ashford, *Crisis in the Workplace*, p. 254.

25. Ibid., p. 298.

BIBLIOGRAPHY

Ashford, Nicholas A. *Crisis in the Workplace. Occupational Disease and Injury: A Report to the Ford Foundation.* Cambridge, Mass.: MIT Press, 1976.

Bardach, Eugene. *The Implementation Game: What Happens after a Bill Becomes a Law.* Cambridge, Mass.: MIT Press, 1977.

Bardach, Eugene, and Robert A. Kagan. *Going by the Book: The Problem of Regulatory Unreasonableness.* Philadelphia: Temple University Press, 1982.

Berman, Daniel M. *Death on the Job: Occupational Health and Safety Struggles in the United States.* New York: Monthly Review Press, 1978.

Bollier, David, and Joan Claybrook. *Freedom from Harm—The Civilizing Influence of Health, Safety, and Environmental Regulation.* Washington, D.C.: Public Citizen and Democracy Project, 1986.

Brodeur, Paul. *Expendable Americans.* New York: Viking Press, 1974.

——. *Outrageous Misconduct—The Asbestos Industry on Trial.* New York: Pantheon Books, 1985.

Bureau of National Affairs. *The Job Safety and Health Act of 1970.* Washington, D.C.: Bureau of National Affairs, 1971.

Eastman, Crystal. *Work Accidents and the Law.* Philadelphia: Russell Sage Foundation, 1910. Reprint. New York: Arno, 1969.

Freedman, Audrey. *Industry Response to Health Risk.* New York: Conference Board, 1981.

Goldsmith, Frank, and Lorin E. Kerr. *Occupational Safety and Health: The Prevention and Control of Work-Related Hazards.* New York: Human Sciences Press, 1982.

Hamilton, Alice. *Exploring the Dangerous Trades.* Boston: Little, Brown, 1943. Reprint. Boston: Northeastern University Press, 1985.

Hawkins, Keith, and John M. Thomas, eds. *Enforcing Regulation.* Boston: Kluwer-Nijhoff, 1984.

Interagency Task Force on Workplace Safety and Health. *Making Prevention Pay: Final Report of the Interagency Task Force on Workplace Safety and Health.* 1978.

Kelman, Steven. *Regulating America, Regulating Sweden: Comparative Study of Occupational Safety and Health Policy.* Cambridge, Mass.: MIT Press, 1981.

McCaffrey, David P. *OSHA and the Politics of Health Regulation.* New York: Plenum Press, 1982.

Mintz, Benjamin W. *OSHA: History, Law, and Policy.* Washington, D.C.: Bureau of National Affairs, 1984.

Moran, Robert D. *How to Avoid OSHA.* Houston: Gulf Publishing, 1981.

National Safe Workplace Institute. *Failed Opportunities: The Decline of U.S. Job Safety in the 1980s.* Chicago: National Safe Workplace Institute, 1988.

Nelkin, Dorothy, and Michael S. Brown. *Workers at Risk: Voices from the Workplace.* Chicago: University of Chicago Press, 1984.

Northrup, Herbert R., Richard L. Rowan, and Charles R. Perry. *The Impact of OSHA: A Study of the Effects of the Occupational Safety and Health Act on Three Key Industries: Aerospace, Chemicals, and Textiles.* Philadelphia: Industrial Research Unit, Wharton School, University of Pennsylvania.

Nothstein, Gary Z. *The Law of Occupational Safety and Health.* New York: Free Press, 1981.

Page, Joseph A., and Mary-Win O'Brien. *Bitter Wages.* New York: Grossman Publishers, 1973.

Rosner, David, and Gerald Markowitz, eds. *Dying for Work: Workers' Safety and Health in Twentieth-Century America.* Indianapolis: Indiana University Press, 1987.

Ruttenberg, Ruth, and Randall Hudgins. *Occupational Safety and Health in the Chemical Industry.* New York: Council on Economic Priorities, 1981.

Scott, Rachel. *Muscle and Blood.* New York: E. P. Dutton, 1974.

Smith, Robert Stewart. *The Occupational Safety and Health Act: Its Goals and Its Achievements.* Washington, D.C.: American Enterprise Institute for Public Policy Research, 1976.

U.S. Congress, Office of Technology Assessment. *Preventing Illness and Injury in the Workplace.* Washington, D.C.: Office of Technology Assessment, 1985.

Viscusi, W. Kip. "Reforming OSHA Regulation of Workplace Risks." In *Regulatory Reform—What Actually Happened,* edited by Leonard W. Weiss and Michael W. Klass. Boston: Little, Brown, 1986.

Wilson, Graham K. *The Politics of Safety and Health—Occupational Safety and Health in the United States and Britain.* New York: Oxford University Press, 1985.

INDEX

Embalming, use of formaldehyde in, 178, 179–96
Emergency eyewashes, 194–95
Employee interviews with inspector, 3
Employee representatives at informal conferences, 224
Employee rights, 1
 appeal system and, 4
 to confidentiality, 201
 to file complaint, 201, 204–5, 233n5
 problems in exercising, 203–6
Employee witnesses at appeal hearings, 205–6
Employers
 British versus U.S., 207
 discrimination against complainant, 205
 incentives to control hazards, 211
 opposition to government regulation, 206–10
 reasons for noncompliance, 208–11
 rights of, 1, 200
 ways OSHA works for, 211–12
Enforcement
 federal and state procedures, 2
 policy, decisions subject to differences in, 213–14
Enforcement through deterrence, 227, 228–29
 appeals and policy of, 217–18
 compliance and, 217–21
 forced consultation versus, 214–17
 need for, 212–21
 penalties and, 217, 218–19, 228–29
 potential drawback of, 221
Engineering controls, 87, 105–6, 201, 202
Environmental Protection Agency (EPA), 10, 12, 115
Enzyme system, lead exposure and, 117

Exposure to contaminants, 5–6. *See also specific contaminants*
Eyewashes, emergency, 194–95

Factory Inspectorate (Britain), 207
Federal Aviation Administration, 53
Federal enforcement procedures, 2
Fines. *See* Penalties
Fire hazards, 66–67
First-aid training, 234n11
Flammable solvents, 65–69
Fluorinated hydrocarbons, 46
Follow-up inspections, 216
Food and Drug Administration, 45
Forced consultation policy, 214–17, 221
Formaldehyde, 175–96
 effects of exposure to, 175, 176
 inspection involving, 179–96
 OSHA exposure limits for, 175–76, 177
 uses for, 177–78
Freons, 46
Funeral homes, formaldehyde exposure in, 179–96

Gasoline
 lead in, 115
 refineries, carbon monoxide exposure in, 142–61
Gleason, John M., 218
Glycol ethers, health effects of, 46
Good faith, reductions based on evidence of, 219

Halide meters, 77
Health hazards, 4–6
 examples of, 4
 hierarchy of controls for correcting, 201–3
 incentives for employers to control, 211
 OSH Act's effect on, 197–98
 See also specific hazards

Money management, compliance
and, 208
Morale, employee, 210
Mortuaries, formaldehyde exposure in, 179–96

Naphtha, 46, 148
National Institute of Occupational
Safety and Health (NIOSH),
1, 10, 72, 135, 175, 176, 199,
203, 219, 227
National Research Council, 11
N-butyl ketone, 46
Nervous system, effect of lead ex-
posure on, 117
Nitrogen dioxide, exposure level
of, 6
Noise, 83–113
effect of exposure to excessive,
83–84
inspections involving, 89–113
instruments to analyze and
quantitate, 84
OSHA standards on, 84–88
Noise dosimeters, 106
Nonabatement penalties, 216
Noncompliers, 219

Occupational Safety and Health
Act (OSH Act), 27
aims in formulating, 1–2
assessing impact of, 197–99
problems in achieving compliance with, 206–11
provisions of, 1
Occupational Safety and Health
Administration (OSHA), 1,
228
asbestos limits, 9–12
benzene exposure limit, 45–46
carbon monoxide exposure limits, 140
consultation services, 219
difficulties in early years of, 207
effect of presence as institution,
199

formaldehyde exposure limits,
175–76, 177
influences on policies of, 212–14
jurisdiction of, 65
noise standards, 84–88
response to criticism of, 199–203
rights under. *See* Rights
at work for employers, 211–12
Occupational Safety and Health
Commission, 1, 221
Office of Management and Budget, 201
Opening conferences, 2–3
Organic solvents, 43
Ovens, carbon monoxide poisoning from, 162–74

Paints, lead content for, 115
Penalties, 3, 4
deal-making in informal conferences and, 222–25
under policy of deterrence, 217,
218–19, 228–29
under policy of forced consultation, 214
nonabatement, 216
power of appeal judges and
board or commission to re-
duče, 224–25
Penalty schedule, 212, 218–19
Perchloroethylene, 46
Peripheral nervous system, effect
of lead exposure on, 117
Personal protective equipment,
202–3
Philosophical or political objections
to compliance, 208–9
*Preventing Illness and Injury in the
Workplace* (U.S. Office of
Technology Assessment), 211
Prevention, concept of, 210–11
Prevention programs
accident, 66
comprehensive, 226–27

Reagan, Ronald, 214
Reagan administration, 176

Don J. Lofgren is an industrial hygiene regional supervisor for the state of Washington OSHA program. *Dangerous Premises* is based on his experiences while working for the California State OSHA program. Before joining OSHA, Lofgren worked as a biochemist for the University of California, San Francisco, and for the Lawrence Livermore Laboratory. He holds a master's degree from the School of Public Health, University of California, Berkeley.

JU